ORANGEFIELD REMEMBERED

A SCHOOL IN BELFAST
1957–1990

EDITORS

Ken Stanley, Thompson Steele, Jack Eaton, Raymond King

in association with

The East Belfast Historical Society

2016

DEDICATION

To

The thousands of people who
are not mentioned here
but are part of the Orangefield we remember

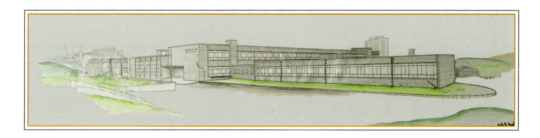

Pencil Drawing of Orangefield Boys' Secondary School by former pupil Neil Hunter [1985-1990]

FINDING WORDS

We scramble Orangefield. The letters fold
    into old autumns, falling leaf by leaf
on lost Septembers, where the red and gold
    linger on long horizons and the grief

of roads not taken and a role not read.
    Our presences and absences define
the texts we file, and how remembrance fled
    beyond the range of words in every line.

We type our alphabets again, a finger
    on keys of loss and hope, on buds of fear
that somewhere in the spaces we will linger
    too long on losses when the hopes are near.

    We scramble Orangefield. The letters fold
    into old harvests: red and ripe and gold.

Trevor Scott: Orangefield Press Christmas Card.   Douglas Carson: Finding Words.

ISBN 978-1-909751-62-0

The authors/editors gratefully acknowledge the permission granted to reproduce the copyright material in this book. Every effort has been made to trace copyright holders and to obtain their permission to use the copyright material. The authors/editors apologise for any errors or omissions in the list of acknowledgements.

CONTENTS

1	Prologue	11
2	The Blakiston-Houston Estate *by Thompson Steele*	13
3	Starting Out in 1957: The Official Opening, 3rd May 1958 *by Ken Stanley*	16
4	In memoriam: Arnold Clarke	23
5	Beginnings and Endings: 'The Malone Road' [1982], Tom Kerr [1957-1964]	25
6	Memoirs: Set 1	
	(a) Sam Reilly: *'A Proud Orangefield Boy'*	29
	(b) Alex Redpath: *'The Big Smoke'*	31
7	The Orangefield House System *by Jack Eaton*	34
8	Memoirs: Set 2	
	(a) David Lynas: *A Good Deed and a Handshake*	43
	(b) Billy McKee: *'Memories are made of this …'*	45
	(c) Ken Smyth: *Travels to East Belfast*	50
9	Counselling and Careers Education *by Jack Eaton*	52
10	Sport at Orangefield: Part 1	
	(a) Football	56
	(b) Basketball	69
	(c) Cricket	75
	(d) Swimming	81
11	Memoirs: Set 3	
	(a) Daly Maxwell: *Learning and Living*	85
	(b) Gerry Dawe: *Lucky Man*	89
	(c) Bruce Cardwell: *'Desperados waiting for a train …'*	92
	(d) Gavin Robinson: *An Orangefield Experience*	96

| 12 | Time It Was *by David Craig* | 99 |

13	Explorations: Stories from the Field	
	(a) Whinlands Field Centre *by Thompson Steele*	102
	(b) Beyond Chalk and Talk *by Matt Maginnis and Stead Black*	113

14	"All the world's a stage"	
	(a) Orangefield Dramatic Society 1961-1965	120
	(b) All right on the night *by Wilfie Pyper*	123
	(c) Saints and Sinners *by Sam McCready*	126

15	Musical Journeys and Frontiers	
	(a) Denis Totton	134
	(b) The Belfast Operatic Company	141
	(c) John Anderson	143
	(d) Van Morrison	146

| 16 | A Southerner in Orangefield *by Jonathan Bardon* | 149 |

17	Memoirs: Set 4	
	(a) Trevor Poots: *History in Room 7*	155
	(b) Fernie Glenfield: *Time flies!*	158
	(c) Philip Monks: *Sport and other things*	160

| 18 | Reflections on OBSS *by Gordon Topping* | 163 |

| 19 | The School Certificate and some more … *by Billy Burnison* | 166 |

20	Sport at Orangefield: Part 2	
	(a) Rugby	176
	(b) Hockey	190
	(c) Athletics	195
	(d) Badminton	201

| 21 | Room 14 *by Walter Rader* | 205 |

| 22 | The Orangefield Observer *by Raymond King* | 209 |

23	Memoirs: Set 5	
	(a) John Grayden: *"Life is often about perceptions …"*	229
	(b) Ian Simons: *Maths is Fun!*	231

24	Clubs and Societies	
	(a) Chess Club	233
	(b) The Young Farmers' Club	235
	(c) Italic Handwriting and Printing Clubs	237
	(d) The Motor Cycle Club	238
	(e) Film-making and Cinema	242
	(f) Scripture Union	245
	(g) Canoeing	247
	(h) Guitar-making	248
25	Memories and Appreciation *by Joan Scott*	249
26	The Orangefield Old Boys' Association	251
27	Staffroom Capers *by Jimmy Clements*	254
28	The Orangefield Library Resource Centre *by Tom McMullan*	255
29	Retrospect: Brian Weston [1957-1988] *by Robert Crone*	258
30	A View from the School Office *by Margaret Vance, Ann Crawford and Hazel Beesley*	265
31	Memoirs: Set 6	
	(a) Alan Galbraith: *Moving On*	267
	(b) Richard Beckwith: *The Last Homework*	269
	(c) Stuart Laffin: *The OBS Bard*	272
	(d) Rodney Brown: *I Remember*	273
32	Epilogue *by Ken Stanley*	276
33	Elegy: The Bright Field *by Douglas Carson*	280
	Acknowledgements	296

1.
PROLOGUE

THE EDUCATION ACT [Northern Ireland] 1947 made available free, full-time schooling to all young people of secondary school age irrespective of social background, ability or religious denomination. Officialdom's attitude towards pupils who failed the Qualifying Examination for entry to grammar schools, around 78% of school children aged eleven, was set out by the Ministry of Education's Committee on *Secondary School Examinations,* HMSO, 1955, chaired by Professor Alexander MacBeath C.B.E.

In respect to the recently created *"experimental"* secondary intermediate school sectors, placed ambiguously between grammar and technical schools, the MacBeath Report observed that *"there was no external examination specially conducted for pupils in these schools."* The Report added:

"... we are assured that only a small proportion of pupils in these schools could sit any examination, which would be instituted, and this would have the unfortunate psychological effect on those who could not take the examination, and cause an undesirable division in the school community."

A number of pioneering secondary intermediate schools challenged the educational orthodoxy of the time. Bearing in mind the contribution Orangefield Boys' School, 1957-1990, made to education in East Belfast and beyond, a small group of former teachers felt it important that the name and work of the School should be kept alive in the form of a book. More than anything else, we have attempted to preserve the human endeavour and spirit of Orangefield in its time and place.

The following narrative has been made possible only by the generous support and commitment of many members of staff and former pupils who made available their stories in various forms: memoirs, verbal anecdotes, written reminiscences, newspaper articles, artefacts, photographs, letters, certificates of achievement, and programmes of school events.

We would like to thank Robert Crone and Robert McNair, former pupils of the School, for their secretarial, graphic design and editorial support in the making of *Orangefield Remembered*.

Inevitably, there remain stories untold. If any upset or offence has been caused, we trust you will understand the difficulty of the task we faced and accept our sincere apologies. Any mistakes are ours, and ours alone.

Ken Stanley, Thompson Steele, Jack Eaton and Raymond King

— 2. —
THE BLAKISTON-HOUSTON ESTATE

IN AN ARTICLE written by Francis Joseph Bigger entitled 'The Romance of the O'Neills', which appeared in the Belfast Telegraph on 17th March 1925, reference is made to the *"rich O'Neill meadows of what is now Orangefield."* In 1603, this O'Neill land was confiscated by the Crown. The vast tract of land was then divided into three huge estates.

O'Neill was granted the lands around his castle, which was very close to the site of Castlereagh Presbyterian Church, and the remainder was divided between two Scottish planters, James Hamilton and Hugh Montgomery. Hamilton acquired North Down and settled at Bangor, whilst Montgomery planted the Ards and settled at Newtownards and, later, Greyabbey.

The unfortunate O'Neill still ruled over a fairly considerable acreage of land, and continued to live a lavish lifestyle which was no longer within his means. Gradually, he sold off parcels of land for ready cash, and most of these were snapped up by Moses Hill of the future Downshire family. He was an English planter, and a henchman of Sir Arthur Chichester.

The first reference we have found to Orangefield House being lived in occurs in 'The Ancient and Present State of Co. Down.' This book, by Walter Harris, was published in 1744, and informs us of *"the new and elegant house and improvements of David Hunter."* It was 60 feet by 40 feet and was four storeys high. It was covered by a flat roof, a fashion he had picked up on his travels to the East Indies. He also laid out gardens, orchards and lawns.

Figure 1: 1858 Ordnance Survey Map

[A revision of the 1834 edition, the map shows the Belfast County Down railway line and in the centre the Blakiston-Houston estate is clearly marked.]

Figure 2: Orangefield: The seat of John H Houston from a plate by Edward K Proctor

[*The illustration shows a windmill in the meadows close to the House, a case perhaps of artistic licence. There was, however, a cornmill on the estate, close to the railings that now surround the park. The mill race was buried when the all-weather pitches were laid out.]*

Over a century later Knox in his 'History of Co Down' (1857) mentions that a Mr Pottinger was living at Orangefield in one of the best houses in the county. He acquired the estate from Thomas Bateson after he took up residence at Belvoir around 1811. There is a fine painting of the Bateson family in the Ulster Museum, dated 1762.

One of the founders of the Belfast Banking Company, Hugh Crawford, lived at Orangefield until 1819. On his death, a fellow banker, John Holmes Houston, purchased the house and estate. John Holmes Houston died on 10th March 1845. His life and public service are commemorated in First Rosemary Street Presbyterian Church, Belfast, where he was a life-long member of the congregation.

Figure 3: By kind permission of First Presbyterian Church: Rosemary Street, Belfast.

John Holmes Houston had no male heirs and when his eldest daughter married Richard Bayley Blakiston, the family name in 1857 became Blakiston-Houston. The eldest son of this union, John Blakiston-Houston, died in 1920 in his ninety-first year.

The last member of the Blakiston-Houston family to live at Orangefield set up a company entitled *'Blakiston Estate Company'* and in 1934 offered to sell part of the 300 acre estate to Belfast Corporation to develop a park, but the price was deemed to be too high.

Figure 4: Orangefield House

The company then applied for permission to sell the land for housing. This was appealed by Belfast Corporation, and the outcome of that was a ruling that some of the land must be preserved for a recreational park. At this point, the City Council agreed at a cost of £20,000 to purchase a parcel of land to create a park. After leaving Orangefield, the Blakiston-Houston family acquired an estate at Beltrim Castle, close to Gortin forest in County Tyrone. The family still live there.

The housing development commenced in the late 1930s but was curtailed by the outbreak of the Second World War in September 1939. During the war Orangefield House and the immediate area around it was occupied by the military. Nissan huts were constructed on the site of Grosvenor High School in Cameronian Drive, and for a period this site as well as Orangefield Public Elementary School, became a prisoner of war camp. A very young John Ritchie recalls seeing when he was a small boy the prisoners being transported by lorries up the Castlereagh Road. On the 4th December 1946, the school was returned to the Belfast Education Authority and the mansion at Orangefield became a site for various business premises.

By the early 1970s, the old House and the stable block had been demolished to provide an extension to Orangefield Girls' School.

It is interesting to note that the Orangefield Estate was one of the properties the Government of Northern Ireland considered as a site for its parliament building.

The Orangefield name has been known in the barony of Castlereagh Upper since at least 1744, but how did this name come to be associated with the area? According to the Pinkerton Manuscripts, King William's army encamped at this spot on their journey to the Boyne. This popular belief would appear to be the origin of the name Orangefield.

Orangefield Boys' Secondary School

It was in September 1957 Orangefield Boys' Secondary School opened in Cameronian Drive, Castlereagh, on land which had been part of the Blakiston-Houston estate. The family later gave the School permission to use the Blakiston-Houston crest on blazer Honours pockets to be awarded to pupils achieving standards of excellence in various aspects of school life.

Sixty years on, it is worth recording the School was in a semi-rural setting bordered on one side by the Knock River. On summer mornings, the sound of bird song greeted pupils and staff walking through Orangefield Park. Before the fields around the School were landscaped to create all-weather and prunty pitches, the sport of *cross-country* meant just that, and the whole area was much more scenic.

During the academic year 1958/59, one Science class spent a short time each week observing the feathered bird life in the grounds. In the course of that year, the boys spotted fifty-four different species of birds. Some of the more unusual birds were kestrel,

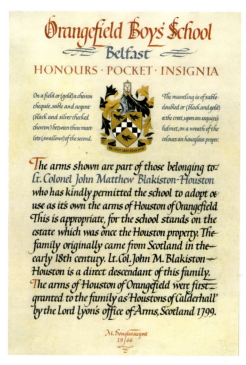

Figure 5: Blakiston-Houston Crest, Used with permission from the Deputy Keeper of the Records, PRONI.

heron, tufted duck, tree creeper, kingfisher, house martin, swallow and corn bunting. It may sound incredible, but in the springtime of the late 1950s, the corncrake could still be heard amongst the rushes and scrub in the marshy area next to Sandhill.

One memorable morning during roll call, Wilson Givan arrived late in class. His excuse for being late was that he had seen a kingfisher on the Knock River. His teacher, Mr Steele, disbelieved him. Wilson remained insistent, and persuaded his teacher to leave his class so that he could take him to the spot where he had seen the bird. This impromptu excursion led the teacher to seeing his first kingfisher.

**Thompson Steele,
East Belfast Historical Society**

– 3. –
STARTING OUT IN 1957

IN SEPTEMBER 1957, Orangefield Boys' Secondary School opened in Cameronian Drive, Castlereagh. Two other schools were to follow on the campus – Grosvenor High School [1958] and Orangefield Girls' Secondary School [1960]. The first Headmaster of Orangefield Boys' Secondary School was John Malone who, prior to taking up this appointment, had established a considerable reputation in teaching and youth work.

Orangefield Boys' School staff comprised a diverse range of individuals. David Francis [Navy], Ronnie McMaster [Army], Barney Megarry [Royal Air Force], and Larry Lannie [Royal Navy], had served during the Second World War 1939-45.

Bill Stirling, the School's first Vice-Principal, pictured Right, had a very distinguished career with the Royal Engineers in Italy, France and Germany. The Editorial of the *Orangefield Observer, Vol 3, No, 9 June 1961*, records Bill being *"awarded the Military Cross for his devotion to duty and gallantry during the operation in which the allied forces crossed the Rhine in 1944."* Later, three other war veterans, Bill Comyns [Merchant Navy], Bob McLean [Royal Air Force], and Max Woods [Army] also joined the staff.

A number of the original staff already had teaching experience, some within the former system of public elementary schooling: Brian

Weston, John Gowen, Jim Parker, Sam Preston, Tony Fleck, Jim Holland, Maurice Scott, Sam Campbell, Jimmy Clements, Billy Hawthorne, Mervyn Douglas and Gerry McClelland. Other members of staff, just starting out on their teaching careers, included Ken Stanley, Duncan Scarlett, Rodney Usher, Jimmy McAvoy and Zeke McCleery.

As Headmaster, John Malone sought to create a school which would challenge the existing concepts of schooling and education. During its lifetime 1957 to 1990, Orangefield Boys' School under his leadership, and successors Brian Weston and Ken Stanley, earned a reputation for liberal educational ideas and practice.

Unfortunately, in some quarters, secondary intermediate schools were regarded as *"dead end schools"* offering their pupils few, if any, opportunities to take public examinations. Jim Holland tells a story from the 1950s of teaching in a post-primary school where no external examinations were made available to some very bright pupils. He approached the Headmaster to suggest that some members of his class might be entered for the Junior Certificate examination. *"In that case"* he was told, *"they are in the wrong school."*

John Malone was determined to change such beliefs and practices: he wanted Orangefield to become a learning community that would offer a new beginning to *all* pupils enrolled at the School. Many of his ideas proved to be ahead of their time, whilst his commitment to pupils and staff became legendary. He encouraged everyone to make the most of his talents.

John Malone saw his first task as providing suitable courses for the various levels of ability,

PREFECTS
1964-1965

Back Row:- I. Millar; S. Spence; H. Moneypenny; P. Wilson; D. McGall; D. Dalton; C. Morrison; I. Davidson; S. McCurry
2nd Row:- Mr. Weston; W. Bleakley; G. McConnell; T. Kerr; I. Scott; A. Kennedy; D. McClure; A. Kirker; F. Donnan; A. Fitzsimmons; S. Reilly; D. Vance; M. Adamson; D. Harvey; Mr. Malone
3rd Row:- R. Freeburn; J. Crone; J. Hagen; M. Russel; R. Moore (Head Boy); R. Bunting; N. Pickles; J. McAllister; M. Watson.
Front Row:- H. Kelham; J. Magennis; F. Truesdale; S. Young; I. Dunbar; K. Seawright; R. Atkinson.

Starting Out in 1957

aptitude and interest of the pupils. He believed in the potential of each child and he was determined to see every boy receive an education best suited to his abilities and interests. From the outset, the most able pupils in Orangefield were prepared for the old Junior Certificate, a public examination normally taken in grammar schools. In addition, boys were also entered for the Junior Technical Certificate, while College of Preceptors examinations provided further vocationally-based qualifications. 'Failure' was not an acceptable label when it came to engaging the potential of every boy. The front-page Editorial of the *Orangefield Observer, Vol 3, No 9, June 1961*, reported that 180 boys were sitting public examinations.

As the Junior and Senior Certificate system of public examinations was phased out, John Malone, along with other secondary intermediate school Headteachers, helped to persuade a reluctant Ministry of Education to allow pupils attending their secondary intermediate schools to sit the new system of G.C.E. 'O' Levels followed by G.C.E. 'A' Levels. By the late 1960s and early 1970s, Orangefield had established a large sixth form and many pupils undertook the study of 'A' Level courses in a wide range of subjects across the school curriculum.

Orangefield's initial enrolment of approximately 570 pupils was drawn almost entirely from seven primary schools — Avoniel, Elmgrove, Euston Street, Harding Memorial, Orangefield, Robert Bell and Strandtown. By the late 1960s, Orangefield's intake comprised children from twenty-five primary schools. Pupil numbers increased to more than 1100, an enrolment figure that required the use of mobile classrooms, and a further extension to the School building.

A major innovation was the introduction of a pastoral system based on the guidance and counselling of boys throughout their time at the School. An experienced member of staff was appointed as a Counsellor for each year group and stayed with the boys from Forms 1 to 5. Older pupils often required specific guidance about possible future careers and, as a result, a separate Careers Department was established.

The four School Houses were named after major firms based in East Belfast — *Bryson, Davidson, Hughes* and *Musgrave* — and helped to establish closer links with local industry. Each firm took a keen interest in its House and supported the School in many ways, for example by providing trophies for inter-House competitions, offering work placements and, on occasion, full-time apprenticeships.

John Malone believed education should not be confined to the classroom alone. The idea of a school-owned residential Field Centre had long been his ambition. Since Orangefield was located in industrialised East Belfast, he believed time away from school should be spent in rural surroundings. Members of staff searched Northern Ireland looking for a suitable building. In 1965 Whinlands, a large house in two acres of land on the outskirts of Annalong, was purchased by the School.

Extra-curricular activities at Orangefield were many and wide-ranging. Sport played an important part in the life of the School. Over many years, football teams at all levels were very successful in the various Leagues and Cup competitions. Players were chosen regularly for the Northern Ireland Schoolboys' International team, and numerous tours took place to various countries. Rugby was played throughout the School. Orangefield's 1st XV competed in the Schools' Cup and also provided players for Ulster and Ireland. Other sports offered to boys included Athletics, Basketball, Hockey, Cricket, Tennis, Swimming, Cross-Country and Badminton. The Orangefield archive contains comprehensive records of pupils' participation in annual inter-House Sports Days and Swimming Galas.

The many after-school clubs and societies reflected the various interests of the staff and pupils. They included among others, the Motor Cycle Club, Young Farmers' Club, Aircraft Recognition Club, Radio Club, Oxfam Group, Film Society, Duke of Edinburgh Award, Student Christian Movement, Scalextric Club, English and Geography Societies, Printing and Italic Handwriting Club, Gymnastics, Table Tennis, Fishing Club, Stamp Club and Scripture Union, while a thriving Chess Club had upwards of two hundred members. Annual trips abroad undertaken by the Ski and Travel Clubs were always over-subscribed.

The Arts also flourished. Drama was very strong and, during the decade of the 1960s, Orangefield earned a deserved reputation for its outstanding productions of plays by Molière, George Bernard Shaw and Brian Friel. Subsequent productions were directed by Paul Acheson and Michael Fieldhouse. For many pupils and parents, a highlight of each year was the musical evening, where large numbers of performers participated to a high standard as members of the School's orchestra, choir, brass band and instrumental groups.

In October 1958, the first copy of the *Orangefield Observer*, edited by David Hammond and a team of boys, appeared price 2d. Later editors included Jim Stevenson, Douglas Carson, Henry Sinnerton, Bob McKinley and Eileen Gardner. This monthly newspaper was produced by a member of staff and an editorial committee of pupils. The *Observer* kept the School community informed as well as entertained. It gave boys experience of writing news reports, articles and letters as well as providing encouragement to budding photographers.

From the outset, good relationships were established with Orangefield Girls' School, and many opportunities were taken for boys and girls to engage in educational activities of mutual benefit. For example, the Music Departments collaborated in a number of highly successful public performances; *"News of the Girls"* provided a regular feature of the *Orangefield Observer* which enjoyed a wide circulation in both schools; shared sixth-form courses were undertaken at GCE "A" Level; outdoor pursuits such as sailing and hill-walking were only two of many joint extra-curricular activities. Special mention is also needed of the major contribution staff and pupils from the Girls' School made to fund-raising activities for Whinlands as well as the provision of furnishings for the Field Centre.

There was never a dull moment in the Boys' School. For example, every Christmas, for many years, Anne Preston and Billy Burnison helped in organising dinner for local senior citizens in the Assembly Hall. The rest of the School however, had to endure the delightful aroma coming from the Hall, while they had to make do with school dinners or packed lunches. The Music Department supplied the entertainment and guests were very appreciative of their efforts.

None of these activities would have been possible without the co-operation of a committed and dedicated staff. John Malone appreciated and valued everyone who worked with him, be they teachers or ancillary staff and, in return, he won their loyalty and support.

The School Library, with David Francis as Librarian, was a valuable asset. Individual pupils and classes made use of it for help with teaching assignments as well as recreational reading. The School was very fortunate to have for many years the services of Mrs Sylvia Stewart and Mrs Doyle as Library ancillary staff.

Staff circa 1965
Squatting: *Mervyn Douglas, David Craig, John Allen, Bob Ashe, John Gowen, Moore Sinnerton, Don McBride, Alex Cunningham.*
Front Row: *Ronnie Horner, David Francis, Brian Weston, John Malone, Barney Megarry, Brian Sloan, Jim Holland.*
1st Row Standing: *Ronnie McCracken, Thompie Steele, Raymond King, John Ritchie, Eric Twaddell, Dessie Taylor, Ronnie McMaster, Nicholas Watson, Douglas Carson, Roy Napier, Ken Stanley, John Mercer, Ted McClelland, Jack Gallagher, Duncan Scarlett, Bill Comyns, Larry Lannie.*
Back Row: *David McKeown, Sam Preston, Jonathan Bardon, Jack Eaton, Jim Leckey, Jim Clements, Bert Caldwell, Rodney Usher, George Hayes.*

For several years, the School Library was a branch of the Belfast Public Library Service and proved popular with readers in the neighbourhood and wider community.

A Visual Aids Room was constructed in the School's quadrangle by Larry Lannie, ably supported by a group of senior boys. This new facility proved very popular for showing films to classes during the day and also for extra-curricular use by the Film Club after school hours. Ross McQuarrie, Jimmy Morrow and Alan Hunter were very involved.

A Pre-Fab was purchased at a reasonable price, and was used largely by the Science and Heavy Craft Departments before it became a mini zoo housing, among other creatures, a snake which aroused some excitement when it was stolen on one occasion. The Science Department's technician, Brian Johnston, looked after the animals in addition to his other duties.

As "The Troubles" developed in the late 1960s, the Ministry of Education invited John Malone to carry out an investigation of ways in which schools might contribute to improved community relations in Northern Ireland. From 1 January 1970, he was seconded from Orangefield to become Director of the Schools' Project in Community Relations [SPICER]. This government initiative was undertaken under the auspices of a newly-established Community Relations Commission based in Bedford House in the centre of Belfast.

By this time Orangefield, along with a number of other pioneering secondary intermediate schools, had done much to raise the educational expectations of parents and the aspirations of pupils across the province. John Malone resigned officially as its Headmaster on 31st August, 1971. Brian Weston, who had served as Vice-Principal [1961-69] and Acting Principal [1970-71], was appointed Headmaster on a permanent basis, a position he held with distinction until his retirement in 1988.

The Official Opening

Although Orangefield opened its doors to the first pupils in September 1957, the Official Opening did not take place until May 3rd, 1958. During this period, pupils and staff were getting to know each other and making themselves familiar with the geography of the new school. Moving from classroom to classroom for different subjects was a fairly new experience for the boys, and probably for some of the staff!

In addition, work was still going on to complete the school building and, with all the various distractions, concentration on lessons was not always easy.

Eventually, the day of the Official Opening arrived. The date, May 3rd was the day of the English FA Cup Final – Manchester United and Bolton Wanderers – and this presented a clash of loyalties for some soccer-loving members of staff and their television sets! However, loyalty to the Headmaster won the day, no doubt influenced by the thought that absence from the ceremony would not look too good when staff promotion openings appeared in the future!

The day dawned bright and sunny and, shortly before 3pm, parents and pupils had taken their

seats in the School Hall. The Lord Mayor Sir Cecil McKee was received in the entrance hall by Rev. W.G. Whittaker, St Columba's Parish Church, King's Road, who, as Chairman of the School Management Committee, then presented the Headmaster and members of the Management Committee.

The Headmaster, in turn, presented the members of staff to the Lord Mayor following which all the dignitaries, invited guests, Management Committee and staff proceeded to the main entrance led by the School Choir under the direction of James McAvoy.

Mr R. McKee, the representative of the builders accompanied by the architect Mr. H. Lynn, presented a Key to the Lord Mayor who formally opened the building. All the guests then took their seats in the hall and a short service followed conducted by the Rev. Eric Gallagher and the Rev. A.M. Parke.

A plaque was then unveiled by the Lord Mayor and he and the headmaster addressed the assembly. Mrs. Hilda Wilson, Chair of the Belfast Education Committee, proposed a vote of thanks to the Lord Mayor which was seconded by Mr. A.C. Williams, Chief Secretary, Department of Education.

The whole afternoon was a great success and Orangefield Boys' Secondary Intermediate School was well and truly launched.

Ken Stanley *was a member of staff from 1957 to 1990. A graduate of Queen's University Belfast, he was made Head of History in 1962 and served as a Housemaster and School Counsellor. In 1972 Ken was appointed Deputy Headmaster and in 1988 Acting Principal prior to the merger of the Boys' and Girls' Schools in 1990.*

— 4. —
ARNOLD CLARKE 1957–1958
IN MEMORIAM

Under 14 XI with John Malone and Ken Stanley. Arnold Clarke, captain, is seated holding the ball in the front row.

ARNOLD CLARKE'S career at Orangefield Boys' School was terminated by a tragic accident. On 1st September 1958 prior to the commencement of his second year at the school, John Malone had invited a group of senior boys to a prefects' meeting at Orangefield. Arnold Clarke was one of the boys who attended that meeting.

As he was returning by bicycle to his home in Jonesboro Street Arnold was struck by a lorry and killed. The accident happened at the Loopland area on the Castlereagh Road. John Malone when recalling this tragedy in an interview he gave in January 1982 said, "The saddest thing was the death of one of those boys on his way home from our very last meeting. It was an awful experience for all of us. But in a peculiar way it brought the school together. The Arnold Clarke Memorial Cup became a kind of symbol of the unity of the school from the beginning."

Arnold Clarke was a very popular boy at school and was a keen member of Ken Stanley's Under 14 Soccer Team [1957/58]. His death was a great shock and tragedy to his family and contemporaries in school.

The Clarke family were members of the Mountpottinger No 1 Corp of the Salvation Army. Wilfie Pyper, who is still in contact with the Clarke family, has been able to recall this memory of Arnold Clarke's funeral.

"The pavements around Jonesboro Street and the lower Castlereagh Road were thronged with people as the cortege left the family home. Being a Salvationist, Arnold was buried in true Salvation Army style. At the head of the procession was the Mountpottinger Corps flag bedecked, for the occasion, in white ribbon tied at the top in a large white bow representing the Crown of Life and flowing from this were two white ribbons of varying length, the shorter representing the life on earth and the longer that of eternal life. In the parlance of the Movement he was not to be mourned but it was a celebration of his 'Promotion to Glory.'

Following the flag were senior members of the corps, the Corps Officers (ministers), senior officers of the Ireland Division, and behind them the Band of some forty musicians, who played suitable music at a slow march pace to the heavy beat of a muffled drum. Next came the hearse which was flanked by an escort of the 88th Scout Troop which was attached to the Corps on the Mountpottinger Road and whose leaders acted as marshals.

This was followed by the family, columns of young and old uniformed Salvationists, representatives of Orangefield School, local councillors and many hundreds of mourners. Such were the crowds that a police escort lined the pavements.

At a given point on the Castlereagh Road, close to where the accident had taken place, the Band split to form a guard of honour and as they played the coffin, followed by the family, slowly processed through their ranks on its way to the newly opened cemetery at Roselawn on the Ballygowan Road."

— 5. —
BEGINNINGS AND ENDINGS

IN A SPECIAL Silver Jubilee edition of the *Orangefield Observer*, 1982, edited by Bob McKinley, John Malone was interviewed on site by four pupils from Class 3MY: Alan Kirkpatrick, Colin Shaw, Jim Hillis and Stephen Thompson. Reading the article, *The Malone Road*, is to be reminded again that it contains John's last thoughts about his time as a school Principal. He died suddenly a month later, on 14 February, 1982, from a heart attack. The *Observer* interview ended with two questions:

Do you think your time was well spent at Orangefield?

"That is for others, and history to say. Looking back, I can see that some decisions were wrong, but largely I would do it the same way."

What do you think Orangefield has achieved?

"The best achievement was, and is, setting standards for other schools — I think you need a school that sets standards. For instance, no other school in the Province has, at present, such a good Resources Centre, and no one else is as well ahead with Computers as you are at the moment. Orangefield has always been like that. I like to think that Orangefield has been — and continues to be — a kind of standard bearer for a certain quality of education."

Brian Weston recorded in the Orangefield Magazine, *33 OBHS, 1990*, that when the School opened, it was one of thirteen schools built by the Belfast Education Committee between 1948 and 1959 following the passing of the Education Act [Northern Ireland] 1947 at Stormont. Orangefield attracted pupils from across the city for a variety of reasons. For example, Ken Stanley recalls in 1957, approximately twenty "qualified" pupils, due to *"an administrative error"* in the 11+ procedure, failed to gain entry to a grammar school. They found themselves part of the School's enrolment in its first year. In the lifetime of Orangefield, this proved a unique event, and was never repeated as the numbers of "qualified" pupils soon tailed off.

Early Days

Tom Kerr [1957-1965] was a member of the first class in Orangefield to sit the Junior Grammar Certificate, GCE 'O' and 'A' Level examinations. Tom was also Head Boy, and the first pupil from the School to go on to University. Tom writes:

"It was summer 1957, and I had got the results of the 11+ exam (possibly titled 'the Qualifying' at that time).* The good news was that I had passed, which was quite an achievement as I was in the first class in our school ever to sit the exam, with only six of the class obtaining a pass.

I said school, but in actual fact 'school' was held in two local churches in the Shankill area of West Belfast: John White Congregational and St. Matthew's Church of Ireland. Classes were held in different-sized rooms with class-size of about forty pupils, and sometimes three classes in one hall separated only by curtains.

There was also bad news that summer, or so it seemed at the time, as my application for a place in Belfast Royal Academy was turned down. It later emerged that a number of children had passed the exam but had not been given places in grammar schools.

Orangefield was breaking new ground as, to this point in time, public examinations had been reserved mainly for grammar or technical school pupils. As well as Junior Grammar streams, there were also Technical streams, and after completion of the Junior Grammar and Technical Examinations, those pupils who had achieved good levels of success were enabled to become the first class at Orangefield to start a GCE 'O' Level course, the new examinations that replaced the old "Senior" as a Group Certificate. So 4T and 3G1 pupils formed 5A, and started a two-year course.*

It was the vision and determination of Mr Malone, and his staff, that created the educational opportunities for all the pupils in 5A. We sat the English-based A.E.B. 'O' Level examinations, and eventually went on to take GCE 'A' Levels. These public examinations, for the first time, opened up the possibility of University entrance for boys attending secondary intermediate schools.

The progress, at times, was not straightforward. For example, the 'Tech' streams had not taken a second Language study which was then a requirement for university entrance. One pupil, Jim Caughey, took GCE 'O' Level French in one year and received a high mark.* In an 'A' Level Chemistry Practical, we were hampered by the School's lack of some essential laboratory equipment. I remember that as part of an experiment, we were required to filter a solution, and the filter paper dissolved. We should have been using a sintered glass filter which was not available in our laboratory. There was also a problem with inferior fume cupboards that had no extraction fitted. However, in spite of these and other problems,

I still managed to obtain a Pass. I was able to complete my GCE 'A' Level exams and obtained a place at Queen's University, Belfast, to study for a B.Sc. degree in Civil Engineering.

During my time at University, I used to call in at the School to update Mr Malone on my progress. I was always well-received, and often would be invited to accompany him on his lunchtime walk around the School. It was impressive, once again, to observe his knowledge of every pupil in a school population of around one thousand pupils. Not only did John Malone know "wee Jimmy", but also that his mum had been ill, or his granny had been in hospital.

I had the honour to be captain of the 1st XI football and cricket teams. In my GCE 'A' level year, I had a serious accident when I was struck in the eye by the cricket ball resulting in an internal haemorrhage and a stay in hospital. My two eyes were bandaged for a period after the accident. The timing was unfortunate as my 'A' level exams were to start in the following two days.

I missed the exams and had to re-sit the following autumn. During the period in hospital, and before it was clear I would not be able to take the exams, the Science teachers, organised by Mr Clements, came each day and read my notes so that my exam preparation could continue. That was an example of the dedication of the staff, and was much appreciated by my family and me. Years later, when my final exam results were posted at Queen's University, I was pleasantly surprised the very next day to receive a congratulations card from Mr Clements.

With much encouragement from Mr Malone and Mr Usher, the Orangefield Old Boys' Association got started around 1966. The Association met weekly and was based mainly

1963-64.

Back Row:- W. Bleakley; R. Bunting; D. McGall.
Middle Row:- Mr. McKeown; I. Scott; J. Crone; D. McClure; H. Moneypenny; A. Redpath; N. Boyd; Mr. Clements
Front Row:- A. Reid; T. Patterson; S. Nelson; T. Kerr; D. Wylie; R. Best.

Tom Kerr, Captain, 1st XI, 1963-64

in the gymnasium. There was great support from the School staff as was evidenced by their attendance at our Annual Dinner Dance and Football dinners. Mr Usher, in particular, was very involved in the Old Boys' Association. In 1970, Mr Lannie and I met with the Northern Amateur Football League and our application was successful in gaining entry to Section 2B. The first match, in August 1970, was played at home against Sparta FC from the Lisburn area, and we managed to get a draw.

Initially, the team was made up exclusively of ex-pupils, but over the years, due to the availability of players, it has become an open club. The team now play in Section 1A, which is the second highest in the League. Some years ago, Orangefield Old Boys' FC combined with Cregagh Cricket Club to form Cregagh Sports Club. They have their own ground and club house with bar facilities. Both sports retain their original identities. In 2016, Orangefield OB FC are planning a fiftieth anniversary formal dinner which they hope will be held in Belfast City Hall."

*Eds. Notes:
In the following years, this examination class was added to by a group of fourth-formers who had followed the College of Preceptors course. Two names spring to mind: Barry Spence, who later obtained a PHD, and Frank Truesdale, who

worked in administration at the University of Ulster, Jordanstown.

Jim Caughey wrote about his time at Orangefield [1958-1962] for the Silver Jubilee edition of the *Observer* published in 1982:

"Memories are happy of that period 20 years ago when I was a pupil at Orangefield. At that time 'A' Level students were rare – we studied in a small group with texts provided, sometimes by request, by Mr. Malone. Encouragement to study was a characteristic of school life. Outside activities such as the Duke of Edinburgh Scheme also figured prominently. The teaching staff was impressive, and vitally important in generating a happy and relaxed atmosphere. Folk songs from David Hammond, and gentle Woodwork classes from 'Pop' Megarry, are just two examples of the good atmosphere. The School was "distinctive", and I believe this arose from the relationships established between staff and pupils. On leaving Orangefield I spent seven years at Queen's University, before joining the Meteorological Office, where I have been carrying out research on boundary layer and cloud physics topics. In 1981, I returned to N. Ireland to take charge of meteorology here."

Subsequently, Dr. S. J. [Jim] Caughey worked as Director of Observations at the United Kingdom Meteorology Office, and as Programme Manager for EUCOS, the European Composite Observing System (for weather), involving both satellite and ground-based equipment. Currently, Dr. Caughey is a Consultant to the World Meteorological Organisation.

The Qualifying Examination, 1947-1965, awarded scholarships to those pupils judged "suitable" for grammar school courses. The procedure comprised written examinations in English [2 papers] and Arithmetic, and a Verbal Reasoning test used for allocating border-band pupils to grammar schools.

Grades A and B, 20 to 25% of the year group, were allocated to Qualified and Border-band qualified candidates. Grades C and D, 75-80%, were given to Border-band *not-qualified* and Unqualified pupils. Fee paying places in grammar schools were available to Grades C and D only. Fee paying was abolished eventually in 1987. The Education Reform (Northern Ireland) Order 1989, ER[NI]O, gave legislative effect to the policy of *open enrolment*, or 'physical capacity' transfer, to selective schools in post-primary education across the Province.

– 6. –
MEMOIRS: SET 1

'A Proud Orangefield Boy'

The title is Sam Reilly's own from his memoir of the Boys' School 1960-67. As Sam adds "You can take the boy out of Orangefield but you can't take Orangefield out of the boy."

MY ORANGEFIELD STORY began in another school, Elmgrove Primary on the Beersbridge Road. The Principal was Mr Clemitson, a tall and very imposing figure. He summoned me and my mum and dad to a consultation in June 1960 about my future secondary schooling. It was a very stressful encounter for my parents. They were told I was not clever enough to sit the Qualifying exam and that Orangefield, a new secondary modern school led by John Malone was the place for me. With hindsight this was a fabulous decision; other secondary schools were available at this time but fate decreed that Orangefield was to be my new school.

In August 1960 my mum and I visited Gowdys School Outfitters on the Woodstock Road (still trading today) to purchase a new school uniform. This was a humorous occasion as a large number of terrified boys were dressed in blazers much too large for them in the hope that this expensive purchase would last at least three years at Orangefield.

It was also at Gowdys that I was told that Orangefield operated a House system. My House was Davidson and a red colour flash was added to my blazer pocket. The other Houses were Bryson, Hughes and Musgrave; all four were well-known businesses, now sadly no longer trading in Northern Ireland. This school involvement with local industry and commerce was a visionary idea introduced by John Malone well in advance of educational practice at the time. Orangefield also developed in the 1960s an Honours Blazer for pupils who made a great contribution to school life through sport. I have to this day got my blazer badge for Rugby and Basketball with the school motto *"Be Just and Fear Not"* emblazoned in gold thread. Cricket and Swimming were also sporting passions of mine. I remember the frantic dash of the whole class down to Templemore Avenue baths to change, swim and dress again within the time slot of a double period!

In the junior school in Social Studies, a combination of History and Geography I benefitted from the wise and wonderful teaching of the late Brian Weston. My two main Geography teachers were Duncan Scarlett and Raymond King, complementary but very different personalities. If it wasn't for Raymond King asking me to consider doing GCE 'A' Levels and also encouraging me to think about going to university, my life would have taken a completely different path. My dad had arranged for me to take the prestigious apprentice examination at Harland & Wolff's which would eventually have meant a career in shipbuilding.

My mum and dad took a brave decision to support me through University. This economic decision was made much easier because I was an only child and their meagre resources were invested in me. No one in my extended family or anyone I knew had ever gone to university, so this was a ground-breaking event. So with my parents' support and my teachers' efforts, in September 1967 I went with two other Orangefield boys – Ronnie Bunting and Jim McAllister – to Queen's University Belfast to study Mathematics, Physics and Geography.

This was an unbelievable experience illustrated by the fact that on my first day at Queen's I boarded a bus opposite Ritchies Fish and Chip shop on the Castlereagh Road. The bus left me at C&A's store in Royal Avenue – present day location of Marks & Spencer – where I had to ask a friendly bus inspector how to get to Queen's University. He guided me up Bedford Street, through Shaftesbury Square and on to University Road. There I saw for the first time the wonderful QUB Lanyon building – the Geography Department in the 1960s was based there – and this would become my home for the next five years.

My father was very proud that I attended Queen's University in Belfast and would tell his mates in Harland & Wolff of his son's great adventure, usually over a few pints of Guinness in the Farmers' Rest on the corner of Templemore Avenue and Castlereagh Street.

After graduating from QUB in 1971 with a 2.1 Honours degree in Geography, I enrolled for a post-graduate Diploma in Education and as part of my teaching practice I spent six weeks in Grosvenor High School. This was memorable because as a seventeen year old pupil at Orangefield studying Physics, I was sent somewhat self-consciously to Grosvenor High School, to the back door of the Physics Block to borrow an oscilloscope. This was needed for an "A" level practical exam and Orangefield did not have such an expensive piece of equipment of its own. It was ironic that I was now entering Grosvenor through the front door as a student teacher in a Grammar School.

My subsequent career in education was always influenced by John Malone's principles and for the need to give pupils in my care the same educational opportunities I had received in Orangefield. I joined the teaching staff of Dundonald Girls' High School in 1972 and there was re-acquainted with another Orangefield teacher, the late Alec Cunningham. Alec was the Vice Principal in Dundonald and was very good to me as a raw young teacher and as a good friend.

I loved teaching Geography and later became Head of Department and much later Principal of the School. In the 1980s, I was fortunate to be seconded for two years to Seacourt Teachers' Centre in Bangor to develop a new syllabus in Geography called Geography for the Young School Leaver [GYSL]. I also became Chief Examiner/Moderator for CSE Geography and marked GCE "A" Level for the Northern Ireland Examinations Board.

'The Big Smoke'

Alex Redpath [1961-67], a self-described "wee country boy from the sticks", remembers his Orangefield days as well as the 'Big Snow' of February 1963.

THE CULTURE AND ethos fostered at Orangefield during the 1960s did much to form my philosophy, character and attitude to so many aspects of life, while also giving me sufficient qualifications to gain entrance to Stranmillis College where I trained to become a primary school teacher. I owe so much to this fantastic East Belfast school, led by a legendary educationist and visionary, John Malone. Here was a man who combined heart and soul with a true philosophy that **all** children must have an equal opportunity for a good education as a platform for their future lives – no ifs, no buts – a comprehensive package aimed at meeting the needs of each and every child – admired throughout the city and beyond. I will be forever grateful.

Arriving into the *"Big Smoke"* in the August of 1961 – a *"wee country boy from the sticks"* outside Cullybackey – this could have been quite an intimidating experience. Yes – I was called "farmer" for a while, but this soon dissipated – probably because I was fairly athletic and that gained a bit of respect! Mind you, Bill Comyns did admit to asking me loads of questions in the class – just to hear how I pronounced the words. There wasn't much "Ulster Scots" dialect in East Belfast in the 1960s; Jack Eaton was the only teacher who understood me!

Everyone probably feels their era or year was the best, but when you hear of some of the successes there might be some credence to this claim. We were outstanding in several sports. The Under 15 soccer team, coached by Bob Ashe and captained by Walter Bleakley, just failed to win the NI Schools Cup at Solitude on Easter Monday, having previously won the Belfast Cup at Seaview. Walter, a "Bobby Moore" type player, spent the summer at Manchester United and could have stayed, but on his return he was talking only of a *"wee lad"* from Cregagh who that Autumn had made his debut – I wonder who!! Billy Rea (Linfield) was our "Denis Law" while George Lennox, Billy Hoey and Ian Scott went on to play for Crusaders and Distillery. Two boys who didn't feature too much at school but had good Irish careers were Jim Martin (prolific striker) and George Bowden (centre half).

Meantime, the Medallion team brilliantly coached by Jim Stevenson (Instonians, Ulster, Ireland) reached the semi-final of the Shield before losing to Ballymena Academy. Little wonder, when you have Gordon McConnell (QUB, CIYMS and Ulster) and Dermot (Dinky) Dalton (Malone and Ulster) supported by boys like Glen Rogers (Civil Service) and Alan (Killer) Kennedy amongst many others.

We were simply the best Irish school at basketball (coach Bob Ashe) where Walter Bleakley and Ian Scott, joined by Ian Davidson and Richard McAlpine, were all Irish Schools' players. Walter Bleakley eventually became an Irish international. Michael McBride (Great Britain Olympic Squad) came to the school from RBAI for Sixth Form studies, and made a great contribution to the school not just in

Basketball but to Orangefield's rugby team as well. In Athletics, Johnny Moreland raced to victory in the N.I. Schools' Cross Country at the Belfast Castle grounds. As I ran in 25th, I couldn't quite follow Don McBride's excitement until the great news was relayed to me. We also had many successes at the annual Schools' Athletics Championships.

Mind you, we already had those boys who preceded us to aspire to, for example Eric McMordie (Middlesborough and Northern Ireland), Roy Coyle (Sheffield Wednesday and Northern Ireland), Adrian Roberts, George Robinson and Jim Stokes (all Malone Rugby RFC). Jim was a great all-rounder, and served in the Northern Ireland Youth team as reserve keeper to Pat Jennings. Jim later became for many years a rugby correspondent for *The Belfast Telegraph*. There were also some outstanding talents who were just after my year group: in rugby Willie Duncan (Malone, Ulster, Ireland), Joe Miles (Malone, Ulster); in soccer Victor Moreland (Derby County, Northern Ireland), Barry Brown (Linfield), Billy Hoey (Distillery), Billy Murray (Linfield) and Stephen Baxter (Linfield) come readily to mind. No doubt, there are many others that I cannot recall!

All the teachers in Orangefield at this time really responded to John Malone's leadership and vision. Certain members of staff had a huge influence on my development and life; thanks so much for that. Teachers such as Raymond King, Duncan Scarlett and Jim Stevenson encouraged my pursuit of Geography/Geology and, likewise, Ken Stanley with History. Don McBride (N.I. Sprint champion on several occasions) coached me from an average middle distance runner into a reasonable sprinter, and I have no doubt this gave me a great basis for a future sporting career. The sessions we did after school were awesome – really, really tough. Rodney Usher, Bob Ashe, Jake Gallagher, and many others, really did set out to give us every opportunity in sport. I also remember Tony Fleck really making English Literature interesting. Brian Weston and Alex Cunningham for making Maths "enjoyable" and David Hammond (folk singer, BBC producer and presenter) was a real character in the building ... what a place it was.....

These are some memories of my time at Orangefield Boys' School, an insight from a pupil's perspective. It was a uniquely vibrant school for its time. Orangefield was blessed by an outstanding headmaster who enthused an incredibly committed teaching staff to go the "extra mile." They were multi-talented and really did strive to put the name Orangefield "on the map" both academically and in the areas of sport, music and drama. It was a special place for me in the 1960s, buzzing in all fields of activity, so thanks so much for that privilege.

Flashbacks

Walter Bleakley coming in and complaining about "the boy next door" who was keeping them all awake at night with his music. I wonder who – Van Morrison of course.

Duncan Scarlett easing our Oxfam coffee group out of his room (too many spillages I guess) and Brian Sloan letting us set up in his lab. By the way, this group led to the establishment of the South & East Belfast Oxfam Group which made £1000's for many years thereafter.

Playing "Shove halfpenny" in Duncan Scarlett's room at lunchtime.

The inter-class 5-aside football (at lunchtime) organised by Eric Twaddell – it was really great fun and our team won it once. Prize – a football ... brilliant!

The Geography "A" Level field study in the Mournes based at the developing Whinlands field centre in Annalong. An interesting activity organised by the teachers (Raymond King and Duncan Scarlett) was attacking us with several buckets of water from a perfect vantage point allowing no chance of a riposte!! What would John Malone have thought!

Cycling the whole way from South Belfast (3.6 miles) every day to be there for the football before school – it was brilliant. I remember 'Mousey' was the 'controller in chief.' Where is he now?

Robert Freeburn (Molière's The Miser) scoring an "own basket" in P.E. – incredulous.

Norman (or Noel) Kelly scheming his way as if "rocket-fuelled" around Bob Ashe's very difficult Obstacle Course in the gym – awesome!

Jim Holland invited Seamus Heaney into our English class – he recited many of his poems including "Mid-Term Break". I have been a reader of his poetry ever since. None of us knew the greatness of the man in our midst that day. Thanks Jim.

There was snow outside, so Don McBride decided to organise a sprint session indoors – starting at the library right along all the entire top corridor to David Craig's Art room and back (3 times). It was brutal, character-building, with a real sense of achievement at the end – he even had a stop watch on each run! I'll never forget lying on the cold, stone floor at the library totally drenched in sweat, feeling both shattered and exhilarated at the same time!

Memories

The great Sports' Days co-ordinated by Rodney Usher, firstly at Ormeau Park, and then at our own track on the hard-core at Orangefield. I have some of the old programmes – brilliant times!!

In February 1963, just before the mid-term break, there was an unforgettable blizzard. I remember sitting in Room 1 watching the snow pile up on the Castlereagh Hills and then the playground. Watching snow fall had always been fascinating to me but I had never witnessed anything quite as spectacular as this before. The flakes were massive and this accompanied by a howling gale certainly made it a freak weather event. Mr Malone came round advising those who lived a fair distance from the school to go home early. As we were going home, Rodney Usher, Bob Ashe, Jimmy Clements and Thompie Steele, who all lived on the other side of town, arrived at school around 10.15 at breaktime. I cycled home to South Belfast, but on reaching the Ormeau Bakery, I had to give up and walk as the ice clogged up the wheels. We haven't had a snowfall like that to this day and that includes March 2013 ... a day I'll never forget!!!

Alex Redpath attended Buick Memorial Primary School in Cullybackey. After leaving Orangefield, he trained as a teacher at Stranmillis College Belfast and taught in Inchmarlo, Seymour Hill and Moneyreagh. Alex served as Vice Principal of Stranmillis Primary School before his appointment as Principal of Bangor Central.

— 7. —

THE ORANGEFIELD HOUSE SYSTEM

House captains with their flags. From left—R. M'Elrea with the flag presented by Mr. E. Bryson, Loopbridge Weaving Factory; A. White (Davidson House), R. Hogg (Hughes House —named after Hughes Tool Company) and J. Welsh (Musgrave House).

School's house system has link with industry

Jack Eaton was the Davidson House Master from 1963 to 1970. He then served as Senior House Master from 1971 to 1974 ...

THE OPENING HOUSE Ceremony took place on Friday, 9th November, 1957, only two months after Orangefield opened, and some six months before the School's official opening on the 3rd May, 1958. This early link with industry underlined the value John Malone placed on the local community as an educational resource, and the fact the School never lost sight of the practical grounding secondary education provided in helping young people acquire knowledge and skills for finding a job. Remembering his time at Orangefield, Gerry Dawe writes:

"The City and Guilds and technological approach that had produced generations of skilled artisans – and underpinned the visual art of a city that only recently is beginning to recover from critical neglect – sat alongside an appreciation of the burgeoning of

administrative and managerial positions available in the civil service, manufacturing and the 'new' technologies."

The four School Houses were linked to major local industries, each of which provided financial support for a wide range of curricular and recreational activities within the School as well as offering valuable work-related experience and apprenticeship opportunities for boys. These firms were:

Bryson
(Loop Bridge Weaving Company)

Davidson
(Davidson & Co., Ltd. – Sirocco Works)

Hughes
(Hughes Tool Co. Ltd.)

Musgrave
(Musgrave & Co. Ltd)

In this way, John Malone, a practical innovator, took a traditional idea, the House system of the English Independent public and grammar school systems, and adapted it to engage more meaningfully with the lives of boys attending a secondary intermediate school close to the industrial heartland of 1950s' East Belfast.

Each School House had a House Master whose role was to encourage the boys to participate in a wide range of in-school activities.

Trees were planted and house flags presented yesterday to Orangefield Boys' Secondary School, by representatives of local industrial firms. Mr. E. D. MaGuire planting a tree on behalf of Messrs. Davidson and Co. (Sirocco Works), of which he is chairman. Also in the picture are, Mr. J. Malone, M.A. (headmaster); Mr. J. R. Holland (house master) and Mr. R. C. Brown, who also represented Sirocco Works.

Participation could range from team membership to organisation behind the scenes as well as team support. The House Master was ably supported by a House Captain, whose drive and enthusiasm was a key factor in promoting House loyalty and encouraging a sense of responsibility. The overall supervision and co-ordination of House activities were the responsibility of a Senior House Master, who worked closely with individual House Masters as well as the staff of the Physical Education Department.

Orangefield's first Senior House Master was Brian Weston who, after a short period, was followed by Jim Holland. House Masters who served in these first years were Sam Campbell **(B)**, Bill Comyns **(D)**, Gerry McClelland **(H)**, Ronnie McMaster **(M)**, Jim Stevenson **(B)**, Ken Stanley **(H)**, and Jack Eaton **(D)**. During the mid to late 1960s, the House Masters were Bert Caldwell **(B)**, Ted McClelland **(B)**, Alex Cunningham **(D)**, Ronnie McCracken **(H)**, and Eric Twaddell **(M)**.

Musgrave House **(M)** became McNeill House **(M/McN)** in 1970, and in 1981 became Scott House **(M/S)**, and in 1984 Stewart House **(M/S)**. By the late 1980s, Davidson House had become Howden – Sirocco **(D/HS)**.

From the early seventies, the House Masters were Robert Clarke **(B)**, David McCullough **(D)**, James Morrow **(H)**, Tony Sherlock **(M)**, and Stead Black **(M/McN)**. After 1974, they were succeeded by Bob McKinley **(B)**, Gordon Topping **(D)**, Philip Hewitt **(H)**, and Jeff Turkington **(M/McN)**. House Masters who served during the 1980s, were Drew McFall **(B)**, John McLaughlin **(D)**, Jim Chambers **(H)**, Norman Johnston **(M/S)**, Maurice Johnston **(B)**, Albert Patterson **(H)**, Henry Blakley **(M/S)**, and Steven McAteer **(D/HS)**.

Senior House Masters who followed on from Jim Holland were Jack Eaton, Alec Cunningham, Stead Black, Jeff Turkington and Philip Hewitt. Looking back over half a century, Jim Holland remembers finding himself responsible for organising evening House Parties at the School. At that time, he was engaged in a constant search for pupils with 'talent' to put on stage to entertain the boys before they let off steam by making as much noise as possible! Jim recalls:

"One boy in particular was a great success: he was John Toan, a diminutive, four-foot tall second former who commanded total silence as he sang a popular Jim Reeves song of the day: "Put your sweet lips / A little closer to the phone / Let's pretend that we're together all alone / I'll tell the man to turn the jukebox way down low / And you can tell your friend there with you he'll have to go." In applause, John brought the house down. [John was called 'semi-tone', because he was smaller than his brother Harry].

Another unforgettable performer, Robert Haskins, played a golden trumpet. He was as good a record-maker as Eddie Calvert, and his rendition of "Oh Mein Papa" was brilliant. Even now with the benefit of YouTube, I can still hear the sound of Robert's magnificent trumpet-playing as it resonated around the Assembly Hall. Robert joined the RUC Police Band.

But there was one incident I will never forget. Many pupils got wind of the fact that I was in search of performers for the House parties, and John Rodgers came up to me and told me he had a friend who had a great band. I asked him to see if he would play at the party on Thursday night. He returned later to say he would, but how much would we pay him? I had no budget to pay any pupils and had to decline the offer. To regret something at the time is bad enough without suffering it again in retrospect. But that boy with the band was Ivan [Van] Morrison later to become a global superstar. Do I feel a fool?"

However, most inter-House activities were team sports providing valuable opportunities for the boys, their House Masters and the Physical Education staff to work together in support of their teams. Jim recalls, *"Over on the pitches between us and Grosvenor High School, at Laburnum, on sunny days with John Malone there, younger staff like myself would shout, yell directions, or encouragement to our House teams while we tried vicariously to be part of the battle taking place before us. How we didn't get our death of cold standing in shirt sleeves in a fresh breeze is amazing."*

The annual Swimming Galas and Sports Days were major events organised by the P.E. staff on an inter-House basis. The Orangefield House Firms presented the School with a range of silver trophies.

The McNEILL Cup for Cross-country was presented in 1970 after the company replaced Musgrave and Co. which having closed in 1963, had left the School House unaffiliated to any local firm. However, their House Captain in 1970 was Bob Nesbitt, who warmly welcomed the McNeill group, assuring the company that they were affiliating with *"probably the most successful House in the School."*

In 1981, McNeill House had been replaced by Scott House (Hugh J Scott Ltd, Ravenhill Road, later to become Thrige-Scott Ltd), before finally becoming Stewart House (Stewarts Supermarket).

From Hughes engineering to Stewarts supermarket, tells its own story of radical change in employment opportunities for boys in East Belfast over the lifetime of Orangefield School.

Other House trophies, not directly associated with local firms, included the McLEAN Cup for Swimming. This award was designed and crafted in memory of Robert (Bob) McLean who died in late December, 1963. Bob taught Woodwork and was also a House Master who had a particular interest in swimming.

The Bryson Cup for Basketball; The Davidson Cup for Cricket; The Hughes Cup for Rugby; The Musgrave Cup for Athletics

Then, of course, there was the ARNOLD CLARKE CUP awarded annually to the House gaining the highest points score for House activities throughout the year.

Arnold Clarke Cup

Former boys and staff will remember the various House trophies displayed in a large, glass-fronted case in the Entrance Hall with the Arnold Clarke Cup having pride of place and adorned with the Colours of the winning House. Indeed this trophy, strongly contested and cherished, came to represent all aspects of House membership.

Many boys will remember the wooden display board where the House points were updated regularly to show the current score for each House. This valuable information-display was initiated by Jeff Turkington during his time as Senior House Master in the late 1970s.

In the Orangefield archive, there is a hard-backed Science laboratory notebook dating from 1958 with green-coloured graph paper opposite a page with a margin and 24 blue-lined spaces. On the blue/grey front cover is printed *OBSS School Records Athletics, Swimming*. Here, long before the computer age, can be found meticulous, hand-printed annual records of 28 Sports Days held from 1958 to 1985, and 26 Swimming Galas dating from 1959 to 1984.

In this *OBSS Records* book, three members of staff, Jim Parker, Rodney Usher and Billy Lawther, year after year recorded the names of competitors, the different events set in various age groups, times achieved by individuals, the number of records broken, and the overall points tally achieved by individual Houses.

Ormeau Park was an early venue for Sports Day and a contemporary newspaper report records the first Athletics *meet* held there being 'baptised' in a rain-storm. The Mary Peters Track [1976-1978] and the Laburnum pitches were also venues for the annual event. The first Sports Day, held in 1958, records Davidson as the Inter-House champions. The *28th Annual Sports Day*, held in 1985 and documented on the following page, details Hughes House as the victorious winners with 499 points, followed by Bryson (420 points), Stewart (382 points) and Davidson (371 points). These yearly Inter-House Athletics competitions were won 10 times by Musgrave/Stewart, 9 times by Davidson, 7 times by Hughes, and 2 times by Bryson. It is worthy of note that Musgrave had a run of 7 successive wins from 1964 to 1970.

The first Swimming Gala in 1958 was held in Templemore Avenue Baths and was won by Davidson. The 30th Swimming Gala, held in 1988 at the Robinson Centre, records Stewart as Inter-House champions with 87 points followed by Howden Sirocco (formerly Davidson House) with 77 points, Hughes 74 points and Bryson 72 points.

28th Annual Sports Day, 1985

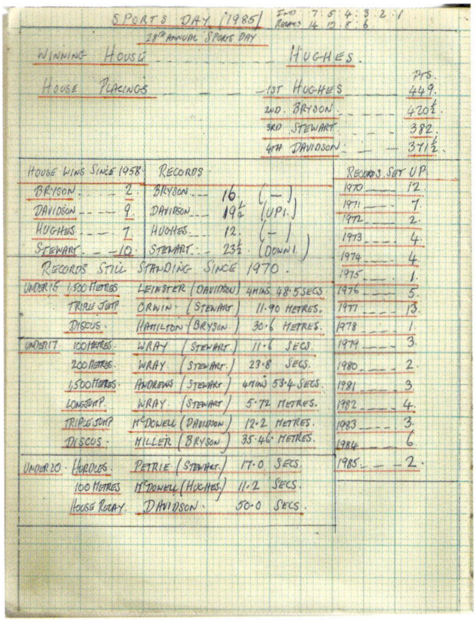

SPORTS DAY (1985) IND 7 : 5 : 4 : 3 : 2 : 1
RELAYS 14 : 10 : 8 : 6

28TH ANNUAL SPORTS DAY

WINNING HOUSE – – – – – – HUGHES.

HOUSE PLACINGS – – – – 1ST HUGHES – – 449. (PTS.)
2ND. BRYSON – – – – 420½.
3RD STEWART – – – 382.
4TH DAVIDSON – – – 371½.

HOUSE WINS SINCE 1958		RECORDS			RECORDS SET UP	
BRYSON	2.	BRYSON	16.	(—)	1970	12.
DAVIDSON	9.	DAVIDSON	19½	(UP 1.)	1971	7.
HUGHES	7.	HUGHES	12.	(—)	1972	2.
STEWART	10.	STEWART	23½.	(DOWN 1.)	1973	4.
					1974	4.

RECORDS STILL STANDING SINCE 1970.

UNDER 15	1,500 METRES	LEINSTER (DAVIDSON)	4MINS 48·5 SECS.	1975	1.
	TRIPLE JUMP	ORWIN (STEWART)	11·90 METRES.	1976	5.
	DISCUS.	HAMILTON (BRYSON)	30·6 METRES.	1977	13.
UNDER 17	100 METRES.	WRAY (STEWART.)	11·6 SECS.	1978	1.
	200 METRES.	WRAY (STEWART.)	23·8 SECS.	1979	3.
	1,500 METRES.	ANDREWS (STEWART)	4MINS 53·4 SECS.	1980	2.
	LONG JUMP.	WRAY (STEWART)	5·72 METRES.	1981	3.
	TRIPLE JUMP	McDOWELL (DAVIDSON)	12·2 METRES.	1982	4.
	DISCUS.	MILLER (BRYSON)	35·46 METRES.	1983	3.
UNDER 20.	HURDLES.	PETRIE (STEWART.)	17·0 SECS.	1984	6.
	100 METRES	McDOWELL (HUGHES)	11·2 SECS.	1985	2.
	HOUSE RELAY.	DAVIDSON.	50·0 SECS.		

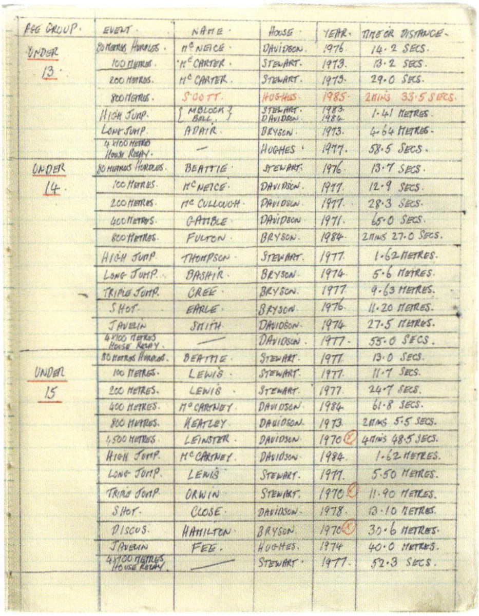

AGE GROUP.	EVENT.	NAME.	HOUSE.	YEAR.	TIME OR DISTANCE.
UNDER 13.	80 METRES HURDLES.	McNEICE.	DAVIDSON.	1976.	14·2 SECS.
	100 METRES.	McCARTER.	STEWART.	1973.	13·2 SECS.
	200 METRES.	McCARTER.	STEWART.	1973.	29·0 SECS.
	800 METRES.	SCOTT.	HUGHES.	1985.	2MINS 33·5 SECS.
	HIGH JUMP.	{ MBLOCK / BELL. }	STEWART. / DAVIDSON.	1983. / 1984.	1·41 METRES.
	LONG JUMP.	ADAIR.	BRYSON.	1973.	4·64 METRES.
	4 x 100 METRES HOUSE RELAY.	—	HUGHES.	1977.	58·5 SECS.
UNDER 14.	80 METRES HURDLES.	BEATTIE.	STEWART.	1976.	13·7 SECS.
	100 METRES.	McNEICE.	DAVIDSON.	1977.	12·9 SECS.
	200 METRES.	McCULLOUGH.	DAVIDSON.	1977.	28·3 SECS.
	400 METRES.	GAMBLE.	DAVIDSON	1971.	65·0 SECS.
	800 METRES.	FULTON.	BRYSON.	1984.	2MINS 27·0 SECS.
	HIGH JUMP.	THOMPSON.	STEWART.	1977.	1·62 METRES.
	LONG JUMP.	BASHIR.	BRYSON.	1974.	5·6 METRES.
	TRIPLE JUMP.	CREE.	BRYSON.	1977.	9·63 METRES.
	SHOT.	EARLE.	BRYSON.	1976.	11·20 METRES.
	JAVELIN	SMITH.	DAVIDSON.	1974.	27·5 METRES.
	4 x 100 METRES HOUSE RELAY.	—	DAVIDSON.	1977.	55·0 SECS.
UNDER 15	80 METRES HURDLES.	BEATTIE.	STEWART.	1977.	13·0 SECS.
	100 METRES.	LEWIS.	STEWART.	1977.	11·7 SECS.
	200 METRES.	LEWIS.	STEWART.	1977.	24·7 SECS.
	400 METRES.	McCARTNEY.	DAVIDSON.	1984.	61·8 SECS.
	800 METRES.	KEATLEY.	DAVIDSON.	1973.	2MINS 5·5 SECS.
	1,500 METRES.	LEINSTER.	DAVIDSON.	1970 (x)	4MINS 48·5 SECS.
	HIGH JUMP.	McCARTNEY.	DAVIDSON.	1984.	1·62 METRES.
	LONG JUMP.	LEWIS.	STEWART.	1977.	5·50 METRES.
	TRIPLE JUMP.	ORWIN	STEWART.	1970 (x)	11·90 METRES.
	SHOT.	CLOSE.	DAVIDSON.	1978.	13·10 METRES.
	DISCUS.	HAMILTON.	BRYSON.	1970 (x)	30·6 METRES.
	JAVELIN	FEE.	HUGHES.	1974.	40·0 METRES.
	4 x 100 METRES HOUSE RELAY.	—	STEWART.	1977.	52·3 SECS.

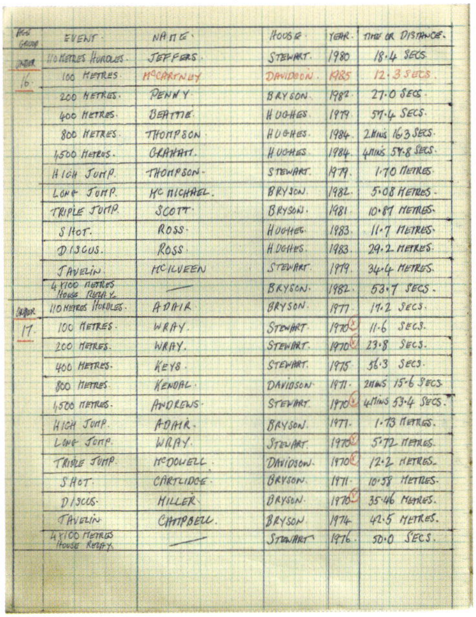

AGE GROUP	EVENT.	NAME.	HOUSE.	YEAR.	TIME OR DISTANCE.
UNDER 16.	110 METRES HURDLES.	JEFFERS.	STEWART.	1980	18·4 SECS.
	100 METRES.	McCARTNEY	DAVIDSON.	1985	12·3 SECS.
	200 METRES.	PENNY.	BRYSON.	1982.	27·0 SECS.
	400 METRES.	BEATTIE.	HUGHES.	1979.	57·4 SECS.
	800 METRES.	THOMPSON.	HUGHES.	1984.	2MINS 16·3 SECS.
	1,500 METRES.	GRAHAM.	HUGHES.	1984.	4MINS 57·8 SECS.
	HIGH JUMP.	THOMPSON.	STEWART.	1979.	1·70 METRES.
	LONG JUMP.	McMICHAEL.	BRYSON.	1982.	5·08 METRES.
	TRIPLE JUMP.	SCOTT.	BRYSON.	1981.	10·87 METRES.
	SHOT.	ROSS.	HUGHES.	1983.	11·7 METRES.
	DISCUS.	ROSS.	HUGHES.	1983.	29·2 METRES.
	JAVELIN.	McILVEEN	STEWART.	1979.	34·4 METRES.
	4 x 100 METRES HOUSE RELAY.	—	BRYSON.	1982.	53·7 SECS.
UNDER 17.	110 METRES HURDLES.	ADAIR.	BRYSON.	1977.	17·2 SECS.
	100 METRES.	WRAY.	STEWART.	1970 (x)	11·6 SECS.
	200 METRES.	WRAY.	STEWART.	1970 (x)	23·8 SECS.
	400 METRES.	KEYS.	STEWART.	1975	56·3 SECS.
	800 METRES.	KENDAL.	DAVIDSON.	1971.	2MINS 15·6 SECS.
	1,500 METRES.	ANDREWS.	STEWART.	1970 (x)	4MINS 53·4 SECS.
	HIGH JUMP.	ADAIR.	BRYSON.	1977.	1·73 METRES.
	LONG JUMP.	WRAY.	STEWART.	1970 (x)	5·72 METRES.
	TRIPLE JUMP.	McDOWELL.	DAVIDSON.	1970 (x)	12·2 METRES.
	SHOT.	CARTLIDGE.	BRYSON.	1971.	10·58 METRES.
	DISCUS.	MILLER.	BRYSON.	1970 (x)	35·46 METRES.
	JAVELIN	CAMPBELL.	BRYSON.	1974.	42·5 METRES.
	4 x 100 METRES HOUSE RELAY.	—	STEWART	1976.	50·0 SECS.

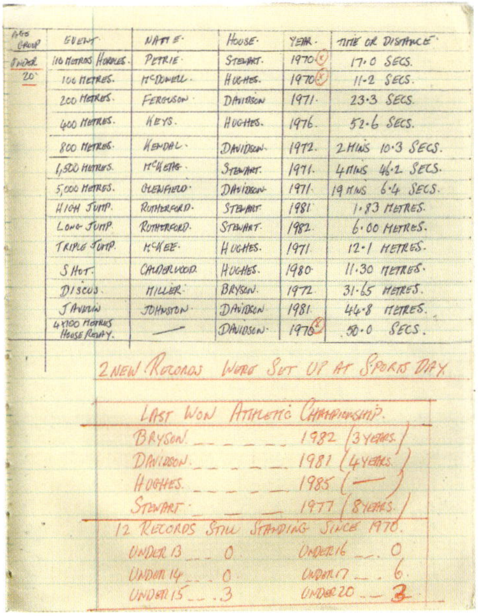

AGE GROUP	EVENT.	NAME.	HOUSE.	YEAR.	TIME OR DISTANCE.
UNDER 20.	110 METRES HURDLES.	PETRIE.	STEWART.	1970 (x)	17·0 SECS.
	100 METRES.	McDOWELL.	HUGHES.	1970 (x)	11·2 SECS.
	200 METRES.	FERGUSON.	DAVIDSON	1971.	23·3 SECS.
	400 METRES.	KEYS.	HUGHES.	1976.	52·6 SECS.
	800 METRES.	KENDAL.	DAVIDSON.	1972.	2MINS 10·3 SECS.
	1,500 METRES.	McKEAG.	STEWART.	1971.	4MINS 46·2 SECS.
	5,000 METRES.	GLENFIELD.	DAVIDSON.	1971.	19MINS 6·4 SECS.
	HIGH JUMP.	RUTHERFORD.	STEWART.	1981.	1·83 METRES.
	LONG JUMP.	RUTHERFORD.	STEWART.	1982.	6·00 METRES.
	TRIPLE JUMP.	McKEE.	HUGHES.	1971.	12·1 METRES.
	SHOT.	CALDERWOOD.	HUGHES.	1980.	11·30 METRES.
	DISCUS.	MILLER.	BRYSON.	1972.	31·65 METRES.
	JAVELIN	JOHNSTON.	DAVIDSON	1981.	44·8 METRES.
	4 x 100 METRES HOUSE RELAY.	—	DAVIDSON.	1970 (x)	50·0 SECS.

2 NEW RECORDS WERE SET UP AT SPORTS DAY.

LAST WON ATHLETIC CHAMPIONSHIP.

BRYSON	1982	(3 YEARS.)
DAVIDSON	1981	(4 YEARS.)
HUGHES	1985	(—)
STEWART	1977	(8 YEARS.)

12 RECORDS STILL STANDING SINCE 1970.

UNDER 13	0.	UNDER 16	0.
UNDER 14	0.	UNDER 17	6.
UNDER 15	3.	UNDER 20	3.

'Neat Diving' as well as diving for tin plates, which were thrown into the pool by Mr Usher, proved very popular events at the Gala. Records show that the Inter-House Swimming Gala was won 11 times by Hughes, 9 times by Musgrave/McNeill/Stewart, 7 times by Davidson and 3 times by Bryson.

McLean Cup for Swimming

There was considerable Inter-House rivalry in other major sports, especially during the 1960s and 1970s. In Rugby, Musgrave obtained four wins (1964-67), followed by a draw with Davidson (1968). Davidson House then won three times (1969-71). The following year (1972), Bryson and Hughes decided to end this Musgrave/Davidson dominance and secured a rare four-way tie in Inter-House Rugby.

During these years, the Inter-House Basketball results showed a fairly even distribution of wins, and indeed the number of shared results indicates just how competitive Basketball had been. The most successful House in Cricket was Hughes, while additional activities in Chess, Golf, Table-Tennis, Badminton, Cross-country and Ten-Pin Bowling provided further competitive opportunities for boys whose individual interests lay outside team games.

It is interesting to note in 1958, the first year of Inter-House competition, as well as in 1990 Davidson House (by then called Howden Sirocco), won the Arnold Clarke Cup. In the last

24th Annual Swimming Gala, 1982

year of the Boys' School, Hughes House were runners-up with Bryson third and Stewart placed fourth. A school magazine titled **OBS – 33,** published in 1990 produced by Eileen Gardner, Yvonne McKelvey and Stephen McAteer, included the following reports of the Inter-House year to mark the end of an era.

Bryson House – House Master – Mr M. [Maurice] Johnston

The year began well with Bryson winning the football section of House competition, but we were narrowly defeated in table-tennis and chess and came runners-up. The swimming gala was our worst event because of poor attendance on the day and commitments of others to the school play, hence our position, fourth. Bryson golfers proved successful again, and just managed to clinch the winning position over Howden.

With the cricket and athletics still to play for, the year's activities are far from over. The second form cricket team has won both their games and the fourth form team is showing potential. Hopefully, we will have victory here as well.

I would like to take this opportunity to thank Mr. Chambers for all his hard work in organising the events, the other House Masters and the P.E. staff.

Hughes House – House Master – Mr A. [Albert] Patterson

In this, the final year of the school as we know it, of the 8 events organised thus far, Hughes House has won four of the events, the cross-country, chess, table-tennis and athletics.

The thing that has pleased me most as House Master this year, is the fact that so many boys have taken part in a least one event, for example every boy in third year, and all but three boys in second year.

In the cross country event, 1st places were obtained in 1st, 2nd, 3rd and 4th years which must be something of a record, but on the other hand, the swimming gala was less successful because some boys did not turn up to compete as promised and valuable points were lost.

Stewart House – House Master – Mr H. [Henry] Blakley

It's been a very mixed year so far for Stewart House in general. As yet, the House has still to win an event, but hopefully this will be rectified during Sports' Day.

The two second places in Badminton and Ten-Pin Bowling have been the best results to date with third place in swimming.

As yet, the House doesn't appear to have any aspiring Ronan Raffertys as golf proved our weakest activity! Individually there have been some good performances from A. Stevenson and R. Lee in swimming, while Campbell, McAllister, Simons and McMullan all did well in their respective years in the cross-country.

Perhaps, with a little more luck in one or two events, the overall position of the House would be better but if most boys are making the effort to participate, little more can be asked.

Howden/Sirocco – House Master – Mr S. [Stephen] McAteer

This has been another successful year. We have come first in Badminton, Ten-Pin Bowling and Swimming, second in Soccer, Cross-Country, Golf and Athletics, and third in two other events.

Our success has been due to the dedication and hard work of many boys with the following being especially worthy of mention: Keith Walker first in Cross Country, two firsts in the

Swimming Gala and a first in Athletics. Other first-place swimmers were Alan Foster, Philip Gray, Samuel McMurray, and Scott Campbell. Bobby McMaster won the Cross-Country event while Richard Hagan had first places in Swimming and Athletics. Richard Beckwith won his swimming event for the third year in a row.

Fourth Form was particularly strong in swimming with Dak Lun Lam, Robert Patton, Mark Tollerton, Neil Whiteside all winning events.

I would like to commend Colin Gallagher, Nigel McQuillan, Don McCann, Neville McCormick, and Marty Wright for their commitment to the House over the last five years.

Richard Beckwith won the award for the best overall junior, with Marty Wright best overall senior. Colin Gallagher received the Company Award.

McNeill Cup for Cross Country.

– 8. –
MEMOIRS: SET 2

A Good Deed and a Handshake

David Lynas, who attended Elmgrove, came to Orangefield Boys' Secondary School the day it opened in September 1957. He was placed in the second form year group and Mr Stanley was his form teacher. While a member of Musgrave House, David did not display an aptitude for team games. He recalls being asked to write 100 lines and a memorable handshake ...

IT WAS A cold, frosty December morning, 1958, as I left Woodlee Street on my two-mile walk to school. I made my way along Abetta Parade on to the path that runs alongside the Knock river which flows all the way through Orangefield plantation. At that time, a new foot bridge was being built across the river connecting Dunraven Avenue to Dixon Park playing fields.

As I passed, I heard a call, "Help!" and discovered the bank of the river had collapsed. A workman lay underneath the partly-built bridge, buried up to his chest in mud. His workmate asked me to call an ambulance. In those days, there were not many phones around. Then I remembered that the TipTop bakery was only a few hundred yards away, so off I went, as fast as I could. Knowing the ambulance was on its way, I continued my journey to school.

Unfortunately, I was now late and was apprehended by two Prefects who put me on detention. At 3.30pm I reported to the detention class and tried to explain to the teacher my ordeal that morning but was told to sit down and write one hundred lines *I must not be late for school.*

It may have been a small price to pay for my good deed, but I felt in my heart I may have helped save a man's life that day.

Duke of Edinburgh Award

In September 1959, all pupils in fourth year were invited to participate in the newly established Duke of Edinburgh Award scheme. After many months of different activities, including a 30-mile walking expedition, spending two nights in the open under canvas, and performing a public service such as helping blind or deaf people, thirty boys attained the Silver Award.

In June 1960, Sir John Hunt, the First Director of the Duke of Edinburgh Award Scheme, was welcomed to the school to present the successful pupils with their Awards. Sir John was a tall, handsome man but at the time looked a little jaded as he had just returned from another heroic mountain expedition.

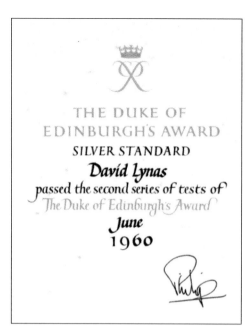

Before the ceremony, all the boys were told when it came to the handshake, "*Just hold out your hand and Sir John will shake your hand.*" His hands still had frostbite scars from past ordeals on Mount Everest.

Mr Malone was extremely proud of the successful pupils and the teachers who gave their time and support to the Duke of Edinburgh Award.

David Hammond, John Malone and Sir John Hunt: David Lynas, suited, in the front row.

Eds. Note: *On leaving school at the end of his fourth form year, David Lynas went to work for S.D. Bell in their Ann Street shop where he learnt about aspects of the grocery trade, in particular tea-blending and bacon-curing. From S.D. Bell's, David moved to a Finance Company, and for the past thirty-one years has managed his own Financial Services firm.*

Memories are made of this …

Billy McKee [1964-1971] writes
"We belonged to Orangefield, but more importantly it also, very much, belonged to us."

HAVING FAILED the 11+, and being informed by my primary school headmaster that I had achieved 100% in Mathematics but murdered the English, I was told *'When you go to Orangefield, Mr Malone will look after you."* How true this proved to be of my secondary schooling under JMM's direction, and of course, its many magnificent, dedicated and caring teachers who had a firm belief in individuals.

I have often heard many people in education stating that John Malone was too far ahead of his time, but I would much prefer to say what a great pity it was that too many were too far behind him. Considering many of his proposed educational initiatives were pursued in later years, and still are, must be interpreted as a vindication of his philosophy. Being known by name by JMM, was an exciting and reassuring part of school life for an eleven year old; I can recall discussions among contemporaries as to just how he managed to know everyone by name, and concluded how marvellous he was to be able to do so.

As pupils, I think our success and of course that of the School as a whole, was in no small way created by the staff who gently invited us into their various rooms of learning, believed in us, and endlessly nurtured us. As an exemplification of this, I vividly recall a Maths teacher, Ronnie McCracken, keeping several of us behind one day to declare his intention to see us enter university to study Mathematics and realise our potential in this field. He left for fresh fields the following year but was replaced by equally capable teachers. His aspirations for us did materialise.

As a pupil, I always felt that I belonged to the School, but on reflection and more importantly, I feel subconsciously that we felt the School belonged to us and our contributions were very much an integral part of it. Just one humorous case in point! Under the guidance of science teacher Frank Loan, assisted by Charlie Stewart the lab technician, our form class set up a Tea/Coffee Bar in Lab 1 which operated at break and lunch times. This was my first financial loan, and it was from one Thompson Steele who provided a sum of £50 (I think this is correct) to allow the purchase of goods such as biscuits etc from the Speedway Wholesale on the Newtownards Road.

The success of the venture saw Frank Loan and two of us make weekly visits to the wholesale outlet to fill his car with goodies and the empire grew! We were given free access to a crate of "dumpy bottles" (1/3 pint) on a daily basis and boys in the class were given two packets of Mary Baker bun mix to have their mums (more likely in those days) create the offerings which sold very readily; boys carrying tins of buns to school would have been more in keeping with Home Economics and the Girls' School! Alas, resurrection of the School Tuck-Shop after two years of trading laid our enterprise to rest!

Again, the largely pupil-directed, Inter-Class 5-a-side football competitions held in the playgrounds at lunchtime each day, provided a great source of friendly banter, fun and entertainment. The fixture lists for the week ahead were immediately scanned when posted for two main reasons, the teams involved, and the referees. Noel Clingan, who went on to be an Irish League referee, always attracted a large crowd, and this ensured a huge amount of banter because of his officious approach. Noel, coupled with certain classes, generated so much entertainment, both on the pitches and sidelines, you could, I suspect, have charged a nominal spectator fee.

Boys climbing downspouts to retrieve the ball from the rooftop was not uncommon and, on occasions, there was a race between two on the downspouts cheered on by the spectators. This was all well and good until a member of staff appeared or, worse still, JMM ("the Boot"). Attempts were made to ensure the ascent went undetected and on such occasions the return journey was via the trap door beside Room 13 on the top floor! Of course, some unfortunate individuals did get caught, but on a positive note, I can recall positive ascents and no one suffering an injury.

Extra-Curricular Activities

Extra-curricular activities played a major role in the life of the school, and with personal experience now behind me, I now fully recognise and appreciate the commitment provided by staff. I know for a fact, having met many staff in other schools on the games field, that Orangefield's commitment to extra-curricular work was exemplary and to be aspired to. There was always an activity there for all and sundry to engage with, ranging from the main individual and team sports to the Chess and Italic Handwriting Clubs. With experience of such work, it is now fully appreciated why Friday afternoon was by-and-large free of sports, which in my case, as I am sure it was for others, carried into university and beyond.

Many pupils were very privileged indeed to have had such committed teachers who gave so generously of their time and talent, often continuing to map your progress after leaving. One stand-out activity was in 1st Form, when Thursday afternoon saw Round-the-School Relay, organised by Don McBride and company, when each class had to supply at least one team – many supplied two competitive groups – of six boys and the winning team was presented with Don's International Running Vests (at least, this was what we were told) to run in the following week. This was a very much cherished reward.

Thus I had after school sport available, Monday to Thursday as well as on Saturday morning, and this most certainly played a major role in my all-round development. Success here definitely transferred into the classroom. Saturday mornings for away games within the city boundary entailed meeting at the City Hall while more rural away games were serviced by the frequent arrival of buses at the School. On these occasions, Orangefield seemed more like a small bus station often with enquiries among boys as to where they were going!

In my own case, I managed to access Swimming, Rugby, Cricket, Athletics and Basketball, with the latter allowing me to travel across Great Britain and the Republic of Ireland when playing for Ulster and Irish Schools' Teams (along with others from Orangefield) and subsequently to continental Europe while attending Queen's University in Belfast. On one occasion, three of us waited in Dublin's O'Connell Street until around 10.00 pm on a Saturday evening until a set of parents picked us up. We had arrived back in Dublin from Wales around 6.00 pm, after being sprayed with disinfectant in Rosslare because of the outbreak of Foot and Mouth Disease on the mainland and planted ourselves into a not-too-expensive eatery to pass the time away. These opportunities, that would simply not be permitted today, allowed us to accept responsibility for our own well-being, grow up and mature. We arrived home safely!

On another occasion, with Brian McKeown, a fellow peer, I was dropped from the U13 Cricket XI. This followed an away match at Regent House when the team had gathered in The Square, in Newtownards, to await the bus. We had been victorious and asked our coach Henry Sinnerton if we could visit Cafolla's to gather some sweets for the journey home which in those days seemed a rather long journey. This was denied us but he later relented of his own accord and gave us permission to go on a 2 x 2 release.

Brian and I were the last in the queue and emerged from the shop just in time to see the bus depart with other team members and Henry peering in disbelief from the rear window; goodness knows how we appeared to them. We chased the bus but it had a much greater pace and Henry decided to alight the bus and await arrival of the next bus some 30 minutes or so later. He admonished us rather sternly, or so we thought, and duly administered a one-match ban, but if my recall is accurate, this match was lost without us!

Whinlands

The purchase of Whinlands was an immense event for pupils and I can recall very clearly the focal point it provided for the school as a whole at that time and in subsequent years. There follow some of my recollections of those days…

The production of household furniture in the Heavy Craft Department, and the construction of a prefabricated 'Audio Visual Aids' building in the school quadrangle undertaken as part of classroom work, after school hours and during half-term breaks. A real team effort pervaded the whole project, and of course many pupils had the privilege of using the final products. In today's terms, it may have been equivalent to 'Sweat Shop' conditions, but it certainly never felt like it!

Then there was the purchase of the *Bedford* School Minibus with its wooden, bench-type seats and the journeys down to Whinlands with stop-offs for tuck supplies at Brennan's on the roadside just outside Ballynahinch.

My first visit to Whinlands was in February 1966 with Moore Sinnerton and Duncan Scarlett and wives. It was during a very prolonged cold spell and Slieve Bignian had huge icicles overhanging. In those days Health and Safety was an unknown entity and we all piled on to a frozen Blue Lough to throw large stones/small boulders from head height in an attempt to crack the ice.

Thankfully, the ice held firm and we progressed with our walk when one of the boys – David 'Shorty' Sayers if my memory is correct – strayed off the well-trodden path to find himself waist-high in a piece of bog. This extracted a response *"Well son, we can head back which will take about an hour or we can head on which will take about an hour"*, and we continued on…

Travelling as a 6th former with a junior class, I can recall a particular and very wet weekend when one rather unfit individual approached the last one hundred feet of a summit on his hands and knees whilst being urged to go for it by class mates and staff alike. He made it!

Every trip to Whinlands had its own tale to tell, and in the very early days, along with washing in cold water in the wooden shed, I can recall a group of us being asked if we believed in ghosts. We vehemently scoffed at the whole idea, and after being offered £1 if we would run around the surrounding graveyard of a church, situated off the main road through Annalong one dark evening, the rather jerky movement of the tower clock minute hand was brought to our attention causing us to reassess the situation. No one attempted the run!

Before Whinlands, Ballagh Cottage without any running water, gas or electricity was also a treat to be savoured! My first visit, probably in 3rd Form, was in the company of Frank Loan and Charlie Stewart, lab technician, who appeared to be well-versed in the art of Ghost Stories. On this occasion Charlie spoke of the next-door neighbour and his black and white sheep dog who had died some years previous but often returned to visit the area.

On exiting the cottage, in the darkness of the evening prior to bedding down for the night, what should be outside the door but a black and white sheep dog. A group of very brave young men made an instant re-entrance and did not emerge until Saturday morning to avail of the open air garden latrine facilities when the dog once again appeared to greet us from the adjacent property.

Flashbacks

In 1st Form (year 8) I was taught science by Jimmy Morrow when he gently managed to make suggestions as to how I might make improvements to my write-ups of experiments, some of which remain with me today and also throughout my own teaching career.

Mr McMaster, Maths teacher, who always had every window in his room open, sat with his anorak on, while boys had to remove their blazers. Apparently, this was healthy and kept the boys awake. It also necessitated a shoulder to be put to the door in order to gain access on very windy days.

"Wild Bill" Comyns, who often climbed on to a stool and spoke to fictional characters in the adjoining store through the heating ventilator grill.

'Pop' Megarry with his innate woodworking skills plus French Polishing in which everyone strived for perfection.

Bert Caldwell, who stood as a NI Labour Party candidate for Bloomfield, and in the process was paraded around the streets on the back of an open lorry to deliver his manifesto through a loudspeaker. He had many fans urging him on but, alas, too young to vote for him.

Dessie Taylor, who always managed to maintain a high degree of classroom order via his quietly spoken comment or a simple disparaging look, and of course, his steely determination never to be defeated by a mathematics problem.

Jimmy Morrow ran a Chemistry Club after school. On one occasion, he managed to drop a winchester of concentrated sodium hydroxide and immediately leapt into the air in an attempt to avoid it but unfortunately landed in the outflow of the rather greasy contents, slipped in it and fell flat onto it. Unfortunately, his trousers began to disintegrate almost instantly much to the amusement of those present.

On another occasion, Jimmy was attempting to form hydrochloric acid by reacting hydrogen and chlorine gas on the lab bench in full sunlight, which I think is a catalyst for the process. The resulting explosion saw his shirt and abdomen lacerated by shards of glass from the confining glass flask. He proceeded to pick the glass out of his body and lamented his ruined shirt.

Probably around 1970, there was a group of us completed a midnight hike around Scrabo

Tower and the surrounding area. Accompanying staff were Frank Loan, Dessie Taylor and Alan (Soupy) Campbell. Again, if my memory is accurate, Dessie Taylor managed to find himself astride a barbed wire fence in the darkness, ripping his trousers.

The walk culminated with us all arriving at Alan's house – in reality his parents' house – where he provided us with refreshments and we talked in hushed tones for several hours. At this stage the "Troubles" were very much to the fore and police had to be informed of our route and timing details. Goodness knows how many parents slept soundly that night!

Billy McKee studied for an Honours degree in Physics and a Diploma in Education at Queen's University Belfast. He was Head of Science at Dunmurry High School 1976-86. From 1986 to 2012 Billy served as a House Master, Head of Physics and Senior Teacher at Campbell College.

Eds. Note: Billy Steenson [1964-1970] studied jewellery and silversmithing at the University of Ulster. In the early 1970s Billy set up a workshop in Toberwine Street, Glenarm, crafting unique contemporary jewellery designs. More than forty years on, the family-run business is Northern Ireland's leading contemporary jewellers. Their Glenarm workshop is open to visitors, while Steensons in Bedford Street, Belfast, displays one of the finest selections of hand-crafted jewellery in Ireland. Steensons have produced crowns, brooches and pendants for the *Game of Thrones* television series.

Travels to East Belfast

Ken Smyth [1964-1971] recalls his travels Eastside to Orangefield from the Donegall Road.

WHEN I FIRST joined Orangefield Boys' School as a first form pupil in 1964, I had no idea that this was to be the start of an association that would include seven years as a pupil from 1964-1971, and fourteen years as a teacher from 1976-1990.

I was one of four boys from the Donegall Road area of Belfast in my first form class [Mr Horner's 1H]. There were also boys from various other parts of Belfast, such as the Lisburn Road, Stranmillis, Malone, Shankill and Crumlin areas, as well as boys from all parts of the greater East Belfast area. Each morning in the city centre, it was normal to see Orangefield boys waiting for the Castlereagh, Braniel or Bloomfield buses. After just 7 years, from the school opened in 1957, it had established an excellent reputation throughout Belfast under the wonderful leadership of its first Principal, Mr John Malone.

At this time, there were approximately 1000 boys in the school with classes often having over 30 pupils. The school building was packed and corridors filled with boys especially at period changes, break-time and lunch-time. I recall the lane leading to the dining centre being full of boys running to get to the top of the queue. After eating, it was usually a quick return to school to try and find somewhere in the playground or all-weather pitches for a game of football. Every piece of ground seemed to be occupied by groups of boys mad keen on kicking a ball.

Even in my early days I was amazed at the amount of extra-curricular activities taking place at lunchtime, after school and at weekends. Who can ever forget the inter-class five-a-side matches at lunchtime or the basketball practices in the gymnasium? There really was something for everyone at lunchtime. I can easily recall activities like table-tennis, basketball, badminton, chess, Scripture Union, motor-bike club and so much more.

After school the place was a hive of activity with all sorts of practices and matches in the various sports like football, hockey, rugby, cricket etc. Is it any wonder why Orangefield established such a good reputation for sporting success? I can recall my first football matches for the Under-12 team coached by Mr Thompson Steele, and the success that many of the school teams had in those early days. One crucially important feature was the number of teachers who so willingly gave of their time to take teams or clubs etc. Possibly my fondest memory of the school football was winning the Under-15 Belfast Senior Cup at the old Grosvenor Park on St Patrick's Day 1968 when we beat Dunlambert in the final. The team was coached by Mr Bert Caldwell and Mr Tony Sherlock (two members of the Science Department).

In my time as a pupil, I can recall the great enthusiasm of teachers like Bob Ashe, Jake Gallagher, Larry Lannie, Ken Stanley, Billy Lawther, John Reaney and many others. My other great enjoyment was the basketball teams and again Orangefield produced many excellent players and successful teams. I personally will never forget the basketball trip to Scotland (based in Lasswade near Edinburgh) and the tournament we took part in based in Liverpool. I will never forget the tremendous enthusiasm of the staff who took these teams. People like

Bob Ashe, John Allen, Trevor Cully, Billy Lawther and Rodney Usher spent many hours in the gymnasium coaching their respective teams. Undoubtedly the enthusiasm, commitment and coaching ability of so many teachers contributed to the success that many pupils achieved in their own sporting careers.

The Inter-House competitions held for the Arnold Clarke Cup gave opportunities in a wide range of sports for lots of boys who possibly could not get on to a school team but were able to represent their House team. Two big highlights of the House system were the Swimming Gala and Sports Day held each year. Again this was a whole school effort with virtually all members of staff officiating or helping in some way at the Sports Day. It was really only when I returned to teach in the school that I realised the tremendous amount of organisation required for this event by the P.E Dept. and House Masters.

Perhaps it would be appropriate for me at this point to pay tribute to the late Mr Alec Cunningham, my old House Master who was also my Form teacher for two years. I had the highest regard for Alec Cunningham as a very capable Maths teacher, Form Master and a person. Likewise, I could say the same about Bob Ashe [known affectionately by boys as Ernie] who was also my Form teacher for two years .... a man of great enthusiasm and commitment, who made a big impression on me, not just for the encouragement he gave me regarding sport, but also as an English teacher. Thinking back, it reminded me that the Boys' School had grown so much that our English classes were held in a room in the Girls' School.

Ken Smyth *attended Donegall Road Primary School. At Orangefield, he was the goalkeeper in all the teams he played for and a member of the 1968 Under-15 Senior Cup team which defeated Dunlambert at Grosvenor Park on St Patrick's Day, 1968. Ken went to Stranmillis College in 1971 and after graduation was appointed to the P.E. Department in Orangefield School.*

— 9. —
COUNSELLING AND CAREERS EDUCATION

Jack Eaton writes:

BOYS TRANSFERRING TO the new Orangefield Boys' Secondary School in September 1957 were entering an educational environment which aimed to address all aspects of their development over the next few years. Their new Headmaster, Mr Malone, believed passionately in the worth of each and every boy — failure was not an acceptable term in his educational thinking.

Furthermore, he recognised that if the boys were to be adequately prepared for entry to adult and working life, then the school curriculum must address all aspects of their development rather than concentrate on academic excellence alone.

This would mean extending the traditionally held view of the curriculum and introducing a richer variety of teaching/learning methods and locations in which teaching/learning could take place. In pursuit of these wider educational goals, the concept of counselling and guidance was introduced as a means of enhancing the life chances of individual pupils.

The programme of counselling in Orangefield was based on a number of key elements which underpinned its effectiveness:

- it focused on individual development as a continuous process rather than on problems of adjustment as they arose;

- it was structured as an integral part of the curriculum in which ALL teachers had a counselling / guidance role;

- each year group had its own Counsellor who remained with them for at least five years thus ensuring better continuity of concern;

- the Counsellor and Form Teachers within each year group worked closely with each other and with the Subject Teachers to provide a well co-ordinated counselling process;

- the support of parents was an essential part of this process and early parental contact was a major part of the first year transition programme;

- a well co-ordinated link between Counselling and Careers Guidance was established especially from 3Rd form;

- the support of outside agencies such as Education Welfare, Social Services, Educational Psychology and Vocational Guidance provided valuable professional support and advice both directly and indirectly. In particular acknowledgement is made to Educational Psychologists Janet Irwin (nee Gallagher), Mrs Miller and Frank Fee as well as Education Welfare Officers Cecil Gray, Marlene Howes and Robert

Little. Ronnie Orr, from Social Services also provided invaluable guidance and support.

The effectiveness of these key elements is perhaps well-illustrated in relation to the growing problem of absenteeism during the 1970s when "The Troubles" created such an insecure environment especially for young people. During this time Orangefield developed a new counselling approach which concentrated on the early identification and prevention of issues related to non-attendance at school.

These issues were examined at the upper primary and lower secondary level and focused on home circumstances, parental support, anxiety and relationships with peers, parents and teachers. The research programme involved local as well as national schools and secured wide coverage in journals, radio and television. The findings were presented to the National Association of Chief Education Social Workers at their annual conference in 1980.

Two important factors were especially significant:

- gaining parental interest and concern whatever the home circumstances. We believed that poor home conditions did not, of themselves, cause poor attendance but only insofar as they contributed to parental lack of interest and concern;

- providing opportunities for boys to establish good relationships with their peers and with their teachers, especially during the post-primary years.

If this preventive approach was to be successful, then the counselling process had to begin before transition to Orangefield and continue throughout the first form. This ensured that transition was structured as a continuous process rather than an event.

The process began with early Primary School visits when the first year Counsellor would meet the P7 teachers to identify the strengths and limitations of those boys coming to Orangefield. This initial profile would help to provide a first year programme suited to individual pupil needs. Any difficulties relating to his relationship with peers or teachers was of particular value in coping with possible non-attendance issues. The counselling process at this early stage centred on four key elements:

- the First Form counselling team was composed of very experienced Class Teachers, who with the Form Counsellor co-ordinated the key counselling role of the Class Teachers and Subject Teachers. Class teachers met their classes each morning and taught them for at least one subject;

- the pre-enrolment contact with the Primary schools which enabled early contact with the P7 teachers provided a useful profile of each new pupil;

- the pre-enrolment meeting at Orangefield when parents and pupils had an opportunity to meet the Staff and the Headmaster. A supplementary meeting was arranged for those parents who couldn't attend and such was the importance of parental contact that parents who hadn't attended either meeting were followed up on an individual basis;

- the residential visit to Whinlands by all first year pupils provided a most valuable experience for Class Teachers and pupils to get to know each other and to establish good working relationships.

These key structures helped provide each pupil with a sense of security in knowing there was a member of staff who would help him address any problems, whether personal or educational in a sympathetic and confidential manner. As one First Form boy wrote in an *Orangefield Observer*:

"Mr Eaton is the first form counsellor this year. He helps us if we have a problem. Recently he has helped me out with a lot of problems.

When my mum was in hospital he arranged for my brother and me to go and see her.

I had a problem when I lost my glasses and I could not see my school work. Mr Eaton arranged for me to have two pairs of glasses — one pair for home and one pair for school.

So you see if you have a problem at school there is always someone there to help you solve it."

The general ethos of Orangefield and its excellent attendance record reflected the value of a secure educational environment, good peer and teacher relationships and constructive parental support. A General Inspection report [1982] stated:

"That the school attendance figures are so outstandingly good is in no doubt attributable in large measure to the effectiveness of the home/school contacts and relationships developed through all aspects of counselling."

The effectiveness of our counselling programme during the transition from Primary school provided a sound preparation for each pupil to develop a better understanding of his strengths and limitations. This aspect of self-awareness was a key element in preparing for the other major transition — from School to adult and working life. It was therefore essential that Counselling and Careers Guidance became increasingly co-ordinated. In Orangefield, the basic purpose of Careers education was to help pupils understand the range of post-16 opportunities available to them, and to plan their way towards a preferred occupational future. The narrow concept of Careers Information alone, however well presented, was not enough. Boys needed guidance in how to relate the information to their individual abilities, interests and personal characteristics.

Subject choice at the end of 3rd year presented a valuable opportunity for each boy to start thinking about possible post-16 opportunities and the demands that these opportunities would make upon them. Over the next two years, the boys would receive lots of guidance from many different sources both formal and informal — schools, parents, local firms, youth organisations, further education, individuals and many others. All of these greatly enhanced the guidance process but it was too readily assumed that the boys would understand the information and could relate it to their own needs and aspirations. This aspect of guidance in Orangefield sought to involve boys more actively in their own guidance process rather than being passive recipients. This underlined the value of a broad cross-curricular approach in providing boys with the basic skills needed to help them manage their futures, and with social and personal skills, e.g. getting on with others, oral communication, being able to listen carefully, filling in forms, self-presentation skills, working as part of a team, unsupervised work skills.

Many of these skills were addressed within the school itself but the worth of these skills in the workplace was realised through our Work Experience programme organised by the late Mr. E. McClelland who wrote the following article in the final year of the Boys' School:

"The first Work Experience for examination pupils was held in November 1977 with a pilot of 55 boys.

This year's work experience was in November 1989 when we had approximately 100 pupils taking part, and placings ranged from NI Railways workshop to vet's surgery, solicitor's office and even acting as curate's assistant to the Rector in St Donard's Anglican Parish – a position capably filled by Colin McCormick of 5FE. This was a first and last for Orangefield.

The reports from employers were of a high calibre, with praise almost embarrassing at times.

Organisation for Work Experience starts in April of 4th year with detailed documentation and dealing with administration of applications for placement.

We start again in September checking class lists and contacting some new firms. We usually finish in December dealing with employers' reports.

Orangefield Boys' was one of the first schools to start a Work Experience for examination pupils and over the years we must have sent out 1500 examination pupils.

Our links with industry certainly were clear to see when we organised a Careers Convention two years ago in February 1988. Parents, pupils, firms and Education Authority and visiting teachers were strong in their praise. It was a most successful event."

Every effort was made to organise work experience with the specific needs of the boys in mind. Those boys whose aspirations were more practical than academic followed the School Certificate Course in 4th and 5th year [years 11 and 12]. This course provided pupils with a more protracted period spent in a working environment in which they could contribute meaningfully to the workplace and gain some understanding of its ethos and expectations as well as its demands and satisfactions.

The teachers in charge of this group organised the pupils' work experience with the help of local firms who provided a valuable longer-term experience on a one-day per week basis. The longer-term opportunity provided individuals with the basic work-related skills and attitudes needed to cope with adult and working life, and in many cases resulted in pupils securing regular employment.

The assertion that all pupils should leave school with something to show for their efforts reflected Orangefield's belief in the worth of every boy. Every school-leaver has achieved something in which pride can be taken – even if the outcomes are not strictly academic – and his self-esteem raised.

The School's record of achievement was developed so that every boy would have a record of his achievements to show an employer. This document provided a range of vocationally relevant achievements as well as performance in traditional school subjects. The record provided opportunities for boys to talk about their progress, achievements and aspirations with all their teachers and thus contribute to their own self-awareness – the core element of a good Guidance and Counselling programme.

Jack Eaton *was a Year Counsellor from 1963 to 1974 and Senior Counsellor 1975-1990. He obtained an Advanced Diploma in Guidance and Counselling from the University of Ulster [1972] and studied full-time for an M.Ed degree at Birmingham University during 1974-75. In 1983, Jack was seconded as Research and Development Officer for the E.C. Transition programme which focused on the preparation of young people for Adult and Working Life (TRAWL). He returned to Orangefield in 1987 and was Acting Vice-Principal from February 1989.*

— 10. —
SPORT AT ORANGEFIELD: PART 1

Football

Billy Lawther, a member of the PE staff from 1966 to 1990, tells the story of football at the School over three decades. Billy was in charge of football at Orangefield for 21 years.

IRISH SCHOOLS SENIOR CHALLENGE CUP 1962

FROM THE DAY Orangefield opened, sport was recognised by John Malone to be important. The Physical Education Department, headed by Rodney Usher, was given a generous allocation of periods on the timetable to encourage and develop a wide range of sporting activities. Mr Malone, and the headmasters who followed him, Brian Weston and Ken Stanley, showed a genuine commitment to sport by their regular presence at football, rugby and hockey matches played at the Laburnum on Saturday mornings, attendance at mid-week games and, on occasion, dropping in to watch physical education activities in the school gymnasium. Many young teachers, with and without expertise, were encouraged or motivated to organise and coach after-school teams in a variety of sports. For some pupils, playing individual or team games was the highlight of their sporting lives, while for others it marked just the beginning of future successful careers in the game[s] of their choice.

Orangefield is fortunate that, over the years, a large number of team photographs in many sports have been preserved. While attending the School, boys noted with pride their photographs on display, and in later years as past pupils, took pleasure in remembering their glory days.

While photographs record membership of school teams for posterity, many boys also enjoyed sport by taking part in the annual inter-House competitions, joining in weekly class, five-a-side, football league matches at lunchtime, or playing daily in the many small-sided games organised on the surrounding pitches. Tom Kerr, for example, recalls:

"One of the most popular activities at lunchtime was a five-a-side football tournament which attracted the majority of the pupils as players and spectators. Pitches had metal goalposts, made by Larry Lannie of the Heavy Craft Department, and were marked out on the school playground.

Competition between classes in each year was quite fierce with most of the school looking on. These lunch-time matches, I think, had a major part to play in the production of many great footballers and the strong performances of the school teams.

I had the privilege of captaining the 'over-age', or Colts' team in a year when Orangefield won four of the six Cup competitions run by the Belfast and NI Schools' Football Association, reaching the final of another, and being a semi-finalist in the remaining competition."

Thankfully, many pupils who participated in sport during their schooldays can still enjoy the memories of success, disappointment, good team mates, great sportsmen, trips away and characters met over the years. Hopefully, personal memories will be stirred from the following account of football life at Orangefield Boys' School, 1957-1990.

Inevitably, apologies must be made to former pupils whose sporting endeavours, in name and achievement, have not found their way into these pages because of fading memories, records mislaid over the years, or destroyed in a fire at the School.

"Footballers are born; they are not made." How much of that statement is true is debatable, but it certainly is a fact that many good footballers were born in East Belfast and came to Orangefield School. Football was the school's most popular game and competitive 'A' and 'B' teams were fielded annually at Under-12, Under-13, Under-14, Under-15 and Under-18 Levels.

Over the years, teams won Minor, Intermediate and Senior Cups as well as League titles. A large number of boys played for the South Belfast & District team each year. From 1962 to 1988 many pupils achieved representative Honours at Under 15 Level with the Northern Ireland Schoolboys' team.

The first Cups were won in 1960-61 when the Under 12, 13, and 14 teams won the Minor, Junior and Intermediate Cups respectively. The 1960s and 1980s were particularly successful years, while over the lifetime of the Boys' School, almost fifty trophies were won. Notable success was achieved in various Finals of the Northern Ireland Senior Cup:

1962	Orangefield	3	Ballygomartin	1
1965	Orangefield	2	Lurgan Tech	0
1967	Orangefield	4	Dunlambert	0
1981	Orangefield	5	Deramore	1
1986	Orangefield	2	La Salle	1
1990	Orangefield	5	Ashfield	0

UNDER 12 XI
WINNERS OF MINOR CUP — 1962-63.

BACK ROW:- Mr. GALLAGHER; B. SIMONS; D. STEWART; A. BROWN; Mr. MILLS.
CENTRE:- B. BROWN; L. COBAIN; R. MORTON; B. GORMAN; J. TATE.
FRONT ROW:- J. NELSON; J. CREE; J. KANE; A. HANNA; B. HORNER; D. HOEY; B. BROWN.
(capt)

INTERMEDIATE XI 1962-63.
INTERMEDIATE CUP WINNERS.

BACK ROW:- B. DUNBAR; W. CURRIE; R. BURROWS; R. STEWART; W. MILLEN; J. WHALLEY.
FRONT ROW:- D. GRAHAM; G. KERBY; W. HOEY; M. STEWART; S. STOTHERS; P. BICKERSTAFF; J. ROGERS
STAFF:- Mr. STANLEY   (capt)   Mr. EATON.

MINOR "B" SOCCER XI
1963-64

Back Row:- T. Holland, R. McNerlan, R. O'Neill, W. Bleakley (5th Form Asst.), I. Scott (5th Form Asst.)
Middle Row:- D. McWilliams, R. Conway, R. Hamilton, J. Lilley, J. Gorman.
Front Row:- V. Kane, S. Downes, W. Morgan (Capt.), T. McCarter, W. Boal.

UNDER 14 XI A
BELFAST AND DISTRICT UNDER 14 SHIELD.
1964-1965.

Back Row:- Mr. J. M. Malone, D. Haggen, B. Brown, B. Gorman, A. Hanna, P. Woods, Mr. J. Gallagher
Middle Row:- B. Simons, R. Crone, V. McKeown, R. Morton, J. Cree, A. Brown
Front Row:- J. Nelson, J. Kane, B. Horner (Capt.), D. Hoey, B. Brown.

UNDER 15 XI SOCCER
WINNERS, IRISH SCHOOLS' CUP AND BELFAST AND DISTRICT UNDER 15 SHIELD
1964-1965

Back Row:- B.Brown; J.Cree; R.Archibald; J.Kane.
Middle Row:- Mr R.Caldwell; J.Clarke; D.Stanfield; A.McCune; D.Steele; L.Walker; B.Gorman; Mr R.K.Ashe.
Front Row:- S.Shaw; J.Brown; G.Robb (Capt); W.Kilpatrick; B.Best.

UNDER 15 XI SOCCER
1966-67

Back Row:- E.Lemon; S.Jamison; J.Raymond; J.Hall; W.Murray; R.Lowry; J.Rowan.
Middle Row:- Mr K.Stanley;   Mr J.M.Malone.
Front Row:- V.Kane; A.Lyttle; P.Woods; T.Kingon (Capt); B.Todd; W.Kelly; D.Gibbons.
Winners, Under 15 Belfast Cup;   Irish Cup.

Orangefield Football teams in 1978: U12, U13, U14, U15, 1st XI with five Belfast Trophies won. Coaches Stanton Sloan, Billy Lawther, Jim Chambers, Paul Acheson, Ken Smyth, David Park

UNDER 15 XI SOCCER
1980-1981

Back Row:- I. Giniff; D. White; M. Rooney; D. Haire; D. Keery
Middle Row:- Mr. W. Lawther; R. Gunn; M. McFarland; L. Noble; R. Sproule; D. Mutch; Mr. K. Smyth.
Front Row:- T. Cousins; S. Baxter; K. Scott; P. Purdy; G. Mills

Treble Winners:- Belfast and District Schools League · Northern Ireland Schools Cup · Belfast and District Cup.

UNDER 14 XI and UNDER 15 XI SOCCER TEAMS — 1985-86.
Winners: Under 14 Belfast and District League   Under 14 Community Relations 5-A-Side
Under 14 Belfast and District Cup; Under 15 Belfast and District League; Under 15 Irish Cup; Under 15 Belfast 5-A-Side Trophy.

Back Row: Mr. J. Chambers; S. Small; D. Lamont; D. Walsh; D. Smith; T. Agnew; R. Houston; S. Ranson; Mr. M. McCambley.
Middle Row: Mr. D. McFall; G. Hillis; R. Wylie; M. Niblock; G. Lightbody; S. McMeekin; R. McComb; S. Stathers; N. Leslie; Mr. P. Acheson.
Front Row: C. McMullan; J. Leman; D. West; A. Spence; G. Blackstock; M. Morrison; C. Phillips; D. Ellis; S. Moore.
Seated: J. Tate; H. Walker; S. Jamison; T. Parker; P. McComb; M. Scott.

1989-1990 Irish Cup Winners
Back Row: Mr. Chambers, Jason McCreight, Alan Agnew, John Fleming, Jason Elliott, Mr Stanley.
Front Row: Glen Davidson, Mark Taylor, Glen Dougherty, Gary Clarke (Capt.), Ray Jackson, Neil Whiteside, Simon Clarke.

Honours Board: Under 15 International Players

In 1962 Randall Taylor was the first Orangefield pupil to play at International level with the Northern Ireland Schoolboys. Other pupils who followed included:

Name	Year	Countries
Noel Gorman	1963	W, E, S
Ken Graham	1963	W, E, S
Jim Whalley	1963	W, E, S
Billy Kilpatrick	1964 & 5	W, S, E
George Robb	1964 & 5	W, S, E
Jim Brown	1964 & 5	W, S, E
Barry Gorman	1966	W, S, E
Jim Kane	1966	W
Jim Hall	1966 & 7	W, E, S
Terry Kingon	1967	W, S, E
Billy Murray	1967	W, S, E
Philip Woods	1967	W, S, E
David Gibbons	1968	RI, W, S, E
Jim Raymond	1968	RI, W, S, E
Ken Wray	1970	RI, W, S
George Dunlop	1971	E (2), W, S
Trevor Thompson	1977	RI, E, S, W
David Beattie	1979	RI, W, E
Brian McVeigh	1980	RI (2), E, H, W, WG
Stephen Baxter	1981	RI, E, S
Gary Mills	1981	RI, E, S
Ken Scott	1981	RI, E, S
Ian Ginnif	1982	RI, E, S, W, WG, SW
David Keery	1982	RI, E, S, W, WG, SW
Stephen Black	1984	E, S, SW, RI
Graeme Lightbody	1987	W
Steven Jamison	1988	RI, BR, E, S, IT
Thomas Parker	1988	RI, W, BR, E, S, FR, SW, IT

CODE

E	England	SW	Switzerland
WG	West Germany	RI	Republic of Ireland
S	Scotland	H	Hungary
IT	Italy	BR	Brazil
W	Wales	F	France

Local Football

From the early 1960s onwards, many Irish League clubs signed past pupils who made a significant contribution to the local game. The passing of the years makes it simply impossible to name everyone who played in the Irish Leagues, the former First and 'B' Divisions and today's Premiership, but there follows a roll call of a number of star players remembered:

Stephen Baxter, George Bowden, Terry Collins, Jim Cowden, Roy Coyle, Joe Cree, Noel Gorman, Barry Gorman, David Graham, Jim Hall, Alan Hanna, Mark Henderson, Billy Hoey, John Kane, David Keery, Bobby Kincaid, Bill Kilpatrick, Tommy Kincaid, Terry Kingon, George Lennox, Stephen McKee, Jim Martin, Billy Millen, Victor Moreland, Terry Moore, Reggie Morton, Billy Murray, Davy Palnoch, Billy Rea, Ian Scott, Brian Simons, Ian Simons, Ian Small, Jim Smyth, David Steele, Roy Stewart, Philip Woods.

Some former pupils became managers of Irish League clubs, most notably Roy Coyle, Stephen Baxter, Tommy Kincaid and Lawrence Walker. Others channelled their energies and abilities into different areas of the game by becoming referees, coaches and administrators.

Quite a few former pupils also became physical education teachers. Walter Bleakley, Barry Gorman, Kevin Balmer and Ken Smyth returned to teach in Orangefield. Ian Davidson, Eddie Heaney, Herbie Barr, Denis Graham, David Thompson, John McKeag, Bob Nesbitt, Noel Gilmore and David Chambers taught in other schools in the Belfast and District area. Ian Scott went to teach in England.

Football Player of the Year

The Northern Ireland Football Writers' Association *Player of the Year* is an annual Award given to the player adjudged to be the best player of the season in the IFA Premiership. There is also an Award made for the Ulster Footballer of the Year.

George Dunlop won both of these Awards. In 1980-81 he was recognised as the Ulster Footballer of the Year, and in the following season became IFA Player of the Year.

Billy Murray, who played for Linfield over a period of eleven years, was voted Ulster Player of the Year during the 1983-84 season when he was playing left wing.

Stephen Baxter won both Awards in the 1996-97 season when he was playing for Crusaders as a striker. Stephen went on to become a successful manager of Crusaders.

Eric Trevorrow, who taught C.D.T. in the school, was Ulster Footballer of the Year in the 1951-52 season when he played for Ballymena United. Eric came from Glasgow and was an outstanding right back for Ballymena. He managed the Northern Ireland Schoolboys' International team for some years.

Northern Ireland International Footballers

Eric McMordie was the first person from Orangefield to gain an International cap for Northern Ireland. He played mid-field for Middlesborough and, from 1966 to 1972,  won a total of 21 caps. Eric as a fifteen year-old, along with George Best from Lisnasharragh Secondary School, had gone to Manchester United on trial. However, both players came home from Old Trafford after feeling homesick. Fortunately, Eric and George soon returned to England to become professional International players for Northern Ireland.

Roy Coyle gained his 5 International caps while playing in midfield for Sheffield Wednesday. Roy played for and managed quite a number of Irish League  clubs winning 50 trophies. He was an outstanding manager at Linfield where he won 31 trophies.

Photographs of George Dunlop and Billy Murray by kind permission of VictorPatterson@me.com

George Dunlop, goalkeeper, won every honour in local football and played for a number of clubs in the Irish League. He spent ten years at Linfield where he  gained 4 caps between 1984 and 1989. George was part of the N. Ireland team at the 1982 FIFA World Cup held in Spain.

Victor Moreland started his playing career in East Belfast with Glentoran who then sold him to Derby County. He won 6 International caps playing in mid-field  during the 1978-79 season. Leaving Derby, Victor emigrated to the U.S.A. and played for Tulsa Roughnecks in the North American League.

American Soccer Journeys

Coach Barry Gorman second left (second from right) gives a team talk during the night game with Neptune High School freshmen team at Memorial Field. Orangefield won 7-1 with Trevor Thompson scoring four goals.

It is noteworthy to record how individual lives were affected as a result of touring America and experiencing at first hand a very different way of life. In total, there were four football tours of the United States undertaken by Orangefield teams. In 1975 and 1977 visits were made to New Jersey (Neptune); in years 1979 and 1983 teams visited Pennsylvania (Myerstown).

The party of 20 pupils from Orangefield Boys' School Under 14 soccer team, and three teachers, Billy Lawther, Paul Acheson and Barry Gorman, who went on a trip to Neptune City, New Jersey for three weeks in September 1975. During a visit to the City Hall, Belfast captain Bobby Emmerson (13) was given letters and a plaque from the Lord Mayor [the late Sir Myles Humphreys}, to present on their arrival in New Jersey.

1977 Orangefield U14 team which toured New Jersey, USA with coaches Jim Chambers, Ross McQuarrie and Billy Lawther.

Subsequently, several Orangefield players went on to make their lives in U.S.A. working as soccer coaches in various American high schools and universities. At the time of writing, what follows is an update on the careers of four Orangefield 'Old Boys' in America:

Barry Gorman won Schoolboy and Youth International caps at school before enjoying a successful career with Linfield. After training at Stranmillis College, Barry returned  to the School to teach P.E. and it was he who organised the first soccer trip to U.S.A. Barry liked the American way of life and left Orangefield and set out on a career as a soccer coach at Loch Haven College, Pennsylvania. Following a successful time there, he moved to Penn State University, where he stayed for 23 years becoming Penn State's most successful soccer coach of all time. Barry's appointment in 2002 as President of the National Soccer Coaches' Association of America [NSCCA] was considered just recognition of his service to the game in his adopted country.

Trevor Adair went to Loch Haven College on a Sports Scholarship and then took up a position of Coach at the University of South Carolina. After nine years, Trevor moved to  Brown College and during his time there he helped coach the Under 18 and Under 20 U.S.A. National Soccer teams. In 1995 he moved to Clemson University as Head Soccer Coach where he stayed for 14 years. At present, Trevor is Associate Head Soccer Coach at Old Dominion College working with Alan Dawson.

Alan Dawson is Head Soccer Coach at Dominion College and has been there for 17 years producing many winning teams. He went to College in Loch Haven and then  took up a position as assistant soccer coach at North Carolina University. He moved to Methodist University where he coached soccer for 9 years. Remarkably, Alan and Trevor Adair participated in the first Orangefield soccer trip to New Jersey in 1975 and today are enjoying working together.

Gary Hamill obtained a Sports Scholarship to Charleston College in South Carolina to play soccer. At present he is the Head Soccer Coach at Wingate University, North Carolina. Gary has been there for 17 years and has brought  great success to the College teams.

It is rewarding to recall how so many young men in various ways benefitted from playing football at Orangefield, not least individuals who with hard work, natural talent and enterprise realised new opportunities in their lives to make successful careers coaching soccer in America.

Eds. Notes: In those days, virtually all young teachers came from rugby-playing grammar school backgrounds. It was unusual, therefore, to have teaching colleagues who were actively involved in soccer. It wasn't until Bob Ashe joined the Department of Physical Education that rugby specialists Rodney Usher and Eric Green, both of whom were Senior League players, were joined by an enthusiastic soccer player.

Bob's arrival at Orangefield in September 1959 coincided with the development of what became a very successful Under 13 team. In 1962 this team, captained by David McWilliams, became the first Orangefield team to win the Irish Schools' Cup by beating Ballygomartin by 3 goals to 1.

To widen the team's experience, during the Halloween break of October 1961, Bob organised a soccer tour to the North West. The team, accompanied by Bob, Eric Twaddell, Larry Lannie, Jake Gallagher and Thompson Steele, travelled by minibus and car to Londonderry to play Clondermot Secondary School. After a successful match for OBS, the team stayed overnight at Learmount Youth Hostel, outside the village of Park, before moving on the next morning to Coleraine, and an arranged match against Coleraine Boys' Secondary School. The outcome of this game was another victory for Orangefield.

In the late 1950s and early 1960s, the School was growing rapidly. Eric Greene left in 1961 to go to Strabane Grammar School. The position in the P.E. Department was filled by Jake Gallagher who, like Bob Ashe, was a soccer player. Jake took the Under 12 Team and assisted Ernie Cave with the Colts. Jake, along with other coaches, was keen to improve the footballing skills of boys taking part in competitive matches played on tour outside Northern Ireland. A visit to the Republic of Ireland saw Orangefield beat off stiff opposition to win the Liam Whelan Cup at Home Farm, Dublin. This competition was organised in memory of the Manchester United player, who was one of the eight 'Busby Babes' killed in the Munich air cash in February, 1958. Jake Gallagher went on to coach the Northern Irish Schools' National squad for a number of years.

Other teachers who coached soccer during the first ten years included: Jimmy Masterson, Zeke McCleery, Bill Comyns, Raymond Mills, Jimmy Clements, Ernie Cave, Ken Stanley, Ted McClelland, David McKeown, John Ritchie, Frank Loan, Bert Caldwell, Thompie Steele and Jack Eaton. Jake Gallagher was responsible for organising football for all the Orangefield school teams, and when he left in the late '60s, Bert Caldwell took over the role for several years.

This position was then undertaken by Billy Lawther (P.E. Department), and he continued in the role until 1990. Other members of the P.E. Department who coached teams were Ken Smyth, Mervyn McQuillan, Raymond McNeill, Walter Bleakley, Barry Gorman, Arthur Corry and Ken Jackson.

Many other staff from different subject departments gave great help and assistance throughout the years. Some had experience of playing Irish league football, while others were qualified Irish Football Association coaches. The lists of names already mentioned, and which follow, are a reflection of the dedication of the Orangefield staff: John Reaney, Eric Trevorrow, Drew McFall, Jim Chambers, Norman Johnstone, Stanton Sloan, Paul Acheson, Michael McCambley, Ross McQuarrie, Derek Ray, Tony Sherlock, Trevor Culley, David McCullough, Noel Spence, David Park and Robert Clarke.

The P.E. Adviser for the Belfast Education and Library Board, Dick Williams, employed ex-professional footballers like Gordon Bradley and Gibby McKenzie, to assist with coaching at Schoolboy level. During these years, Gordon and Gibby were to be seen frequently on the Orangefield Laburnum pitches passing on their knowledge and skills to boys who had a keen interest in soccer.

Basketball

Walter Bleakley attended Orangefield from 1959 to 1965 and was also a member of staff from 1969 to 1974.

ON ARRIVAL AT their new school, two out of three boys wanted to play football for Orangefield and the 1959 intake was no exception. Football's popularity was reflective of their primary school experience of games and the profile of the sport in East Belfast at that time. However, the school curriculum and especially the extra-curricular programme on offer at the new school saw the introduction of new games activities such as volleyball and basketball alongside other, more well-known games such as hockey and rugby. The new boys were spoilt for choice and did not have the distraction of x-box 360 or even television to detract from their involvement in new sporting experiences.

The Physical Education staff were the driving force behind these new sports and activities. Rodney Usher and Bob Ashe, both of whom

UNDER 13 BASKETBALL
1963-64.

Back Row:- R. Morton; G. Copeland; W. Gibson; I. Wilson.
Middle Row:- Mr. Usher; B. Gorman; P. Woods; J. Hall; W. Horner; C. McKibben; Mr. Malone
Front Row:- L. Elliott; J. Miles; A. Hanna (Capt); J. Kane; J. Tate.

UNDER 13 BASKETBALL
WINNERS ALL-BELFAST UNDER 13 LEAGUE 1964-1965.

Back Row:- J. Hall, B. Petrie.
Middle Row:- Mr R.K. Ashe; T. Binns; A. Ruth; B. Rankin; B. Todd; T. Neill; Mr Caldwell
Front Row:- H. Morton; J. Raymond; P. Woods (Capt); W. Murray; S. Patterson.

were playing for a Senior League club *Belfast Dodgers* at the time, were very much the leading staff in the introduction of Basketball at the school. Later on, a Science teacher Trevor Culley joined the staff and he also became part of the Basketball Club that began to develop and later flourish in the school.

One should not under-estimate the difficulty of introducing a sporting activity to a group of boys who had never seen the game being played, and therefore had no *concept* of the game or its laws and structure. However, Bob Ashe had spent a year on a teaching exchange in the USA and had a contact who sent super 8 film of High School and College Basketball games. He used to show them behind the curtain on the Assembly Hall stage at break, lunchtime and often after school.

It was "standing room only" most afternoons quickly followed by practice sessions in the gymnasium where we tried out all of the "moves" we had seen on film. This was a fertile source of ideas and physical challenges for us as novice players and the teaching staff encouraged us to try things out such as the one-handed set shot, the jump shot and the lay-up shot in all of its forms. We learnt from the staff and each other, especially the then senior pupils at that time including Adrian Roberts and Jim Stokes. We ate our packed lunch in *circa* fifteen seconds flat so that the remaining fifty minutes could be spent playing basketball in the gymnasium. This was a daily routine and was supported by structured, after-school practice time formally supervised by the teaching staff who gave of their time and professional expertise to develop us as basketball players.

BASKETBALL CLUB 1962-63
WINNERS OF JUNIOR CUP, 1963; INTERMEDIATE CUP, 1963; BELFAST LEAGUE 1963

BACK ROW (L to R) W. HOEY; R. McALPINE; S. RILEY; G. LAVERY; M. STEWART; R. HARBINSON
MIDDLE ROW: Mr. USHER; R. BURROWS; B. PORTER; G. WALKER; I. DAVIDSON; S. MARTIN; S. GAMBLE; Mr. ASHE
SEATED: D. McGALL; M. CLELAND; I. SCOTT; R. STEWART; W. BLEAKLEY; D. LINDSAY; F. McCULLOUGH
(Capt.)

The time was fast approaching when our new skills and abilities in basketball were to be tested against other school basketball teams. I have a very clear memory of an early game against Knockbreda High School when our teacher Mr Ashe called a time-out and told us that we were not allowed to dribble the ball anymore and, if we did, he would blow his whistle and give the ball to the opposition who, incidentally, were not subject to this restriction.

It was our teacher's way of limiting our scoring ability as we were leading by some 30 points. However, this tactic did not work. The week before he taught us a "5 man weave" which was a means of attacking without bouncing the ball. We simply set this up every time we got the ball and continued to score liberally!

Other abiding memories of basketball at Orangefield were the various modes of travel that we undertook to games. There was Molloy's Motors Bedford mini bus hired for a trip to county Cork in which my only available seat was a basketball balanced against the mini bus door. Then there was Rodney Usher's little Morris Minor that didn't travel much more than 30 miles an hour, perhaps because he had the starting 5 in it at the time!

Occasionally, Mr Ashe's motor-bike was reserved especially for players who were not released punctually from class to play in an after-school game because of some misdemeanour in class.

With increased levels of competitive exposure and dedicated practice, we began to develop

SENIOR BASKETBALL CLUB
1963 – 64
WINNERS, INTERMEDIATE AND SENIOR CUPS

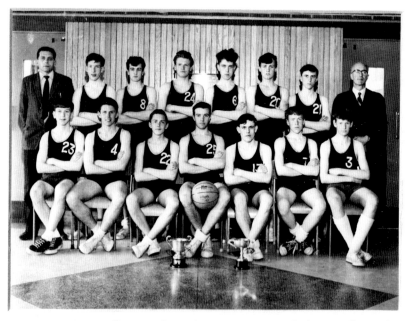

Back Row:- Mr. Usher; S. Reilly; D. McGall; I. Davidson; G. Lavery; M. Cleland; S. Gamble; Mr. Malone
Front Row:- I. Scott; W. Bleakley; R. McAlpine; R. Stewart (Capt.); D. Lindsay; P. McClinton; A. Rodway.

as basketball players and the next level was the challenge of other teams in other countries. Games against teams in the Republic of Ireland and England reaffirmed our competitive abilities at home. For example, in one year Orangefield Basketball teams won all of the Northern Ireland age-group trophies from Under 12 to Under 18.

Playing this new game provided opportunities for travel to the Republic of Ireland and an opportunity for exposure to cultural and religious experience not to be found in East Belfast. Basketball was a largely Catholic game in the Republic of Ireland and managed by the Clerical Orders with lots of the coaches being members of the clergy. One visit to Cork provided a vivid memory of travel to the South in a Mini Bus, being met on a bridge over the River Shannon at Limerick by a Franciscan monk complete with habit on a motorbike and following him to a Catholic Retreat House where we were to stay for the night. Supper was served in the Refectory with grace being said by one of the Brothers and then retirement to individual 'cells' for sleep. In the morning, the Brothers provided a substantial breakfast complete with home-made bread and their own honey, eggs, sausage and bacon completing the feast. This was a unique hospitality experience for young Protestant boys from East Belfast.

A high percentage of basketball players were also successful footballers at the school, especially at Under-15 Level. Indeed, eight of the successful Irish Schools' Football Cup winning side of 1962 were school basketball players, of whom four in that age group represented Ulster Schools, while three

UNDER 18 BASKETBALL
1964 – 1965
WINNERS UNDER 15 BELFAST LEAGUE

Back Row:- Mr. J. R. Usher; D. Steele; S. Reilly; I. Davidson; S. Gamble; Mr. R. K. Ashe.
Front Row:- A. Ralph; R. McAlpine; W. Bleakley; I. Scott; D. McGall.

became full Irish School Internationals. Following the winning on Easter Monday of the Irish Schools' Under 15 Cup played at Solitude beating Ballygomartin 3-1 in the final we went on a tour of Liverpool and Manchester. The team's rich blend of games' talent was to be felt keenly by our Lancashire school hosts! The first match was arranged by Arthur Smith, Treasurer of the National Association of Schoolmasters whilst the games in Manchester were arranged by Bob Porter, the P.E. Adviser in that area. (Before moving to England Bob had lectured in P.E. at Stranmillis College). On arrival in Manchester, we played our hosts who were then the current County champions at football and beat them 4-0.

The following morning we played their Colts side and beat them 2-0.

At lunch, our Tour organiser and coach Bob Ashe noticed another trophy in the Lancashire school's display cabinet. It was the Lancashire Schools' Basketball Championship Trophy. Bob Ashe enquired of the coach of our hosts if he would be interested in a challenge match before we departed. The Manchester coach agreed to the fixture thinking that he might salvage some credibility with a victory at basketball.

The final outcome was yet another decisive victory for Orangefield. While in Manchester, the team visited Old Trafford and enjoyed a conducted tour around the dressing rooms and other facilities at the ground. Our guide noticed one of our players was limping and asked him what was wrong. On learning that he had been injured during the game the previous day, the guide invited him to come to Old Trafford the following morning for physiotherapy treatment. Next morning, as he lay on the couch being treated, he found himself in the company of soccer giants such as Denis Law, Bobby Charlton, Nobbie Stiles and George Best.

Members of staff who accompanied the squad of basketball and soccer players on this tour included Bob Ashe, Eric Twaddell, Larry Lannie, Jake Gallagher and Thompie Steele.

Orangefield's prowess at basketball was being recognised beyond the school with many players being selected for Representative Honours at both Ulster Schools' and Irish Schools' levels. The following is a list of a number of these pupils. It is important to note the names are limited by the author's waning memory and apologies are offered if other individuals are not listed.

> **Ulster Schools Under 15 & 18**
> Walter Bleakley, Ian Scott, Ian Davidson, Richard McAlpine, Billy McKee, George Dunlop and Michael McBride.

> **Irish Schools Under 15 & Under 18**
> Walter Bleakley, Ian Scott, Ian Davidson, David McCracken and Michael McBride.

Eds. Notes: *In December 1974, Walter Bleakley left Orangefield to join the NI Sports Council. In 1977 he was appointed to the staff of the Ulster Polytechnic. When Walter retired in 2013, he was a Senior Lecturer in Education at what had become the Jordanstown campus of the University of Ulster.*

While at Orangefield, Walter attracted the attention of soccer scouts. He was persuaded to go to Manchester United for a trial. United were keen to sign him but his father was keen for his son to continue with his education. The Club arranged for Walter to be trained as an electrician or bricklayer, but his father rejected this suggestion. Walter returned to Orangefield.

Cricket

CRICKET AT ORANGEFIELD was started by a Welshman, David Francis, who played the sport at senior level for various clubs in Belfast including St Mary's and CIYMS. A grass roots Inter-Class Cricket league was set up initially. The Orangefield Observers of the 1960s report on Cricket team performance and results at U-13, U-14, U-15, 1st XI and Colts Levels.

Matches at different levels were played against various teams representing Annadale, Ballyclare High, Ballygomartin, Bangor Grammar, Belfast Model, B.R.A., Campbell College, Donacloney, Dunlambert, Edenderry, Everton, Friends' School, Grosvenor High, Inst, Kelvin, Larne, Lurgan, Methody, Portadown, and Wallace High School.

Sam Reilly remembers Dai Francis as the mastermind behind Cricket at the School and how, at the start of the season, the English master's Library store room reeked of the smell of linseed oil which was liberally applied to the bats to stop them splitting. Tom Kerr recalls his time as a player:

"Although our First Eleven Cricket team didn't participate in Cup competitions, we played a mixture of secondary schools such as the Belfast Model and grammar schools such as Annadale and Down High. We won a majority of our matches, but strangely, my most enjoyable match was a defeat against Portadown College, who were a very accomplished side with a number of senior

1st XI in alphabetical order: Billy Davidson, Gary Donaldson, Harry Glendinning, Louis Keery, Andy Morrow, Jim Stokes (Captain, centre of front row), Clifford Quinn.

UNDER 13 XI CRICKET TEAM
1962-63

BACK ROW:- Mr. WESTON; J. KANE; W. HORNER; R. MORTON; B. BROWN; J. REDPATH; J. NELSON; Mr. GALLAGHER
MIDDLE ROW:- T. COFFEY; L. LACEY; J. TATE; L. ELLIOTT; C. DOYLE.
SEATED:- L. COBAIN; I. McMILLAN; H. RICE; B. GORMAN; C. McKIBBEN; A. HANNA; D. HAYES.

UNDER 13 XI CRICKET
1964-1965

Back Row:- Mr. Sinnerton, T. Neill, P. Woods, H. Preston, B. Rea, W. Gorman, Mr. Malone
Middle Row:- N. Hill, J. Ferguson, T. Kingon, W. Murray, R. Conway
Front Row:- P. Holland, A. Telford

UNDER 15 XI CRICKET
1964 - 1965

Back Row:— Mr.E.Twaddell; R.Best; J.Young; W.Alexander; I.Dickson; J.Shields; Graham; J.Clarke; Mr.R.Caldwell
Front Row:— D. Steele; R.Archibald; A. Rolph; R.Harbinson; N. Davidson.

1st XI CRICKET
1964 - 1965

Back Row:— R. McAlpine; I. Scott; S. Young
Middle Row:— Mr D.G.Francis; R.Cole; J.Crone; D.McGall; J.Whalley; Mr J.R. Usher
Front Row:— G.McConnell; G.Robb; I.Millar (Capt); S. Gamble; A. Rodway.

UNDER 13 XI CRICKET
1972-73

Back Row: Paul Osborne; Eric McClure; Mr M Graham
Middle Row: Neil Connolly, Robert Malcolmson, Gareth Murphy, Robin Stanex
Front Row: Thomas Turkington, Ian Patterson, Gavin Kelso, Timothy Horne, Ian Simons.

UNDER 15 XI CRICKET
1972-73

Back Row:- A. Lavery; M. Herron.
Middle Row:- Mr. N Spence; D. Palnoch; B. Smallwood; T. Bell; P. Murray.
Front Row:- M. Hill; M. Gordon; R. Rasool; T. Moore; S. Martin.

UNDER 13 XI CRICKET
1976-77

Back Row:- Mr. P. Gibson; S. Whiteside; K. Surgenor; J. Meaney; I. Montgomery; M. Kennedy.
Front Row:- B. Babb; S. West; J. Dowds; F. Brady; K. Forsythe.

cricketers in their ranks. It was a great game played in a good spirit and I was top scorer for our team.

We never really played the top Grammar Schools; however, we were given a match against Campbell College, who sent their third team to play us, and I think they were surprised when we beat them.

In my last season as Captain of the cricket team, we went through the whole season with few, if any, defeats, and many of our team went on to play senior cricket. Jim Stokes, Andy Morrow, Ivan Miller, Ian Scott, Gordon McConnell, George Robb and Billy Dale are names that spring to mind."

Cricket was very much in competition with other sports in the summer term. The sport at the School also had its difficulties getting suitable cricket pitches to play on.

Undeterred, Head of Physical Education, Rodney Usher, helped organise indoor nets in the gymnasium with bowlers able to run down the corridor outside, through the doorway to deliver the ball to batsmen playing on a mat wicket laid down on the floor!

Eric Twaddell helped David Francis with teams throughout the 1960s. However, fixtures were hard to get as very few other secondary schools played the game. As Tom Kerr recalls, there were occasional fixtures with grammar schools but getting into their fixture lists was not easy.

"What do they know of cricket who only cricket know?"
C.L.R. James, *Beyond A Boundary*, 1963.

The staff also had a team for a number of years and especially in the early days played the school's First XI as well as other staff teams.

On one memorable occasion, Orangefield played a match against the staff of Ballygomartin. Their opening bowler named Campbell played cricket at Woodvale. His fast bowling on the poor wicket was extremely dangerous especially as this was in the days before protective gear for batsmen. One of the Orangefield team, Sam Campbell, before being bowled out had been hit a few times prior to his dismissal. As he left the field, Sam muttered wryly, "If that's what he did to a fellow clansman what would he do to a McDonald or a McKenzie!"

On another occasion, the married men on the staff played the single men. Rodney Usher starred for the single men and David Francis excelled for the married men. There were many hilarious incidents during the game especially when David Hammond, as he approached the stumps to bowl shouted, "*LBW play, hit the wicket and run away.*" This was a well-known chant used by children when they played cricket in the street. The strength of the staff team was greatly enhanced when Eric Twaddell and Moore Sinnerton joined the staff.

Swimming

THE *ORANGEFIELD OBSERVER*, Vol 3, No 4, December 1960 includes an article written by reporter Tom Ross (1G) and photographer John Kane (4G). It provides a fascinating glimpse into a bygone age of innocence in Sport, as the young journalists venture to obtain an interview with Anita Lonsborough, who in the 1960 summer Olympic Games held in Rome was a Gold medallist:

"*I saw a poster advertising a particularly interesting swimming gala in which Anita Lonsborough, the Olympic gold medallist was to take part, so John Kane, our ace photographer and I decided to go along and try to interview her.*

I met John outside Templemore Avenue baths at 7.15 p.m. and we pushed our way in through the crowds of people flocking in to see this great swimmer from Huddersfield. Clutching my reporter's card and holding on to John's sleeve, I managed to get in. Once inside John decided to load his camera but he had quite a job because of the people pressing around him.

I went to one of the gala officials and showed him my reporter's card which had served me well and helped me to get to the officials' box where I asked to see Anita Lonsborough. Nearly at once John and I were led off to another pond where Anita was swimming and she consented to answer my questions.

SWIMMING CLUB 1960-61   RUNNERS-UP INTER SCHOOLS GALA

BACK ROW: MR. USHER, R. McKNIGHT, M. DAVIES, D. HOLMES, A. ROBERTS, T. McCLENAGHAN, R. BUNTING, MR. ASHE
CENTRE ROW: T. THOMPSON, D. PEDEN, P. WILSON, B. HYNDMAN, R. MURPHY, W. GREER, W. CONWAY
FRONT ROW: R. HURST, L. KENNY, D. MONTGOMERY

Anita thinks that all boys should have swimming on their school-timetable because she thinks all people should be able to swim. She would have been a dancer but she was too tall. Anita advises all swimmers to go to a good coach, be willing to do what he tells them and devote all their spare time to swimming. In training Anita likes all strokes except breast-stroke, although it was in breast-stroke that she won the Gold medal.

In 1961 Anita is going to New Zealand with Natalie Stewart. In 1962 she hopes to go to the European games. In 1963 the Huddersfield girl is going to the Empire Games and in 1964 she hopes to go to the Olympic Games.

Anita is a wonderful girl with a charming personality and it was an education to all swimmers as they watched her demonstrate the different strokes in Templemore Avenue baths.

I am sure we all wish her great success in her future swimming career."

The Orangefield Swimming archive comprises no fewer than thirty annual School Swimming Galas and records in detail boys' performances, times and new records set at Under 12, 13, 14, 15 and 16 Levels. A wide range of events participated in include the 50 metres front and back crawl, 50 metres breast-stroke, 25 metres butterfly, diving competitions as well as free-style and medley relay races. The first Gala in 1959 took place in Templemore Baths and the thirtieth was held in the Robinson Centre in 1988.

SWIMMING TEAM
WINNERS, INTER-SCHOOLS' MINOR (U12 & U13) CUP.
1964 - 1965.

Back Row:- Long; H. Kelham; R. Hurst; R. Bunting; G. Copeland; A. Ruth; I. Taylor; T. Robinson
Middle Row:- Mr. R.K. Ashe; Seawright; W. Conway; K. Balmer; Hurst; P. Wilson; Mulloy; Williamson; Beggs; W. Bleakley; Mr. J.R. Usher
Lower Middle Row:- G. Friel; Goody; R. Morton   Irwin; Muir; Matchett
Front Row:- J. Briggs; Graham;   P. Morton; Clarke; J. Cree; H. Morton.

In addition, the O.B.S.S. Swimming archive documents three Inter-Schools Galas from 1962 to 1964 where Orangefield Boys' competed against other Club teams from Ashfield, Ballygomartin, Carrick Tech, De La Salle, Dunlambert, Park Parade, St Patrick's and Templemore Avenue.

Alan Ruth was the most successful swimmer to attend Orangefield. During the years 1963-67, Alan held no fewer than 8 Gala records. He went on to represent Ireland in both Swimming and Water Polo. Spotting Alan's talent from an early stage, the following report from *The News Letter*, was quoted by the *Orangefield Observer*, Vol 6, No 4, in March 1964:

"An evening of top class swimming at the Boys' Secondary Schools' gala on Saturday, produced seven new individual records.

Pride of place went to the lads of Malone School, who captured both the senior and junior championships.

Not far behind them came Orangefield School, who won the Minor championship and were runners-up for the junior title. Their efforts included five firsts, four seconds and one third in individual placings, and four firsts, two seconds, two thirds in the team relay events.

Alan Ruth, of Orangefield, was awarded the Cup for the most promising swimmer at the gala. He had two wins in record times, chopping six seconds off the under-12 25 yard crawl."

SPORTS PROFILE

Orangefield has always been fortunate in that it has consistently produced pupils who have excelled both in the sporting and academic spheres of life. Alan Ruth of 5G is a boy who manages to combine both aspects very successfully. His dedicated determined approach plus a very high degree of natural ability has led to outstanding successes in the swimming world.

Alan slightly shy and modest - the latter quality makes him a difficult subject to interview - consented to answer a few questions.

First of all I asked him if he experiences any difficulty in combining his rigorous training schedule with the more academic side of life. He agreed this was indeed a difficulty and added that he made it his consistent endeavour to fit in as many homeworks as he could always provided that didn't interfere with his swimming.

Alan, commented on the recent controversy in Irish swimming regarding international team-mate's Paddy Graham's decision not to participate in the Irish Championships at Mosney because he felt the holiday atmosphere does not encourage good performances saying that he agreed absolutely with Graham's stand.

Finally Alan said he had no further ambitions apart from giving added emphasis in the future to passing his 'O' levels and planning his marriage for a year after he leaves school.

Observer, Vol. 9, No 1, October 1966.

SCHOOL SWIMMING TEAM
1967-1968

Back Row:- R. Green; F. Cartlidge; G. Dunlop; J. Kelly; B. McKee; G. Millar; E. Millar; P. McMillan.
Middle Row:- Mr. R. Usher; R. Stewart; G. Egner; T. Cairns; G. Brown; B. Fisher; D. Cartlidge; A. Moneypenny; K. Bolmer; Mr. J. D. Allen
Front Row:- D. Irwin; K. Irwin; T. Loughlin; J. Gordon; M. Matthews.
(On floor) A. Beggs, S. Gillespie, V. Shaw, W. Moore.

SCHOOL SWIMMING TEAM
1968-69

Back Row:- P. McConaghie; F. Cartlidge; P. Millar; J. Egner; A. Moore; J. Mullan; P. Catling; P. McMillan
Middle Row:- Mr. W. J. Paul; D. Mathews; K. Fee; D. Bannister; G. Doherty; N. McIlhenney; E. Power; Mr. W. Lawther.
Front Row:- J. Walker; J. Dilworth; W. Gray; R. Hill; P. Meaney.

– 11. –
MEMOIRS: SET 3

Living and Learning

Daly Maxwell [1964-1968] *recalls four years at Orangefield and his transition to adult working life. Daly's story is of a career made as well as a vocation found in helping others.*

AFTER LEAVING MY primary school, I was completely overwhelmed by the atmosphere and warmth I felt at Orangefield. After years of being called 'you' or 'Maxwell', I thought it most unusual to be called by my Christian name. John Malone, the Headmaster at that time, was so caring, supportive and encouraging. Again, he knew the school's pupils by their Christian names. I find this still to be one of the most important things that I remember.

There were some amazing people there who had heart, soul, care and compassion and who encouraged us to flourish. I spent four happy years in Thompie Steele's class where I learnt a lot, perhaps not so much about Maths and Science, but more about getting on with people and communicating with others.

I also developed an interest in political issues, this in no small measure through getting to

Members of Thompie Steele's class, 4SJS, circa 1966 practising Belfast Street songs for a BBC Schools' Broadcast of the poet W.R. Rodgers's radio play, 'The Return Room.' From Left to Right Ronnie Scott, Samuel Graham, George Holmes, Jim Greer, Raymond Drennan, Bobby Pinkerton, Roy Holden, and Daly Maxwell.

know Roman Catholic children. Where I come from, this was almost unheard of.

Another experience that influenced me greatly was the holidays that the school provided. I remember especially visiting Quarry Cottage near Annalong, where we learnt about music, the Mountains of Mourne, and country life. I often think back to these days with really happy memories, of sitting round the fire and singing Irish folk songs and having a truly wonderful time. In my opinion, this was real education, where people could feel relaxed and get to know teachers as people, and where we developed friendships with classmates.

The day I left school I cried. After leaving Orangefield in 1968 at the age of fifteen, I had a variety of jobs. I was a store boy at Stewarts which I hated, but I got a break and was given a job at McNeills in Larne and finally had my own room! My next job took me back to Belfast working in Purdysburn Hospital. It was for people with mental health problems. Back then, over forty years ago, the standards of care at the hospital were appalling, good practice and any kind of respect was non-existent.

This experience had a major impact on me and has stayed with me throughout my career, now always striving and wanting to make life fairer and better for people I've come in contact with. I left Purdysburn to work at Montgomery House in the Cancer Unit for adults and children. This was a wonderfully rewarding job. I felt privileged to have had the chance to work with the children who were unfortunately there, some of whom had a terminal diagnosis.

As we all know, *The Belfast Telegraph* was a great source of information and it was here that I saw an advertisement inserted by the Royal Air Force in West Sussex. They were looking to recruit people to work in a home caring for survivors of the World War who had disabilities.

I applied, got the job and moved to England to start another adventure. It was a great job, and I also met some special people who became life-long friends.

I moved from West Sussex to East Sussex after a couple of years and lived in Brighton where I worked for Social Services as a carer for the elderly.

In 1981, I was offered a job working for the Church of England in London. It was to set up a day and evening Centre for London's street homeless at St Botolph's Church in the heart of the city. At first I was apprehensive as I hadn't taken on anything of this scale before, but thanks to people's faith and trust in me I decided to accept the job and stayed for over thirteen years. I went from being the Day Centre manager to Senior Social Worker and eventually became the Centre's Director of Care.

The Day Centre started almost as a basic soup kitchen with just a handful of volunteers but soon grew into a dynamic environment comprising forty staff, a medical team and over one hundred volunteers. We welcomed up to three hundred clients a day and offered such things as hospitality, food, medical care, resettlement, outreach work, housing advice, art therapy, music therapy, literacy and numeracy workshops and lots more. Most importantly, the Centre gave people a place to feel empowered and an opportunity to think about change.

In 1984, I was approached by the BBC who wanted to make a fly-on-the-wall documentary about the work at St Botolph's to highlight the injustices around homelessness in Thatcher's Britain. It was filmed over a year and televised on BBC 2 as part of a series of documentaries called Present and Imperfect. It was around this time that I was invited to a World

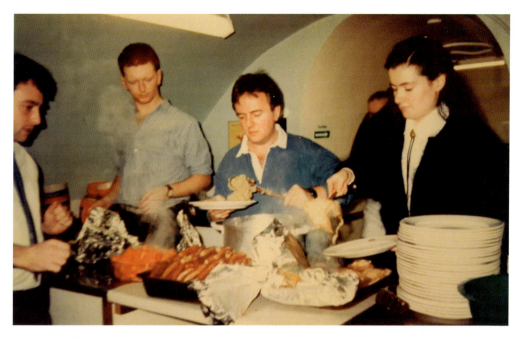

Daly Maxwell (centre) with colleagues serving Christmas dinner for the homeless in the crypt of St Botolph's Church, London.

Conference in Paris as a representative to speak on AIDS and Homelessness in Britain to highlight the struggle for people who were being marginalised and discriminated against, experiencing poverty and unemployment, people with very few rights, no vote and no voice.

Everything I had learned and experienced at St. Botolph's I was able to take with me when offered a month's sabbatical working in New York and San Francisco at some of their homeless projects. When I returned I was asked to write "A Day in the Life of" article for *The Sunday Times* which helped to raise the profile of the project. I was also interviewed by the BBC when "Songs of Praise" was broadcast from the City of London.

Due to its growing reputation, St Botolph's was able to attract some influential speakers, most notably Archbishop Desmond Tutu, who gave an immensely moving and powerful talk to a fortunate and captivated audience. Afterwards, he also spoke with the workers at the Centre.

During my time at St Botolph's, I also formed a link with the University at Jordanstown which enabled youth and community students to work alongside us on placement giving them some insight and valuable experiences into homelessness. Other people who came to St Botolph's on placement were from countries as far away as America, Sweden and India.

My job gave me the opportunity to expand my learning. I studied Counselling and Psychotherapy at the Lincoln College in London and also at Kent and York Universities where I enrolled in a class on psycho-dynamic approaches to drug dependency and alcoholism. With these experiences, I was then able to teach and also work as a freelance trainer helping health professionals develop their skills and techniques in the care and counselling of their patients.

Looking back to when I was just a boy of fifteen, I would never have thought any of this was possible having left school without a single qualification. Some even told me I might just as well get a job in a shop, as that was about all I really was capable of doing. However, Orangefield helped me to develop because of Thompie Steele's and John Malone's style of educating, drawing out the best in their students (often without it being obvious), to which I owe the confidence that allowed me to achieve all of the above. Orangefield taught me how to respect and value people no matter who they are or from what background they come from.

Now, this seems a long way off from 4SJS.

Eds. Notes: *The photograph of 4SJS was taken in the School quadrangle outside the 'Do It Yourself' Visual Aids Room. Ronnie Scott was seen by Thompie Steele running in the first Belfast Marathon. Samuel Graham now lives near Ballynahinch and has his own Painting & Decorating Business. He has taken his workmates behind the former 'Iron Curtain' to decorate orphanages in Romania. Sadly, George Holmes, Jim Greer and Roy Holden are dead. Jim was killed in a car crash. Raymond Drennan's son was enrolled at Orangefield the year Thompie Steele retired. Daly Maxwell now lives on the South coast of England.*

Lucky Man

Gerry Dawe [1963-1969] remembers his upbringing, John Malone, the influence of his first English teacher, David [Dai] Francis, and his colleagues.

I HAD LIVED in a house of women in north Belfast since 1956, when the war-time romance of my parents' marriage hit rocky waters, and eventually they split up. My mother took her two children and resettled in *her* mother's house in Skegoneil, north Belfast. We were to remain there until 1970.

I had been a somewhat solitary and troubled young boy, plagued with asthma and eczema, swaddled in bandages. I lived in the back bedroom most of the time, until I secured the top attic, and began a night-watch over the avenues of the neighbourhood, falling in love with the dusk over the city lights, the whistling and echoing conversations of evening, and the early morning traffic.

After I sat and failed 'narrowly', as an eleven year old, the Qualifying Examination, my mother was not quite sure what I should do next. So, turning to one of her father's relatives for advice, a teacher in one of the city's grammar schools, the name Orangefield was mentioned as a temporary option. She heard great things about what John Malone was doing there. I distinctly remember his name being mentioned. That stuck. JOHN MALONE.

So off I went, four buses a day. One into town and one out to Castlereagh, and back into town after school, on the No 64. Then, I stepped away from the cosseted home life I had known and started the real business of growing up. Orangefield was all part of the process. It was the best thing that happened to me, although that first year was difficult, adjusting and feeling the pangs of separation from an all too cosy home life, as well as leaving Seaview Primary School, a stone's throw from the family home.

For the twelve-year-old I was in 1964, primed that *that* journey to Orangefield would be an *interim* business until I managed to sit 'The Review' of the 11+, it only took one conversation, brief enough, to settle the matter. It would last in my mind, to this very day. Under the stairs, in the corridor that ran off from the school's Assembly Hall leading up to the first floor of Art and Geography classrooms, my mother and I met in an anteroom, or office, with Mr Dai Francis, my first English teacher.

It would have been in the late spring 1964. What was my plan, I was asked? I didn't really know. What did my mother think, now that I had settled somewhat? She was uncertain. After a shaky start, my record was improving. I'd likely be able to move on, if I so wished. But did I want that, or would I prefer to stay? Without a second's hesitation, I said I'd like to stay put if that was OK. And, from that moment on, despite the ups and downs and disappearing acts we knew then as 'beaking off' (to dances in the Plaza on Wednesday afternoons), Orangefield became the most significant guide to a generation of boys growing into young men in a time just before crisis engulfed their city.

I owe a personal debt to Dai Francis for his calm, intelligent nudge in the right direction, not least for the manner in which he conveyed literature as a *living* voice with such peerless conviction. I can still hear his voice recite the General Prologue to Chaucer's *Canterbury Tales*, as the class looked on, caught somewhere between awe and embarrassment:

Whan that Aprile with hise shoures soote
The droght of March hath perced to the rote,
And bathed every veyne in swich licour
Of which virtu engendred is the flour.

Dai Francis recited poetry with an un-indulgent clarity, and made literature not something that belonged elsewhere but very much at the core of everyday life. Though, literature was also special too. And its value came, not from some alluring sense of bohemian lifestyle, but rather from the marvel of working language into a potent life-force.

None of this was explicit, just Dai's voice, reciting a poem or getting his class *to hear* by simply listening to what was written. It seemed so natural then, and yet to a class of (how many boys was it?) twenty or thirty – no easy task *whatsoever*. In one way or another, I've been following in the footsteps of David Francis ever since, in the classroom and lecture hall.

Dai Francis laid the foundations which other mentors took over and encouraged us to think, act, engage and work our way into theatre, politics, and, crucially, into writing itself.

The writers who visited Orangefield such as Stewart Parker, matched the flair and (I can think of no better word for it) sophistication of the teachers themselves: Sam McCready, Davey Hammond, Moore and Henry Sinnerton, Raymond King, Ken Stanley, Jonathan Bardon, David Craig, Jim Holland, Brian Weston, Ronnie Horner, Barney Megarry and Harold Magowan come to mind among others.

I still have my testament to those years. It's right by me now, fifty years later. A copy owned by Gordon Scott (6AWY), of the *Faber Book of Modern Verse* anthology, the set text for GCE 'A' Level in English literature. Along with 'The Use of English' examination we were encouraged to sit – a State experiment, if memory serves me right, long since discontinued – these set me on my way and started the halting stabs at poetry I wrote in science notebooks which would also be filled with quotations I loved from all sorts of sources, including that Faber book's selection of Dylan Thomas:

Light breaks on secret lots,
On tips of thought where thoughts smell in the rain;
When logics dies,
The secret of the soil grows through the eye,
And blood jumps in the sun;
Above the waste allotments the dawn halts.

Like many others of my generation, I am in the debt of what Orangefield set out to prove, providing for an independence of thought and spirit, of getting out *into* the world without fear or favour. We had fun too. And even though I can still recall, with a shudder, those wet industrial mornings in mid-December or late February, and the darkness descending early afternoon, I can also see Mr Malone in his starched white shirt and (was it) College tie, straightening his academic gown (a *gown*, imagine!), the ascetic face with its penetrating eyes, disappearing into the office and the green light going on, as three of us bravely advanced Sixth Form's entitlement for one thing or another, to his watching and alert reception.

There should be a bridge named after John Malone, a bridge between the east of the city

and the city centre because that is what he, and his teachers achieved. They crossed barriers, and made it possible for a younger generation — of which I was lucky enough to be part — to follow, by example, in their own way.

Gerald Dawe *has published nine collections of poetry, is a Professor of English and Fellow of Trinity College Dublin. Prose works published by Lagan Press Belfast include* My Mother-City *[2008],* The World as Province *[2009],* Conversations: Poets & Poetry *[2011],* The Stoic Man *[2015], and* Of War and War's Alarms: Reflections on Modern Irish Writing, *Cork University Press [2015].*

'Desperados waiting for a train'

Bruce Cardwell [1964-67] summons America's Ellis Island, Bob Dylan, Roger Daltrey, St Jude, medieval dungeons, sans culottes, celestial marble halls, the Fureys and David Hammond to the telling of his tale …

AFTER A YEAR of mutual antipathy with one of Belfast's more self-regarding educational institutions, I find myself in 1964 together with my harassed mother, in another Headmaster's office with John Malone.

Could I be accepted into Orangefield?

The school then seemed akin to America's Ellis Island… *"Bring me your poor and your needy, your unmanageable and your recalcitrant, your sullen and your rebellious"* and accommodated a sizeable group of rejects and misfits inherited from the more prestigious academies around Belfast as well as a cohort of local boys from East Belfast.

John Malone is Saint Jude, the patron of hopeless cases, and I am accepted into Orangefield Boys' Secondary School. Accepted by the establishment at any rate, but there is a slight hitch. I have an accent conditioned by time spent in England, and perceived by my new peer group as posh. I soon learn to call the Employment Exchange the "buroo" as in Brian Boru, however, and slowly become integrated with my classmates.

Ashleigh Rodway is reserved and plays the violin, so by rights should be teased and bullied to distraction, but we are secretly impressed by the ability of one of our own to do such a thing. Billy Alexander combs his sandy hair across his brow in a fringe. The Beatles and the Stones are big, and he plays bass guitar in a group. He wears a pinkish striped scarf from an unspecified girls school permanently flung across his throat and over his right shoulder. It is a sign of conquest, meant to impress us.

Eddie Heaney and Ronnie Eadie form a duo, Eddie with the impressive combed back-lick of oiled hair and Ronnie with his distinctive upturned nose. Keen footballers both, they excel effortlessly at rugby when coaxed out to make up the numbers, exciting a mixture of admiration and jealousy from the regular players.

We see ourselves as the rightful inheritors of the brave new post-war world. Bob Dylan is *Freewheelin'* along a snowy road with a conspicuously pretty girl hanging on his left elbow, while Roger Daltrey and the Lord knows Who are telling the world what they need to know about *My Generation*. We realise that the education on offer is in some regard past the sell-by date, but not that it is the only education in town. We rebelliously scorn "O" levels and "A" levels, for we are desperados waiting for a train.

In the face of this precocity, the teaching staff adopt a variety of individualised strategies. John Malone is "The Boss", and sweeps along the corridors periodically from the Olympus of his office in a black academic gown. Brian Weston is his Vice Principal and enforcer, and GBW is also accorded the gravitas of a black gown. It is he who feels the sting of our insolent ingratitude towards the forbearing altruism of John Malone, and takes us to task for it in the good, old-fashioned way. When we are late for morning Assembly, which is not infrequently, we are corralled into Room 7 to receive a single slash of the cane from him on reluctantly extended palms.

Engaging and sporty, Jake Gallagher is invariably attended when on playground duty by a trail of hero-worshipping little boys. They follow him like gun-dog puppies aching to be sent by him on some pointless errand, which he always accompanies by his inevitable catchphrase *"Speed, boy, speed is essential."* On one occasion he takes me to task for a lack of routine application. *"You're a butterfly, boy, you will never settle to anything."* He's not entirely wrong in that assessment, but to compound the injury the gun-dog puppies regard me with silent resentment for having enjoyed his exclusive regard for a while.

Jim "Dutchie" Holland takes a group that purports to be "A" Level English. He can speak French, has been to Paris, eats garlic and wears a green two-piece suit. This is all cutting-edge stuff in 1965, but we are not prepared to be impressed. When he hobbles into a lesson after hurting his back in a surfing mishap, we shamefully and ungraciously howl with derision. Subversion at any price. Dutchie produces a cardboard box of paperback books for us which have been kept separate as being unsuitable for the younger pupils, and to which we are given access. We read the lot in a diligent search for the dirty bits, which we never find. Fair enough, you had us nicely there. Educated *in spite of* ourselves.

In the lab Mr. Brian Sloan takes no nonsense but tolerates my jokes about tropical disease being spread in Africa by the 'teste' fly, possibly on the basis that it means I have at least looked at the big green Biology textbooks he hands out. Mr. Sloan takes us on a field trip down to the foot of the Mournes. We are not fit to be let out, and a complaint is received about raucous renditions of sectarian songs, but after a lecture from The Boss on the social inappropriateness of "party songs", no further action is taken. I genuinely believe at the time that by "party" JMM means a social event rather than a political affiliation.

In 1965, the younger of the Sinnerton brothers joins the school as a teacher, and is tasked with the "short straw" of taking the rugby team to away matches. His friendly and relaxed approach endear him to us, and when he is to marry we have a whip-round to buy him a ceramic tankard embossed with a figure of Finn McCool. He sportingly drains it of beer at a draught as we cheer him and hoot encouragement.

It is the last day of term in Room 7 and the levels of general anarchy are approaching scary proportions; we simply do not know what to do to be more manic. It is time for extraordinary measures. Davey Hammond bursts into the room, a ruddy face topped by disregarded disordered hair. He is carrying a black instrument case from which he extracts a gut-strung Spanish-style guitar.

We *sans culottes* are suddenly quiet, unsure of what is developing in front of us. Davey sheds his tweed jacket and throws the guitar strap behind his neck. Like a General Gordon at Khartoum he manages to hold rolling-eye contact with a whole roomful of adolescent hysterics as he riffles across the notes of a confident opening chord. We hear about a boy hero who swims away from his warship towards *"the Spanish enemy, and with his little augur in her side he bored holes three, and he sank her in the Lowlands, Lowlands low ... he sank her in the Lowlands sea."* The hard cases and troublemakers are impressed and subdued.

I am spellbound by this contact with a raw musical charisma, and intrigued by a live experience of performed ballads. Davey subsequently takes me to the Guinness Festival of Irish Traditional Music in Queen's University where he is playing on a bill with Finbar and Eddie Furey. No audience other than myself turns up – this is 1965 and Country and Western is the big draw. I sit on the stage with a bottle of Guinness while Davey sings. Finbar and Eddie play instrumentals on Uilleann Pipes and guitar. I am completely blown away and it is the start of a love affair that persists until today.

Davey keeps in touch with me through sporadic postcards during my own musical career, encouraging me up until the year before his death. He collected songs from Sarah Makem who, via Tommy Makem furnished the phenomenally successful Clancy Brothers with much of their material. Davey taught me "*The Rocks of Bawn*", and a song called "*I'll Tell Me Ma*" which he collected in Belfast. This was later to become the unofficial anthem of our city. He linked me into a historic train of musical transmission and gave me the confidence to see myself as a continuing extension of it.

Interplay between bolshie sixties' pupils and idiosyncratic staff is not the only drama in Orangefield. It is also manifest through the slight physique and compelling persona of actor Sam McCready. We can see that he is the real deal, a pukka thespian because he projects and pronounces so explosively that we are often sprayed while playing opposite him. Credibility trumps hygiene as far as we are concerned, though, and having the benefit of his professional expertise compels our respect. He casts me as rough diamond Captain La Hire in the School production of Bernard Shaw's "*St. Joan*", and after the initial queasy nervousness it is an enjoyable and positive experience.

He subsequently invites a group of us to The Lyric Theatre in Derryvolgie Avenue to see a performance of "*Juno and the Paycock*" in which he is playing. We are painfully, embarrassingly silly. Pearls, and swine with too much wine. In truth I think that we are nervous when suddenly confronted with proper high culture and do not know how to behave. Perhaps Sean O'Casey would have regarded it as a valid proletarian reaction; in any case we are thankfully not punished or further humiliated.

We are Orangefield, pupils and teachers alike, and we disregard the rulebook. This is a time before there was a requirement for all teachers to be formally trained, and we experience a wide variety of method in the delivery of our education. The great saving grace of this arrangement is the engagement that occurs on a personal and individual basis between students and staff.

Pranks occasionally stray from the robust into the marginally brutal. There is a craze for hanging up great numbers of first year pupils in the cloakrooms by the collars of their new big-school blazers, and the school takes on the appearance of a neo-medieval dungeon. The unfortunate John Malone is inundated with complaints from the parental buyers of said blazers, and he announces sternly in morning Assembly that this practice will cease forthwith.

Another pastime which enjoys a vogue for some time is "Steel Nux", a game for two played with a full deck of playing cards. Each player cuts the cards, and the highest value drawn is the winner. The loser then cuts the deck again, scoring on a range from one to ten. This indicates the number of times that the winner can slash the edge of the full deck across his opponent's knuckles. The process is repeated until blood is drawn, at which point the bleeder is deemed to have lost.

By 2015, it is recorded by those who have strolled among the rubble of demolition that Orangefield has been razed. Not so. It has in fact been *raised* — elevated to the status of myth. There is in some far celestial realm a marbled hall housing the memories of all great human endeavour. On the wide steps of this classical construct, a group of Belfast schoolboys in slightly shabby black blazers are clearly desperados waiting for a train.

Orangefield is an attitude informed by ideas. These do not pass away.

Bruce Cardwell is a musician, photographer and writer.
A Welsh-speaker, Bruce is author of The Harp in Wales, Seren Books, 2013.

An Orangefield Experience

Gavin Robinson writes:

SOME SAY THAT school days are the best days of your life. Some say this is a cliché used by parents to convince children who think otherwise. I only know that they have occupied a large percentage of my life both young and old.

Looking back can be tinged either with nostalgia or revulsion depending on personal experience but ever since I set foot in a school, the first of which was Orangefield Primary, I had the learning bug. I could easily have gone to a Special School considering my profound deafness save for my mum who, on the advice of a teacher friend, decided that a normal school was best. Thus I moved to Orangefield Boys' Secondary School without any stigma that I had failed the 11+ and would not be going to Grosvenor High School.

From 1968 to 1975, I benefited from the dedication, commitment and enthusiasm of a young staff feeling that what I did was important – a sense that only comes when you belong to a large family. The Principal, Mr John Malone, was memorable in two ways – as a considerate disciplinarian and as a dedicated educationalist, even lending for a time his own money to help secure the purchase of a school Field Centre in Annalong so that his pupils could benefit from extra-curricular activities. His zeal was shared by the staff.

Mr Mercer, a dignified and formidable music teacher, would instruct me how to pretend to play the recorder whilst occupying a position in the back row so that the chances of anyone seeing me, let alone hearing me, were slim.

Nonetheless, I still love music and like to sing at home though my wife closes all the doors leading from the bathroom believing that I can be happy on my own without inflicting sorrow on others.

Mr Campbell was our Maths teacher and undoubtedly saved me from complete innumeracy as a result of his careful and repeated explanations of why numbers can be fun. Even now I find Maths fascinating and look at my son's work with awe and admiration, vainly thinking that I must have passed on a talent that I never fully developed.

It was, however, in the practical subjects that I felt most at home where we had a bunch of Wood, Metal and Technical Drawing teachers who were craftsmen – Barney Megarry, Larry Lannie, Eric Trevorrow, Jack Cranston, "Wild Bill" Comyns and Jack Eaton. All of them expected high standards in terms of work and behaviour and were highly respected by their pupils. Exactness, care and the production of quality work were the benchmarks I absorbed and still hold today.

The application of craft skills within and beyond the classroom did so much to inspire my love of the subject. The production of articles for sale at school fairs, the construction of sets and props for school plays and other events and the use of newly acquired skills at home instilled a new-found sense of pride and satisfaction in our craft. On one occasion, Jack

Cranston brought in the instrument panel of his boat and used it as the basis of a lesson where he would enthusiastically sand it down to restore it to pristine condition. It was his unspoken passion which spurred us on to excel. Not that it was all work and no play for on one of our many returns from Whinlands, Eric Trevorrow treated us to a round of Golf – a major passion of his – during which we gained an insight into his sociability and jovial nature. It was, in hindsight, this balance of discipline and sociability which formed our characters and made us realise we were fortunate to be taught by individuals who were masters of their craft and the art of teaching.

Undoubtedly the most impressive project undertaken by the Heavy Craft department was the construction of the Visual Aids room. This project was led by one of my teachers, Mr Lannie, and the following extracts are taken from an article he wrote for the *Orangefield Observer*, Vol 8, No. 2, June 1966:

"Approval was given and in the summer term of last year (1965) the City Architect's Department supplied working drawings and estimated that the cost would be £1,145. Group discussion took place with a G.C.E. woodwork class and we planned the job to suit the Heavy Craft timetable and accommodation. The bulk of the work has been carried out by the same GCE class, assisted by 4S1 and 4S2 …The job is now well on towards the painting stage and we sincerely hope that it will be completed by the end of June, commissioned and operative by September (1966).

These days we are hearing more and more about ' Team Teaching'. The 'Buildin' will, we hope hold around 120 bodies and should provide an opportunity to gain some experience in the techniques of team-teaching. As a Visual Aids room, it will be used by every department in the school. It will also be suitable for form assemblies. The Parents' Association will find it suitable for their meetings and a budding builder was heard to mention 'Saturday Night Hoolies.'

I hope all those who shared in the building of this 'teaching space' (Ministry description) will forgive me if I name three boys who deserve special mention: theirs was a major contribution to the work and their loyalty, cheerfulness and reliability deserves recognition. These boys are Geoffrey Hoskins (6W), Paul Smith (6A) and Richard Cole (6W). Finally, our thanks to Mrs Smith and Mrs Harris who supplied us with hot tea, buns and biscuits during the winter."

Sixth-former Richard Cole, writing in the same *Orangefield Observer* article praised and warned at the same time, "I think the room represents a great achievement for Orangefield and woe-betide anyone who damages, with pen, pencil or penknife, this sacred shrine of industry and skill."

When I returned to Orangefield in 1979 as a teacher of Crafts and English, I was proud to teach alongside many who had taught me, including Mr Lannie whose support and advice I have never forgotten. We had all become a little older but the vigour was still there, the discipline was still there and the sense of purpose was as strong as ever. Orangefield worked because you could focus on the pupils and help them discover the things they enjoyed and were good at. You had a role to play in their success and this was the real job satisfaction. I have seen Orangefield from both sides and both have been founded on support, care, guidance and friendship.

Orangefield has been one of the major influences on who I have become and since time doesn't stand still, since demographics alter, since falling rolls can mean a school's closure, it was so very sad to attend Van's end of school gig. Not sad to listen to the music of an iconic former pupil but sad to think of corridors without sound, classrooms without pupils and teachers with no place to teach.

But it is not the sadness which one should keep. It is the knowledge and memories of what Orangefield did and the sense of purpose it instilled. The football teams whose players are still mates today. The past pupils and former teachers who remember you because of the school and all the stories woven into it. Well, my mamma told me there would be days like this and she was right.

Gavin Robinson [1968-1975] completed a four-year course at Stranmillis College and returned to Orangefield where he taught Heavy Crafts and English from 1976 to 1986. Following a two-year period of self-employment, Gavin joined the staff of Hazelwood Integrated College where he has been teaching since 1988.

12.

TIME IT WAS

David Craig, a member of staff 1962-72, reminisces about his time in the Art Department. David was known to colleagues for his "spring-sprung gait."

HOW DOES ONE encapsulate the memories of the place that was, for ten years, my work place, my learning place, my play place, the place that instilled certain values and attitudes into me that, to some extent, still remain as I enter my fourteenth year of retirement? Why do I still recall, almost daily, something or someone from my time at the school that John Malone created, aided and abetted by a motley crew of teachers, some, like me, wet behind the ears, others experienced and able to bring their knowledge and occasional wisdom to bear? I can't really answer except by jotting down my memories as they occur and hope they trigger some response. I must keep on the move or Ken Stanley will find me and ask me, most politely, to provide cover for someone.

I mentioned John Malone. Everyone contributing, who taught at the School, will undoubtedly have many and varied memories of this most gifted man. I have spoken about him to numerous people since coming to Scotland the year I left Orangefield. I have one particular story which I think says so much about John I have to tell it. John was very approachable and, as I wished to consult him, I knocked on his door and entered to find the Headmaster peeling an orange for one of the youngest pupils in the school. John smiled and asked me to wait while he finished his task. "Run along, Tommy" he said and as Tommy departed John added, "He had a problem and I was able to solve it!" Enough said.

I have two people in particular to thank, as well as John, for making Orangefield the great place it was for me. The first is Mervyn Douglas, my first department head whom I had previously encountered as a teacher of calligraphy in an evening class at the Art School. His organisational skills were second to none and he was always ready to advise; I even occasionally took his advice. We lived in the same street for part of my time, just up the road from Barney Megarry. I still have a souvenir of Mervyn; a small bone folder from my room; anyone on the staff of that time will remember the late arrival of pupils from Mervyn's class following what almost amounted to a strip-search for just such an item if one was missed from the end-of-lesson check. Celia and I enjoyed the company of Mervyn and Vivienne on many occasions.

Brian Weston was a genial man who was always the same and as a fellow Old Instonian shared a number of memories of another place! He was happy to chat if I was on playground duty before directing me back to the busy areas from the quiet sanctuary round the back. When John departed to pastures new Brian took on the position of Acting Head, maintaining the atmosphere and ethos that John had built. When he was rightly made

Headmaster after John's decision not to return, the Staff were relieved that the School was in very good hands. He was kind enough to give me a reference a couple of years later when I applied for a post at St Columba's School in Kilmacolm in Renfrewshire. He obviously glossed over the weaknesses as I got the job and stayed there until retiring 28 years later.

Memories, memories, memories; friends and colleagues on the staff whom I am calling to mind and I cannot think of a falling out except with the occasional pupil! I do remember the Cross Country group I trained because there was a particularly talented runner called Bruce from New Zealand who ran in bare feet. I always enjoyed the enthusiasm of the boys in the sports field although I think the Staff/pupil matches became a bit competitive!

Whinlands was a very special place and Celia always accompanied me on our weekends. While baby Maureen slept in her pram my elder daughter Susan, aged about four years enjoyed playing with the big boys as they 'drilled', a sign of those times. It was customary for wives to provide the culinary expertise! This was the only time in my life that I was involved in hill walking. For some reason best known to the management, the Art Department was chosen to paint the rooms – not murals or decorations, just painting the walls with emulsion to make the place look smart. Just half a dozen sixth year pupils to do the work!

Another special memory was a continental trip to Belgium. Did we have any staff with modern languages? No, only Technical and Art! Jim Leckey was the man in charge aided by Messrs McClelland and Thorpe. Celia was introduced to joys of the rugby tackle as the boys decided this was the only way to capture her in some obscure hide-and-seek game!

They were very considerate as they didn't want to manhandle her. I was the linguist with my schoolboy French.

I could go on for hours but let me finish with a big THANK YOU to all those old men who were the young men I knew on the Staff back then.

We had some very interesting Staff parties – enough said.

Girl with a Lute: Graphite, Ink and Chalk on Paper, 16" x 12".

Sisters: Oil on Panel 18" x 14"

Eds. Note: *Ken Hamilton [1967-1974] enrolled at the Belfast College of Art and Design before moving to England in 1977 to study horticulture and landscape design at Merrist Wood College in Surrey. In 1990, finding in landscape design the means of earning a living, Ken took up once more his original plan to become a painter. He searched in old art books the key to unlock the mysteries of the Old Masters before travelling to Paris in 2002 to teach himself, by first-hand observation and examination, the methods of the great European painters. Setting his easel in the grand halls of the Louvre, he painted the works of the French and Spanish masters, Ingres, Le Valentine and Ribera. Ken has exhibited in Belfast, Dublin, London and New York.*

– 13. –
EXPLORATIONS: STORIES FROM THE FIELD

Whinlands Field Centre, Annalong, 1965–1990

Thompson Steele writes:

THE RE-ORGANISATION OF secondary schooling in Northern Ireland brought about dramatic changes in the education system. Most children, who didn't pass the new Qualifying Examination, went to secondary intermediate schools, or remained at their former public elementary schools. Some teachers in Belfast schools took their pupils hostelling, and also to camps at Dundrum. The Churches' Youth Welfare Council's Centre at Shimna House, Newcastle, also proved a very popular destination.

John Malone, who had taught in Edenderry and Ashfield Boys' Secondary Schools, was one of the teachers who introduced young people to what, for many, was a completely new experience, *school field trips*. At Orangefield, John encouraged his staff to take class groups and school societies to Shimna House and other accommodation such as youth hostels including Bloody Bridge as well as cottages at the Ballagh and Spence's Mountain. This practice continued until Shimna House was sold in the early 1960s.

The loss of Shimna House caused great concern to Mr Malone. Fortunately, it was discovered that the Central Council for Physical Recreation (now the N.I. Sports Council) was vacating its rented house, Ballagh Cottage, on the Old Glasdrumman Road. In 1964, Orangefield decided to rent this house for a trial period to ascertain if there was sufficient interest and enthusiasm amongst the staff to justify obtaining a larger property at some future date. The time spent at Ballagh Cottage proved to be so beneficial and successful that before the end of the first year of use, it was decided to seek a more commodious property.

The first property viewed was the vacant, for-sale Police Station in the centre of Rostrevor. The fact that the station had a prison cell appealed to some staff. In Ballycastle, two properties were viewed, a detached house on the golf course and Corrymeela. Next, the quest returned to the Mournes where two locations were viewed, Ballyardle Cottage outside Kilkeel, and a green field site at Glasdrumman.

In March 1965, John Malone and Thompson Steele went to view the Mullartown Parochial Hall outside Annalong. Later that day, a lady who had been a contemporary of Mr Malone at Methodist College Belfast, called at his home to inquire if it would be possible for her son, Malcolm Kidd, to be enrolled at Orangefield. John Malone remembered that this lady had been raised in Annalong and mentioned to her that earlier that day he'd been in Annalong viewing Mullartown Parochial Hall to assess its suitability for use as a field centre for the School. Mrs Kidd informed him that her uncle's house, 'Whinlands', was for sale for £5,000 and that he should go to Annalong and visit the property.

On seeing the house in two acres of land, Mr Malone realised he had found the ideal spot. He was so enthusiastic, he arranged for interested staff to view the house the following Sunday. Twenty nine staff travelled to Whinlands, and agreed that it would be ideal for the School. However, they all wondered how on earth the school would find the £5,000 asking price.

Unknown to the staff, Mr Malone secured a bank loan for £5,000 and purchased the house. He was convinced somewhere a Trust would respond favourably for a grant. Through the good offices of G. B. Newe, Secretary of the Northern Ireland Council for Social Services, he was advised that the Carnegie Trust might be a suitable body to target for this pioneering project. In August 1965, Mr Lowe, the secretary of the Carnegie Trust UK and Mrs Sharpe, a trustee, came from Scotland to view Whinlands and discussed the project with Mr Malone and some of the staff.

Jim Holland, Jack Eaton and Don McBride, along with their wives and children as well as some pupils from the School, went to stay at Whinlands during the time of the Carnegie Visit. This meant that the house and the grounds were a hive of activity during the visit. In addition, Thompie Steele along with John Malone took Mr Lowe and Mrs Sharpe up the road from Whinlands to the Carrick Track to let them see the proximity of the Mournes to the house.

The visitors were impressed with the house and its potential as well as the charm of the Annalong area. They listened most intently to the plans the School had in mind for improving the property. The house had two main disadvantages: it only had had two toilets, one of which was outside; and it lacked proper washing facilities for the boys. It is interesting to note that for the first two years of its existence as a centre, the young Amazons from East Belfast washed outside in the garage using buckets of cold water. The plans to improve Whinlands included enlarging the kitchen, and building a two-storied shower and toilets block so that the house could cater for parties of boys and girls. From the outset, the staff and pupils of Orangefield Girls' School gave their enthusiastic support to the project.

When Mr Malone and Mr Steele left the Carnegie party to the Glasgow boat, it was apparent the visitors were returning to Dunfermline highly impressed with what they had seen and heard. When School opened again in September 1965, everyone's energies turned to raising money for Whinlands. There was also a tremendous demand from the staff and boys to sample the facilities at Annalong. The house was soon heavily booked by school groups from the Boys' and the Girls' Schools. The first group of Orangefield boys to stay at the centre was from Mr Gowen's class of 1965-66.

In October 1965, Mr Malone received a telegram from The Carnegie Trust saying it was prepared, under certain conditions, to cover the purchase price of the house. These conditions were spelt out in a following letter: (i) the house was to be held in Trust by a body known as 'The Whinlands Trust', (ii) the house was to be extended by the addition of extra toilets and washrooms, and (iii) other groups were permitted to book the house. Mr Malone and his staff readily agreed to these terms.

A School Fair, organised by Rodney Usher and Bob Ashe, was planned for a Saturday in June 1966 and, fortunately, the weather was kind. The Boys' and Girls' Schools were both used for the event and the sward between the two Orangefields resembled a tented village. Marquees were erected on the Friday afternoon, and a group of senior boys volunteered to sleep in them overnight to keep 'prowlers at bay.' On Saturday morning, Mr Gowen toured the district with a loudspeaker inviting everyone to come to the Whinlands Fair at Orangefield. This prodigious event, which was opened by the well-known UTV presenter David Mahlowe, raised £1,000. With the School Band playing conductor John Ritchie's Basin Street Variations on the "Death March" and, by special request of Bob Ashe, Sandie Shaw's Eurovision Song Contest winner "Puppet on a String", a carnival atmosphere was created and greatly enjoyed by the community at large. The following year, a second School Fair was held, and raised a further £1,400.

Attractions at the School Fairs held in 1966 and 1967 included the "Kinnegar Flyer" train, kindly provided as well as staffed by, members of the Royal Inniskilling Fusiliers and the Queen's Royal Irish Hussars; go-kart racing and pony rides; a huge supermarket located within the Assembly Hall; tombola "supervised" by Raymond King; Art and Craftwork Sales in the hands of Messrs. Douglas, Lannie and Megarry; and Book Sales.

In the Girls' School, Fashion Shows and discotheque sessions were held as well as provision made for baby-minding and serving teas; pram-pushing races. Other attractions were Sam McCready's circus activities, Moore Sinnerton's "Motion Picture Palace", and various Fancy Dress competitions. Small children paid sixpence for diving into a big bran tub for treasures such as water pistols, toy trumpets, squeakers and mouth organs; a Plant Sale was held and included specimens from Brian Sloan's garden, augmented by produce from John Malone's town garden at Belmont Park, which was really an allotment. Bean-Bag throwing, coin rolling, hoopla, and throwing table tennis balls into cups, were all under the supervision of Anne Preston and her team. Jack Eaton's singular contribution to fund-raising efforts are detailed elsewhere under the heading *Chicken Fayre*.

Hundreds of people attended the two School Fairs which proved to be among the most memorable days in the history of Orangefield. Fifty years ago, the sums raised appear modest; however, their monetary value today would be in excess of £45,000. Member of staff Billy McKee, then a pupil, remembers how the purchase of Whinlands was an immense event at the time, and provided a focal point for the School community. Billy's recollections include the issuing of Bob-a-Job type cards to each boy, and the intense competition they engendered among pupils:

"For a School Fair, I remember suggesting a Ballot for a tent and this resulted in me being given the bus fare to head to the Scout Shop in town and collect the prize. It proved to be a great attraction and money-spinner, both in the school on the run-up to the Fete as well as on the gloriously sunny Saturday of the main event."

The building of the first extension to Whinlands was completed in September 1967. The builder of the extension was Leslie McCullough, whose son was on the school staff, and the plans were drawn by Mr Douglas' brother, Colin. Whinlands was opened officially on 28th October 1967 by Capt. Terence O'Neill, the Prime Minister of Northern Ireland. The Governor of N. Ireland, Lord Grey of Naunton, declined to do the honours because he didn't work at the week-ends. This grand event was planned to be housed in a huge marquee which had been pitched two days before. Unfortunately, there was an overnight gale and the marquee, like the veil in the temple, was rent in twain!

Whinlands Programme, Official Opening Ceremony, 28th October, 1967.

At very short notice, the ceremony was switched to Kilhorne Parish Church, Annalong.

By the time of the official opening of Whinlands over £10,000 had been raised. However, there was still a debt of £12,000 owed to the bank. This was not paid off until 1970 when Mr Weston was Acting Principal.

In 1976, another extension comprising a classroom, dining room, additional dormitories and a drying room, was completed at a cost of £15,000. On this occasion, the Department of Education, through its Community Relations Branch, gave a 50% grant towards the cost of the work. This phase of the development of Whinlands was opened officially by John Malone.

On the same day, a new set of gates were opened by Mr and Mrs George Doyle, whose son Colin was an ex-pupil. The gates were paid for by the Doyle family. 'Enterprise Ulster' rounded off this phase by landscaping the ground, rebuilding a granite wall on to the Moneydarragh Road, removing the wooden garage and replacing it with a more sturdy structure, part of which became a museum housing local artefacts.

In 1968, Mr Allan Kilgore was appointed to the staff of Orangefield Boys' School as Whinlands Field Officer. The Department of Education was not pleased and questioned the appointment. However, John Malone was not prepared to let the Department's protestations get in the way of the progress of Whinlands. After taking up residence in Annalong in 1969, Mr Kilgore organised and oversaw the varied programmes on offer at Whinlands. Undoubtedly, Allan Kilgore played a vital role in the development of Orangefield's very own field centre.

Between 1965 and 1990, over 1000 young people per year participated in residential courses and activities lasting at least two days. Each year, during July and August, the centre was a popular residential venue used by various church groups as well as young people supported by Friends of the Handicapped, an organisation that had given financial support to the School's endeavour to have its own field centre.

The success of Whinlands can obviously be attributed to the enthusiasm of the pupils and young people who used the centre. However, over the years the commitment and support of so many teachers from the Boys' and Girls' Schools, who so willingly gave of their time to accompany groups to Whinlands, was also a crucial factor.

Headmasters Brian Weston and Ken Stanley maintained unwavering support for the centre's continued existence and well-being. Allan Kilgore held the post of Field Officer for thirty years, and his enthusiasm and commitment to the educational project remained undaunted. The author of this article, for 25 years in the Boys' School, co-ordinated all of the tasks associated with Whinlands, a

Annalong fishermen checking their nets.

vital role carried out by Ken Smyth from 1990 onwards in the newly merged, co-educational Orangefield High School.

Since 1965, many other centres for fieldwork and outdoor pursuits were opened in Mourne country. Some of them were operated and staffed by the Education and Library Boards of the time. What made Whinlands unique was that it was the first school field centre to be established in the Mournes and it was managed by a committee of trustees, the majority of whom had a connection with Orangefield Boys' School.

For many years, the centre was an example of the vision and drive of a unique headmaster, John Malone, [1917-1982]. Unquestionably, he was one of the most remarkable and outstanding men in the field of secondary schooling in the immediate post-war era, whose concept of education reached far beyond the bounds of the classroom and the school environs.

Whinlands museum: More artefacts held in a cabinet made by Larry Lannie, Heavy Craft Department.

A traditional Mourne hearth from Spence's Mountain.

Pupils' Common Room. The Mourne granite fireplace was built in memory of George Hayes, Art Department, who disappeared in 1965 while on an ill-fated canoeing expedition in Canada.

Classroom/Recreation Room. The mural, titled 'Mourne', was painted by Edward Calderbank, a pupil at the School from 1960-1967. The work arose out of an Art Department visit to Whinlands.

Whinlands museum: Artefacts and Photographs on display.

Pupils from Ken Smyth's class refuelling after a day spent in outdoor pursuits.

A group of boys in Annalong Valley with Allan Kilgore, the Whinlands Field Officer.

Boys walking at a frozen Blue Lough flanked by Slievelamaghan, Mournes.

Mr Steele pointing out to Brian Munn, Kevin Balmer, and classmates, geological and geographical features.

Harry Wilson clearing ditch in grounds at Whinlands and filling Mr Steele's wheelbarrow.

Chicken Fayre

Raising money for Whinlands made many demands on the creativity and energies of the School community. Member of staff Thompson Steele and pupil Billy McKee give their respective accounts of the chicken-plucking activity that to this day remains a vivid part of Orangefield lore. John Malone's family home in Downpatrick had its chicken run, the place where a young JMM first honed his skills ...

Thompson Steele: At the Summer Fair 1968, Jack Eaton introduced a novel fund-raiser to the event. He persuaded his mother who lived on a small farm outside Ballyclare to raise chickens for boiling. Orders for the boiling fowl were placed by the staffs of the Girls' and the Boys' Schools.

Jack Eaton and Thompie Steele travelled to Ballyclare after school to collect the chickens which Jack's mother had killed by wringing their necks. From Ballyclare the boxes containing the deceased hens were taken to Crossgar by car where arrangements had been made to have them plucked.

On arrival at Bell's in Crossgar the plucking machine operator pointed out that the machine wouldn't pluck cold dead chickens and proceeded to demonstrate this. What was to be done?

As Jack Eaton and Thompie Steele travelled back to Orangefield Jack was heard to mutter "If my mother had not spent so much time rearing and killing those birds, I'd stop now and throw the whole blooming lot over the nearest hedge."

When the dejected entrepreneurs arrived back at Orangefield, John Malone, some staff and senior boys were making preparations for the Great Fair. John Malone soon solved the problem of the feathered fowl by escorting the senior boys to one of the P.E. Changing Rooms where he proceeded to give a demonstration of how to pluck a dead chicken and then supervised the youthful workforce.

Until the day he retired from Orangefield in 1990, Rodney Usher claimed there were still feathers floating about in that changing room!

Billy McKee: An abiding memory of a School Fete was plucking chickens late into the night and early hours of the morning, on the Thursday preceding the event, after the Schools Sports Night. Along with a number of others, I was approached by Mr Malone (perhaps other staff too) on the Athletics Track asking if we had a phone (I suspect not overly common in those days), and also if we could help to pluck some chickens after the Sports Evening? A positive reply to both and we were assured our parents would be contacted to inform them of the arrangement and a lift home would be provided.

This resulted in a gathering of pupils and some staff in the large changing room along with a large number of still-feathered chicken carcasses. Apparently, the automatic plucking machine had malfunctioned and plucking was best completed whilst the birds had some body heat.

The volunteers were then promptly given a demonstration on how to pluck the same birds to avoid ripping the skin.

This is where my memory fades, but I can definitely remember John Malone and Jack Eaton being present and the demonstration resulting in a ripped skin after which we were promptly told to get started before the birds became too cold.

This occasion also provided me with my first full cup of coffee when Mr Malone asked the

Boys' School mobile classrooms, Assembly Hall entrance, and woodwork rooms. Girls' School playground and gymnasium. Car Park and Marquees for School Fairs, Laburnum. In the distance the newly-built Braniel Flats.

boys if we would like a cup of coffee and took us to the Staffroom. The coffee was so strong you could have stood a spoon in it, but then, it might have been designed to keep us awake. If my recollections are right Rodney Usher, Head of PE, had a few words to say on the use of his Kingdom for such an activity and the reverberations could be detected the next day!

Thompson Steele *joined the Science Department in September 1958. He took over David Hammond's class after David joined the BBC in 1964 as a Producer of Schools Programmes and remained in that department. When the quest for a residential centre in the Mournes commenced, Thompson was asked to look after the pilot project at Ballagh Cottage. After a year, Whinlands was acquired in 1965, and he became "Whinlands Organiser", a position he held until his retirement in 1990. With the raising of the School leaving age [ROSLA] in the early 1970s, Thompson moved to the School Certificate Department to join Sam Preston, Billy Burnison and Austin Hewitt. He succeeded Billy Burnison as head of that department in 1979.*

Beyond 'Chalk and Talk'

Matt Maginnis joined Orangefield in 1966. Matt, a young subject teacher whose boots were made for walking, remembers ...

I JOINED ORANGEFIELD Boys' School in 1966 as a Geography teacher with extras. In those days, subject teachers were expected to teach more than one subject, especially at Junior level. So, I also taught Maths, History and Religious Education [R.E.]. Staff at Orangefield also had other roles to perform as Form Tutors, Sport Coaches, Rugby Referees, and Weekend Leaders on residential trips to Whinlands in Annalong. Indeed, some older members of staff preferred to use the term 'Schoolmaster' instead of 'Teacher' because there were so many aspects to the job at that time.

The Geography Department was well-organised by 'Captain' Duncan Scarlett, and there was a team of graduate specialists, Raymond King and Stead Black, already in place offering the subject at GCE 'O' and 'A' level.

We were all products of Professor Estyn Evans's Geography Department in the early sixties which included some outstanding Geographers such as Noel Mitchel, Robin Glasscock, Nick Stephens, Doc. Common and Rosemary Harris. The Geology Department in Elmwood Avenue, especially Professor Williams and Doc. Preston, also helped mould the Geographers in my student days. The Geography Department had a solid reputation and all of us believed in 'Geography through the soles of your boots.' Whinlands was a very useful location for physical and human topics as well as Geology, Mountain navigation, Map reading and moderate scrambles to the Cave on Cove Mountain.

'Mourne Country', by Estyn Evans, became an essential reference book for all Geographers in Orangefield Boys' School. Fieldwork gave the boys a sense of scale and understanding of the formation of landforms and land use in Mourne Country. Allan Kilgore, the School's Field Officer at Whinlands, provided valuable support, and he also had a wide range of local knowledge of Mourne botany, wildlife, folklore and mountain safety. During the herring season, Allan often provided a supply of fish for the Whinlands' version of a fish supper. The students always produced a field report at the end of the week and this helped them to success in formal exams. Often the report was broken down into chapters, each written by 6th Form students such as Trevor Magee, Jim McIlwaine, Harold Smith, Jackie Redpath, Gordon Smyth, Gordon Copeland, Norman Darbyshire, William Duff, Herbie Barr and Richard Gough, to name but a few.

Orangefield Boys' was comprehensive in outlook and it offered a variety of courses to the pupils of East Belfast. The Extension, in my day, was designed to provide a richer variety of courses in Metalwork and Woodwork given the imminent raising of the school leaving age to 16. By the early 1970s, ROSLA was upon us and new courses had to be devised to motivate and encourage all abilities.

Outward Bound

John Malone, after the official opening of Whinlands, was keen that all Staff had the opportunity to gain training in Outward Bound activities which would enhance the Whinlands experience for all the boys. Orangefield Boys' teachers were an adventurous lot, and there were many instances of planned expeditions and courses organised by individuals with specialist knowledge. For example, there were Mountaineering Courses at the Tollymore Mountain Centre, Canoeing at New Forge, Eskimo Roll Courses in a local swimming pool, Canoe Trails down the Quoile and Strangford Lough, Bill Skelly's Sailing Courses at Killyleagh, and Rodney Usher's Coaching and Rugby Referee Courses held at the school.

One famous staff expedition took place in the summer of 1969, at the time that the Troubles began to take root in Belfast. The GRAND CHASM EXPEDITION was organised by Peter Scott of the English Department and it gave teachers an opportunity to go beyond Whinlands into the limestone cave systems of County Fermanagh. He picked staff of '*proven fortitude, reliability and determination*' to sample pot-holing around Marble Arch, Boho and Blacklion. Bill Skelly, John Allen, Jeffrey Wynne and myself apparently made the grade

and we ended up in the Spartan base camp in Blacklion with bare floorboards and a resident bat on the ceiling. Helmets, lamps, torches, candles, boiler suits, stout boots, woollen jumpers, sleeping bags and airbeds were essential items for all participants.

Other cavers regaled us with stories about 'suds on the roof' after a heavy downpour but Pete was determined that we would have the full underground experience and lined up such delights as crawling along the 'Sewer Pipe' and avoiding being sucked down a sump! The Marble Arch Caves are now a major tourist attraction but, in 1969, it was a privilege to see all the dripstone and flowstones before the system was open to the public. I still have the photographs from the expedition and they provided valuable visual aids for many lessons on Karst Scenery. Thanks for that, Pete! John Malone joked, when we returned, that he found our whole speleological experience *'too Freudian to contemplate'*.

Whinlands

I am sure many pupils and staff have plenty of stories to tell about Whinlands. John Malone was born in Downpatrick and, from the drumlin belt, had a clear view of Slieve Donard and the High Mournes. He negotiated the purchase of Whinlands in 1965 and he saw the potential for introducing urban students to the rural delights of Mourne Mountain, plain and seascape. Academics in Geography, Geology, History and Biology were not the only ones catered for and Art, Drama and Outward Bound were also included in the weekly programmes.

Staff often took their Form Class for a week of planned and structured activities. These included mountain navigation, climbing on Little Bignian, abseiling, canoeing, swimming in the Annalong River and living together. There are many stories about Whinlands and each trip had its own set of adventures and characters.

I used to help Bill Skelly with the Duke of Edinburgh Silver assessment in the late 1960s. One June night we had arranged to inspect a Silver group's campsite at the Hare's Gap, a well-known landmark. We set off at 11pm up the Trassey track to the gap in total darkness. This was a mild summer night and we were armed with torches and whistles and a six figure reference for the campsite. We got to the gap at midnight and gave several blasts on the whistles and flashed our torches down the slopes. We searched the area in a wide circle but there was no sign of the party! Disappointed, we returned to Whinlands, thinking that the group had got lost on the Brandy Pad.

The next day the group walked into Whinlands with tales of their ordeal – blisters, starvation, exhaustion, the only thing missing was an encounter with a yeti! They were completely gunked when we told them we could not find them at the Hare's Gap, the agreed second campsite. It turned out that the group had hidden in a local farmer's barn and the farmer's wife had provided them with food and tea! You could not fault them on initiative but we had to fail them for not completing the planned route.

Near Whinlands, just beyond Longstone, was an area we called 'The Maze' because it was lined by a high density of typical Mourne drystone walls. It was all on the flat and ideal for orienteering exercises. I devised a trail for the boys based on a map with compass bearings and grid references. The idea was that each group of four would go round the rectangular course collecting clues from tins which had been secreted in the stone walls at each junction. Each group handed in their collection at the end of the trail as proof of

Whinlands Group: Peter Scott, Bill Skelly and the back-up team

completion. This exercise worked out well for junior pupils and taught them lessons in team work, map reading, grid references, and bearings. However, one day the whole exercise went badly wrong for two of my colleagues. One group failed to return to base and a search party was mustered to look for them before dark. Fortunately, the group was found safe and sound in the middle of 'The Maze', slightly dejected because they had not completed the route. They had a colourful story to tell. One of the group, let us call him R, had been caught short and he had to dash behind a wall. The only source of paper available was in the tin with the clues and you can guess the rest!

One favourite walk in the Annalong Valley was to the cave on Cove Mountain. The route was usually up the trail past the entrance to the Bignian Tunnel and then to the waterfall and pool. At the cave there was a tight squeeze upwards before you managed to emerge on the top of the spur with a view below of the meanders and the incised terminal moraine. This is one of the best views of the Mournes because there are so many iconic features on show.

One day a group was walking along this trail and they spotted a new form of wildlife. I am not sure if it was an Orangefied group or one from Strandtown Primary. As they approached the waterfall, they disturbed the new species of wildlife. Two naked females had to scamper for their clothes to protect their modesty and retreat from the group's chosen path to the cave. A new term was introduced into Whinlands folklore and, thereafter, the boys would request a return visit to see the 'bobbits' again. Alas, this was the first and only sighting.

Often at night, Whinlands provided a suitable atmosphere for ghost stories. A favourite was the story of *'Herman the German'* with Stead

Black often specialising in the different versions of this tale of Haunted Whinlands. This bogeyman wandered the grounds and his presence was usually signalled by a 'cold spell' in the dorm. One night the storyteller was so effective the teachers in charge heard an almighty clatter and clunking of beds in the dorm above. They raced upstairs and found all the beds pushed together in a corner. *'We are trying to avoid the 'cold spell' sir!'* Silence reigned that night.

Allan Kilgore, the Field Officer of Whinlands, was a great support to all staff. He was and still is part of the local community in Annalong. Steeped in Mourne folklore and neighbourly banter, he often accompanied field groups on mountain walks with his dog, Hans. A vivid raconteur, Allan would tell tales of the peregrines on Buzzards Roost, the herring hogs offshore, the Diamond Rocks as well as the workings of the lowly dung beetle encountered on the trail. He had a wealth of knowledge of Mourne history, industry, planning, rescue and conservation.

Allan often let staff use the centre as a base for the Mourne Wall Walk in the late sixties, 1968 & 1969. Staff and some former pupils attempted this marathon of 22 miles over the High Mournes. Thompson Steele, Stead Black, Frank Loan and myself based ourselves at Whinlands on Saturday nights for our early Sunday morning start. I have more pleasant memories of 1969 when Brian Petrie, an ex-pupil, acted as pacemaker and got us round in 9 hours. This was about three hours faster than the year before. When we picked up our certificates at the end, we were a trifle disheartened to learn that a Swiss walker had completed the walk in 5 hours! Apparently he said, *'These are not mountains, just hills.'*

Allan Kilgore with a group in the Mournes

Stead Black [1965-1990] reflects on classroom teaching and life outdoors ...

I started my Orangefield teaching career in September, 1965. I was absolutely delighted to have been given this opportunity, as I had spent my final teaching practice there, and it was apparent this was a very special place in which to teach.

Duncan Scarlett and Raymond King were the two specialist teachers within the Department. Duncan was an excellent Head of Department, teacher and mentor. I was so fortunate that Duncan helped to shape my teaching career. Duncan's class management was excellent coupled with his firm discipline as well as canny and sincere interest in all his pupils. His blackboard work was something to which to aspire, worksheets produced on the geography of Ireland invariably were of textbook quality, while information and maps provided for field courses in the Annalong area were outstanding.

Matt Maginnis joined the department in 1966. A little later, Harry Adams joined the staff and identified readily with the ethos of the Geography department. In 1972, I was appointed Head of Department when Duncan and Matt left. Over the years, I was lucky to work with very many dedicated teachers within the department. Davy McBride and Gordon Topping were appointed to replace Matt and Duncan. Harry Adams left to move to Newtownbreda, and eventually became Vice-Principal of Donaghadee High School. Gordon Topping became the Chief Executive Officer of the North-Eastern Education and Library Board. Chris Acheson, after a number of years teaching in Orangefield, moved on and eventually became Principal of Beechlawn School in Hillsborough.

Nathan Todd helped introduce the successful application of Techniques of Statistical analysis and the New Geography into the classroom. This enhanced the delivery of fine GCE 'A 'Level Coursework and Individual Coursework. After leaving Orangefield, Nathan taught in Ashleigh House School and from there he was appointed a Field Officer with the Belfast Education and Library Board. David Clarke, a former GCE 'A' Level Geography student at Orangefield, returned to the school after teacher training at Stranmillis College. David helped coach the 1st XV before being appointed to Regent House, where David Spence was Head of Department. [David had spent a year teaching in Orangefield in the early 1970s.]

Jim Chambers, after his appointment, taught in the Boys' School until the merger with Orangefield Girls' School in 1990. Ken Smyth, another former pupil, also returned to the school. Although a specialised P.E. teacher, Ken was a first class teacher of Geography who willingly helped with GCSE fieldwork at Whinlands. As a Head of Department, I also benefitted greatly from many other teachers at the school who willingly taught Geography as a subject to their form classes, and readily bought into the aims and ethos of the department. They delivered the subject with enthusiasm and success, and I truly appreciated their commitment over many years.

Fieldwork was an important part of those taking Geography at examination level. 4th Form classes spent a Fieldwork week at Whinlands. At 6th Form, Fieldwork was undertaken in North Antrim and Whinlands and, on a number of occasions, the GCE 'A' level classes went to the British mainland. The areas we travelled to included South Wales (twice), Devon three times, North Wales and the Highlands of Scotland.

In my first GCE class, there were six GCE Grade 1s [GCE candidates were graded 1 to 9 at that time]. I remember Henry McFarland and the class of long-haired youths who, if not set out in school uniform, would have resembled a Pop Group. My first GCE 'A' Level class included Michael Andrews, David Clarke, Billy Murray, Colin McCool, Harold Foy, Andrew Street, Albert McDowell, Norman Shields, Kevin Adair, Brian Wilson, Brian McKeown, Robert Simpson, Alan Patterson, Noel Gilmore, Gary Dalzell and Janetha Matchett from the Girls' School. There were 22 in the class, and 19 were successful.

In the mid-1970s, the class achieved 100% success at 'A' Level, with 70% gaining A and B Grades – the names of some were David West, Crawford McGrath, the Haire twins, John McFeeters, and 'Gougher' who came to sixth form from Lisnasharragh.

Among the participants of field trips to North Antrim and Devon were Tom McCready, Stephen Brown, Mark Nelson, Brian Anderson, Clifford Gilmore, Andrew Spiers, Bobby Emerson, John Shanks, David Mackey and Robert Hanna. From the Girls' School were Rosemary Bell, Deborah Miskelly, Sandra Chapman and Ann McGagherty.

Brian Anderson was President of the Methodist Church in Ireland 2015/16. In a recent conversation with Thomas McKeown, (Tucker), he recalled being sent to Exeter when he first started work – a place he had visited during Fieldwork. 'Tucker' was a star man as Fagan in the school's production of *Oliver*.

From the 1980s, I remember Alan Stitt, now Professor and Chair of Experimental Ophthalmology at Queen's University Belfast, Michael McGarry, Nigel Carson, Ken Kavanagh, Angela McAlpine and Grace Flack.

Orangefield was a school for real characters, and two I remember from the '80s were Rooster (David Roulston) and Jonesy (David Jones). They were inseparable and always full of fun. Jonesy is now Colonel D.A. Jones, M.B.E. and is working in Kosovo for NATO and the British Embassy.

Stead Black graduated in Geography from Queen's University Belfast in 1964 and then studied for a Diploma in Education [Dip Ed], a one-year full-time course for post-graduates wishing to train as post-primary schoolteachers. Stead joined the Orangefield teaching staff in 1965 and served as Head of the Geography Department from 1972 to 1990.

From 1972 Matt Maginnis taught in schools across Europe. On returning to the UK in 1985, he was appointed to the Girls' Model School as Head of Geography. Prior to Matt's retirement, he had been Acting Vice Principal at the Girls' Model.

— 14. —
ALL THE WORLD'S A STAGE

Orangefield Dramatic Society 1961–1965

THE PLAYS OF 17th century French comic dramatist, Molière (1622-1673), seem today an unlikely choice for performance by a Boys' Secondary Intermediate School located in industrial East Belfast. The Orangefield Dramatic Society, formed in 1961 by Ronnie Horner, Head of Drama, inaugurated an extraordinary decade of outstanding theatrical productions that enjoyed widespread acclaim across the city of Belfast and beyond. Productions included:

1962 "The Would-Be Gentleman", A modern English adaptation of "le Bourgeois Gentilhomme" by Molière (Performed 21-24 March, 1962);

1962 "The Imaginary Invalid", A modern English adaptation of "Le Malade Imaginaire" by Molière (Performed 12-15 December, 1962);

1964 "The Miser", A modern English adaptation of "L'Avare" by Molière (Performed 4-7 March 1964);

1965 "Tartuffe", A modern English adaptation of "Tartuffe" or "L'Imposteur" by Molière (Performed 3-6 March, 1965).

Walter Ellis acted in all of the Molière productions. Walter's review of *The Miser* published in the school's newspaper, *The Orangefield Observer*, is reprinted below:

"After the success of our two preceding plays, Le Bourgeois Gentilhomme and Le Malade Imaginaire we all hoped that The Miser *(L'Avare) would not be a lesser production, especially in view of the fact that we were to be honoured by a visit from the French Consul and other important guests from Queen's and Stranmillis College. We were therefore pleased and proud when we were informed by many authoritative people that it was possibly the best of the three.*

In Le Bourgeois Gentilhomme *and* Le Malade Imaginaire *there was perhaps more raucous comedy;* The Miser *having its comedy in isolated incidents with moments of pathos and tragedy interspersed. There was also in the last scene of the two earlier plays a comedy ballet which was noticeably lacking in* The Miser. *This was, however, remedied by the tremendously high standard of acting throughout the play and the realisation that this was more than a farcical play, one with serious motives as well.*

Robert Freeburn (Harpagon) Derek Sloan (Frosine)

Throughout the play Robert Freeburn gave an outstanding representation of the miser;

especially in his numerous quarrels with Cléante, Élise, Valère, Jacques, his cook and coachman, and the Justice he engages to recover his stolen money. Perhaps the climax of his performance was his "requiem" on discovering his money to have been stolen and each night as he finished it thunderous applause followed him off stage. His was an amazing performance which deservedly won him most of the applause.

Also outstanding amongst the actors were Valère played by Frederick Donnan, whose quick changes from lover to flatterer were delightful to watch; Alan Kirker as Cléante, a young man hopelessly in love for the first time; Ronald Bunting as Jacques a roguish buffoon; Mervyn Watson as La Flèche, a diplomatic worldly-wise Parisien; and Derek Sloan as a languorous Froisine. Walter Ellis, of course, was Master Simon and the Justice of the Peace. (This boy did indeed give a splendid performance, second to none.)

Robert Freeburn (Harpagon), Garfield Coleman (Élise)

The set presented many difficulties in that it was supposed to have the appearance of decaying grandeur, but Mr Thorpe who assembled it and Mr. Douglas and Mr. Craig who painted it are to be congratulated on giving a splendid effect in showing a once-stately home now much cracked and mildewed. Make-up and costumes were again used to the best possible advantage giving (in most cases) normal boys the appearance of senility or striking good looks, or in the case of the males playing girls, the attributes of the fairer sex which made it impossible to detect that they were indeed boys.

A special word of thanks must go to Mr. Horner who produced the play, designed the costumes, designed and assisted with the set, and helped with the make-up. To him the school owes a deep debt of gratitude in that he has succeeded in making ours the best school play in Belfast, perhaps in the whole of Ireland."

Molière presented his comedy *Tartuffe* in May 1664 before Louis XIV, the King of France at Versailles, as part of the festival of 'The Pleasures of the Enchanted Isle'. The theme of the play was a satire on bigotry and religious hypocrisy. Its effect was immediate: it aroused a storm of protest from scandalised clerical and quasi-religious circles, who saw themselves held up to ridicule on the public stage.

Robert Freeburn (Tartuffe), Garfield Coleman (Elmire), Fred Donnan (Orgon)

Molière remarked in his Preface to the 1669 edition of the play, "*People can put up with rebukes but they cannot bear being laughed at:*

they are prepared to be wicked but they dislike appearing ridiculous." The satire, however, went too nearly home and not even Louis XIV dared publically to license an indictment of religious hypocrisy, with which he secretly agreed. King Louis XIV, therefore, found it expedient to prohibit the play's performance.

The play remained banned for a period of five years despite Molière's protests that *Tartuffe* was a satire on false and not genuine piety. After extensive revision to make the text less offensive to religious susceptibilities, permission was granted to allow the play in its final form to be performed at the Palais Royal, Molière's own theatre, on 5th February, 1669.

Robert Freeburn [Tartuffe], Mervyn Watson (Damis), Fred Donnan (Orgon)

Tartuffe was an immediate and prodigious success and it continued to be the most frequently performed and remunerative of all Molière's plays, in his own lifetime and afterwards.

From the cast list of the Molière era at the School Walter Ellis became a journalist, editor and writer working for *The Irish Times, The Sunday Times* and *The Financial Times.* Robert Freeburn taught at Fettes College, Edinburgh, before becoming Director of Drama at Eton College. Robert later accepted a senior post as Voice Coach at the Royal London Academy of Music and Dramatic Art and is Director of the Voice and Speech Centre, London. Fred Donnan was accepted by the Guildhall School of Music and Drama, London, but did not take up the offer. Fred worked as an executive with British Airways in Manchester and New York. In retirement in rural Lancashire, Fred leads a local group of players. Ronnie Bunting trained as a teacher and Alan Kirker, a former Head Boy, became Head of Maths at Kilkeel High School.

The late John Hewitt became a professional actor and starred in many productions at the Lyric Theatre. John was also Director of the Arts Theatre in Belfast and appeared in numerous drama productions televised on BBC and UTV. Mervyn Watson enjoyed a career as an agricultural historian in the Ulster Museum and Ulster Folk Museum at Cultra. Arthur Murdock and John Gallagher qualified as schoolteachers. Derek Sloan trained as a chef at Belfast College of Technology. Subsequently, Derek worked in two London restaurants but, sadly, a promising career as a restaurateur, was cut short by his untimely death in 1973.

Eds. Note: *We are very grateful to Ronnie Horner for providing the photographic, critical and biographical information included in this article. He left Orangefield in 1965 to take up a lecturing post in Drama at Neville's Cross College of Education, Durham, and then Bedford College of Education. Later, Ronnie taught English at Wellington College and Pangbourne College in Berkshire. He also took part in Schools Broadcasts from Belfast.*

All right on the night ...

Wilfie Pyper [1961-68] writes about life as well as his experience of Drama under the direction of Ronnie Horner and Sam McCready.

DESPITE HAVING SPENT a lifetime in theatre, I have never subscribed to the adage *'It will be all right on the night'* because, as those who have worked with me will tell, I believe if a show is not ready well in advance then someone hasn't been doing their work. I have discovered that there are many *'all right on the night moments'*, times when a particular event upsets all the plans you have made and yet as a consequence of these seeming disasters, the resulting outcome opens up hitherto unthought-of avenues.

The first, and perhaps the most formative of these, was in 1960. Shortly before taking my 11+ my mother unexpectedly passed away. In an era when bereavement counselling for children was deemed unnecessary, I rather unsuccessfully muddled my way through my final year at primary school. Consequently, the planned transfer to Grosvenor High School did not take place and my next level of education was to unfold at Orangefield Boys' School. What appeared to be a huge disappointment was to shape the rest of my life in a manner which I could never have envisaged.

We had a reasonably creative household and, coming from a Salvation Army background, I had been well-versed in brass playing, choral singing and getting up to perform from a very early age. This was a fact that seemed to have eluded staff at my primary school but one which I was to discover was to be fully exploited in my new educational home.

It is recognised that among many other factors, John Malone's success as a head teacher was his ability to surround himself with excellent young staff, many of whom went on to carve prestigious careers in education. Among these was a certain Ronald Horner, a somewhat unique individual with a prodigious talent for theatre and in particular at that time, the works of Molière. As a result, this became his writer of choice for the school productions for a number of years. A strange choice many might think for an East Belfast secondary school but, as with so many things in Orangefield, there were no boundaries which dictated or limited what the boys could achieve. These were not school plays in the 'make do' manner but sophisticated productions of an exceptional standard both in terms of their production values and level of performance expected. Such was their reputation, tickets were always at a premium, and indeed the French Consulate regularly included the plays in its diary of events to attend.

Having watched these productions in awe, consider my joy when I was deemed good enough in third year to become part of the cast for the next three years. Working with Ronnie Horner, even at this early stage, was to shape my stage craft for the rest of my life both as an actor and as a director. No expense was spared. Costumes made from specially imported material and hand-made for each actor, wigs of a professional standard, stage sets of the highest order, and an expectation of the actor to perform at the very highest level. This was something which we took for granted, but in later life were to discover was something unique.

It was during this period that one Sunday afternoon Ronnie arrived at our house in Orby to inquire of my father if I might be allowed to audition for a part in an Abbey Theatre production of *Stephen D.* Reluctantly, my father agreed (after all it was Sunday!) and so it was, as a very small boy, I walked out on that vast stage and looked into the abyss of the empty auditorium for the very first time. Little did I realise that one day I would have the privilege of bringing the first of many of my own productions into that wonderful theatre.

It was with a huge sense of shock that we were informed Mr Horner was to take up an appointment at Durham University and as a result would be leaving the school. We were devastated. Was this the end of drama at Orangefield? However, this was to be another of those '*all right on the night*' moments as Mr Malone, in his own inimitable way and foresight, replaced Ronnie Horner with a gentleman who was to become one of the leading lights in Ulster Theatre and went on to establish an international reputation, Mr Sam McCready.

Those of us who had come from the 'Molière School' were a little horrified to discover our next performance involved scaffolding and poetry and a most avant-garde entertainment. *Expression '66*, I believe it was called. Sam had arrived and over the next three years was to open our eyes to a whole new way of looking at acting and theatre. I was introduced to Stanislavsky and the method school. In essence, we were told to stop acting and 'be'. These proved to be momentous and exciting years. Rather than lose all of what had gone on before, our school productions and our acting were taken to a new level. The following year saw an epic production of Shaw's *Saint Joan*

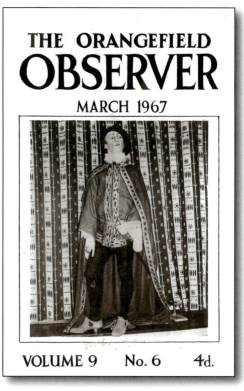

Wilfie Pyper, Earl of Warwick, Shaw's St. Joan, Assembly Hall, 28th February to 4th March 1967.

Wilfie Pyper, Best Director Gilbert and Sullivan Award and Winner of the Tommy Ebbs Trophy.

and after that a ground-breaking production of Friel's *The Enemy Within*.

Sadly, those heady days were to come to an end, but the legacy for me was incalculable. It has afforded me the privilege to work with so many talented people throughout Ireland and the United Kingdom and in a strange sense has come full circle. I have the honour of being resident director of the Belfast Operatic Company, one of Ireland's leading musical theatre groups, not surprisingly founded over fifty years ago by John Mercer, yet another product of John Malone's staffing visions at Orangefield.

All right on the night ... of course it was.

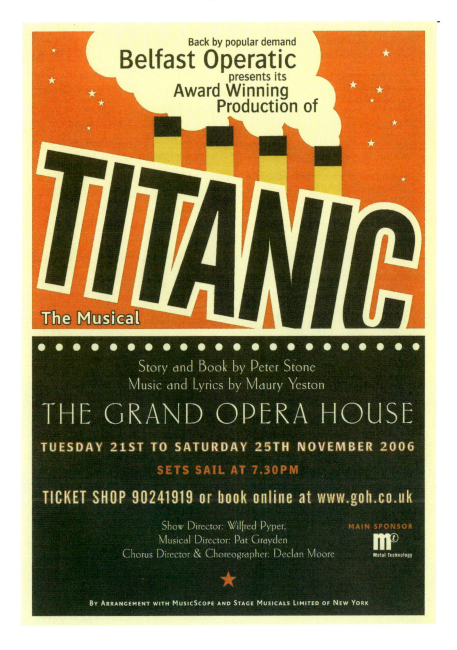

Saints and Sinners

Sam McCready writes:

APART FROM THE first interview I had when he appointed me as Head of Drama, I don't remember ever having a discussion with John Malone in his office; it always seemed to take place in a corridor or in the school foyer. And it was in a corridor that he asked me what I planned to do for the next school production. "I want to do a play with a cast and crew of a hundred," I told him, "I believe drama is not just a show. It's a process whereby pupils can grow socially, intellectually and imaginatively through their engagement with dramatic literature. Every pupil in the school should have the opportunity to take part in a play and that's why I want a cast and crew of a hundred." John Malone was a good listener. His nodding head and continued smile told me I had his blessing.

I decided to do G.B. Shaw's drama about St. Joan. It was on the GCE syllabus; it had only one female character – which could be a boy in the tradition of Shakespearean theatre – and it had over forty in the cast; it was a good start. I chose not to use the conventional school stage in the school assembly hall but to build the stage in the middle of the audience. It would be an innovative 'in-the-round' production, which would bring the action within a few feet of most of the audience. But where would I find a cast willing to risk performing on a stage that made enormous demands on the nerves and the concentration? I was able to cast the major roles but this was a large cast and I needed more. Bob Ashe came to the rescue. "Tell me what you need," he said, "and I'll get them." "I need soldiers, big, strong lads who look as if they could hold their own in a fight. The audience must believe they are putting St. Joan to death." Out Bob went to the playing fields and came back with Barrie Megarry, David Steele, Kevin Balmer, Robert McCord, Lawrence Walker, Fred Halliday and others. I had my mean soldiers!

Photo: St Joan: L-R. Brent Alexander, Brian Munn, Ashley Rodway.

As I write this, I am looking at the programme and I am astounded at the numbers involved. Apart from the 40-plus actors, there were more than fifty staff and pupils responsible for the technical aspects. Bob Ashe was the Assistant Producer, Moore Sinnerton was the Stage Manager, Trevor Scott designed the costumes and setting, John Ritchie was responsible for the music, and Eric Twaddell did the lighting.

A remarkable feature of the production was the period costumes made by Christiane Niclause, Joan McCready, and ladies of the Parents' Association, Mrs. Givan, Mrs. McGookin and Mrs. Scott. The authentic props, swords and halberds made by Messrs. Megarry, Lannie, Comyns, Eaton, McClelland and the GCE Metalwork class also aroused much admiration from the audience. One pupil from another school was heard to remark, "Look, Miss, they're using real swords!"

An enormous effort was also put into the decoration of the foyer, the preparation of the programme, and the exacting task of selling and distributing the tickets, all accomplished to a high standard by Messrs. McBride, Frazer, Douglas, Gallagher, and Holland.

Photo: St Joan: L-R Back row. David Aicken, Brent Alexander.
L-R Front Row: Norman Derbyshire, Roger Doherty, Alec Magee.

The production was a success; capacity audiences of pupils, the majority from other schools, were fully engaged in the trial and execution of the brave Joan of Arc, while everyone who had invested so much in the production, the actors, technical personnel and members of staff, felt a sense of accomplishment.

So many of the performances remain with me to this day: a towering John Hewitt as Bishop Cauchon, a dignified Trevor Magee as the Archbishop, Gordon Copeland as the supercilious De La Tremouille, Wifie Pyper as the manipulative Warwick, Robert Crone as an engaging Dauphin, and Ashley Rodway as a sympathetic Dunois, with his young page played by Brent Alexander, but special mention must be made of Brian Munn who played St. Joan with supreme sincerity and was the emotional heart of the production.

How would I follow *St Joan*? I decided I would change direction; I would not do a play; I would mount an evening of the students' own writing under the title *Expression '66: A Programme of creative writing and spoken English by the boys of Orangefield Boys' School*. A catalyst for this was my developing friendship with Bob Ashe. Bob and I had met at Stranmillis and appeared to have little in common. When I arrived in Orangefield, he barely acknowledged me, but one day he asked me if I would come to his class to talk about the production I was doing at the Lyric Theatre in Derryvolgie Avenue.

In the course of talking about the production, I realised Bob was passionate about teaching literature. He shared that passion with his classes who bombarded me with insightful questions that revealed the depth of Bob's teaching. In his creative writing classes, Bob emphasized writing from a personal perspective. "Tell me truthfully what is in your mind; don't tell me what you think I want to hear." "How do you *feel* about what you are writing about?" "How would I know you are telling the truth and not just making it up?", and with essay titles like "The First Time", his students shared an abundance of personal experiences that were often searing in their frankness and honesty.

I saw the opportunity to showcase this remarkable material in a production. I asked the Head of English, Jimmy Holland, who also placed much emphasis on creative writing, to solicit the best work from a range of classes, and with Bob's help, I made the selection and gave it some theatrical shape. The selections covered particular topics, 'Myself' 'My Family' 'Where I live'. A large number of students in black shirts and pants read and performed on a set made up of scaffolding.

We completed the programme with a performance of W.B. Yeats's one-act play, *Calvary*. *Expression '66* was an innovative alternative to the school play and yielded some talented writers, most notably Brian Keenan, whose ballad "Keep Your Hands off My Generation" was later selected by the *Daily Mail* as among the outstanding poems written in the UK. [Reproduced in Eds. Notes].

At Orangefield there was a focus on local history. This encouraged me to look to Ulster drama as a source for the next school production, and what better playwright to look at in the 1960s but Brian Friel, already making a name for himself with plays like *Philadelphia, Here I Come!* Thus I turned to an earlier play of his, *The Enemy Within*, which tells the story of St Columba's exile from Ireland to the island of Iona. The play had an all-male cast, though much smaller than *St. Joan*. Most of the characters were older, devout monks, well outside the experience of the students who would have to adapt to a time and a lifestyle very different from what they knew growing up in East Belfast. Conventional rehearsals, I thought, would not be especially helpful; how could I create conditions similar to what Columba and his fellow monks endured in Iona?

With the support of other members of staff, Moore Sinnerton, Duncan Scarlett and Trevor Scott, I took the cast to Whinlands, the school's house outside Annalong. There, for some days, they lived as Columba and his monks might have lived. They wore coarse white habits made specially by the ladies of the Parents' Association supervised by Christiane Niclause, and traditional handmade cowhide shoes, called pampooties, which had to be kept in water overnight and put on the feet wet next morning. After breakfast, we went outside and for the rest of the day the students lived as monks, finding firewood, building stone walls (there's a lot of stones around the Mournes) and searching for edible food. They built a causeway at the seashore and discovered how heavy the long white tunics could get as the salt water seeped up the fabric, weighing them down. And putting on cold, wet pampooties was not a pleasant experience. In the evening, after dinner, we sat round a fire and read scenes from the play (and actors also warmed their feet).

This unusual rehearsal process enabled the young actors to experience, to a degree, the hard, austere lives of the sixth-century monks. They also bonded socially and developed the kind of trust evident in the best theatre productions.

Moore Sinnerton joined me as co-director and the production was a model for interdisciplinary co-operation; it was also remarkable for the professional level of the staging, designed by Trevor Scott, with hand-embroidered cloaks made by Christiane Niclause and Joan McCready, the extraordinary soundscape designed by John Page, lighting by Eric Twaddell, House Management by Duncan

The Enemy Within: outdoor rehearsal at Whinlands L-R. John McKee, Ashley Rodway, Brian Munn, Colin Lewis.

Scarlett, Alan Hunter, Jimmy Holland, Henry Sinnerton, and the fine quality of the student performances, led by the dynamic Ashley Rodway as St. Columba. There were equally fine performances from John Hewitt, Colin Lewis, Brian Munn, John McKee, Thomas Trew, Wilfie Pyper, Michael McKnight and Bill McClatchey. And I would like to give a shout to Trevor Scott's beautifully designed programme,

The Enemy Within: L-R John Hewitt, Brian Munn, John McKee, Ashley Rodway.

a model of its kind, and his wonderful blown-up, black and white pictures, on display in the school foyer, of the cast at Whinlands.

To increase the exposure of the school's drama programme to a wider audience and to extend the experience of the students, we entered three of the amateur drama festivals around the province: Newry, Larne and Carrickmore. We won them all and qualified, as a result, for the Ulster Amateur Drama Finals in the Grand Opera House, Belfast, and the All-Ireland Finals in Athlone – the only school drama group in the history of amateur drama in Ireland to achieve such a feat – and we returned to Orangefield with major prizes – John Hewitt, in particular, being singled out for Best Actor Awards.

My final production at Orangefield was a production of John Milton's *Paradise Lost, Books 1&2,* which I had adapted for the stage. Dressed in black, six actors, with silver-backed books in hand, spoke and acted out the demonic actions of Satan and the other devils in what was a *tour-de-force* for young performers. I was teaching the text with my GCE English class and felt the words must be heard to be fully appreciated; I knew the extraordinary text would only come fully to life if we could see and hear it performed. Since such a production did not exist, we had to do it ourselves.

The production was mesmeric and I have to thank the extraordinarily talented group of actors who took part in it and gave me one of my richest experiences as a director and an actor (Yes, I acted in the play as well, playing Satan) – John Hewitt, Brian Munn, Colin Lewis, Michael McKnight and Brian Keenan. The cast's speaking of Milton's powerful verse, often accompanied by the music of the Moody Blues and Pink Floyd, gripped the capacity audiences, a majority of whom were GCE students from all over the province. Among my treasured possessions are letters from 6th Form students at Our Lady's Grammar School, Newry, all praising the production and thanking us for the opportunity of seeing this great work performed.

Paradise Lost: L-R. Colin Lewis, John Hewitt, Brian Munn, Michael McKnight.

Looking back on the black and white pictures of that production, I am astonished that we were doing work of this quality in a school in Belfast in 1968. When word of the production got out, we were invited to perform it in the beautiful Examinations Hall in Trinity College, Dublin for a conference of UK and Irish Teachers of Speech and Drama. Again the response from experienced teachers and performers was overwhelming.

Paradise Lost: L-R. Colin Lewis, Brian Keenan, Brian Munn, Michael McKnight.

At Orangefield, I made lifelong friends among the staff and pupils, and shepherded the acting talents of a number of the students, three of whom were accepted by the Guildhall School of Music and Drama, John Hewitt, Colin Lewis and Brian Munn. Michael McKnight was to follow in their footsteps a few years later, while other in students such as Wilfie Pyper continue to be heavily involved with drama and musicals in the province.

In five years at Orangefield, in choice of plays (two of them were about saints, the other about sinners, hence the title of this article), and in attempts to involve as many students and staff as possible, I had stuck to my belief that the school play is not merely an opportunity to showcase the talents of the staff and best students but an opportunity, through the rehearsal process, to enable everyone taking part to stretch themselves and to prepare socially, intellectually and imaginatively for whatever they might do for the rest of their lives. It is a developmental process, and the success of productions at Orangefield, I believe, was a result of that approach, exemplified by the rehearsal process for *The Enemy Within*. Thank you everyone who was a part of it; I'm enormously proud of what was accomplished and consider the plays we did at Orangefield highlights of my career as a teacher and theatre artist.

Sam McCready's Class: David Ervine is standing, extreme Right.

Sam McCready was a founding member of the Lyric Players in Derryvolgie Avenue, and later a Trustee and Artistic Director of the Lyric Theatre in Ridgeway Street. After leaving Orangefield, Sam lectured at the University of North Wales, 1969-78, and was then Head of Drama at Stranmillis College, 1978-83. He emigrated to the United States in 1984 when he was appointed Professor of Theatre at the University of Maryland. With his wife, the actor and teacher Joan McCready, Sam returns regularly to perform in Ireland.

Eds. Notes: The *Orangefield Observer*, February 1967, Vol 9, No 9, under a banner photo headline, 'Peace in Vietnam', printed fifteen year-old Brian Keenan's protest lyric 'KEEP YOUR HANDS OFF MY GENERATION':

The adult generation look down on us
They don't take us serious
They say our thoughts about bombs mushrooming black
Should be just shattered with a crack.
People try to put us down
But they may not be here when the bomb hits the ground.

Keep your hands off my Generation
They're just thinking 'bout the future nation.

You say you love and slave for us
But why spend your money so ridiculous?
You buy clothes to "Keep up with the Jones'"
But to Hell with the Jones
When Radiation rots your bones.
You say the Lord above gon'a protect us
But the way I see he just neglects us
He lets them mushrooms grow every day.
He's just takin' our life away.

Keep your hands off my Generation
They're just thinking 'bout the future nation.

You just don't understand how we think
No wonder we turn to drugs and drink
When the threat of Nuclear War is all around us.
Someday you're gon'a die riding home in your bus.
You just don't understand us at all
So go back, play bingo in your little Church hall.
It's gon'a snow radiation some day.
Takin' all our grandchildren away.
And humanity's gon'a lie flat on its back
Magnesium burns up to its neck.

Keep your hands off my Generation
They're just thinking 'bout the future nation.

When they drop the bomb you're gon'a die
And it's not gon'a help you to
Weep and cry.
So you grown-ups who think you know it all
Try, try to understand us
'Cause you know nothing at all.

(Selected by the *Daily Mail* as among the outstanding poems in the UK.)

Brian Keenan [1962-1969] *in his childhood memoir titled* 'I'll Tell Me Ma', *Vintage Books, 2010, has written about his time at Orangefield. After spending a number of years in teaching and community development work in Belfast, Brian took up an appointment at Beirut University in 1985. In* 'An Evil Cradling', *Hutchinson, 1992, he tells the story of being kidnapped by fundamentalist Shi'ite militiamen and being held in captivity in the suburbs of Beirut for four-and-a-half years. The award-winning feature film,* 'Blind Flight', *for which he wrote the screenplay, portrayed Brian's hostage ordeal with John McCarthy, and was shown as part of the Eastside Arts Festival in August, 2014.*

Henry Sinnerton's *biography,* 'David Ervine: Unchartered Waters', *published by Brandon, 1992, provides an account of David's school days at Orangefield [1965-1968], his life experiences during The Troubles, and the contribution he went on to make as a political leader to Inter-Party discussions that culminated in the signing of the Belfast Agreement on 10th April, 1998. David Ervine died from a heart attack in 2007.*

— 15. —
MUSICAL JOURNEYS AND FRONTIERS

Denis Totton discovers 'a veritable Tardis with two Doctors', 'Narnia' and 'a sweetie shop without a charge' ...

John Ritchie, John Mercer, Edna Stanley

THE MUSIC DEPARTMENT was very ably managed by the Two Johns ... JS Mercer and JB Ritchie. They proved to be an excellent duo having differing but complementary attributes, styles and personalities. JSM was a tall, dark-haired figure with flowing locks, a neat beard and black-framed glasses who swept along the corridors at tremendous speed. JR was a medium height, slim, dapper man with neatly-trimmed greying hair on three sides and the gait of a genial friar on his way to the Refectory. He had an unflappable manner which co-ordinated quite naturally with the oft-times wearing of a cardigan. Any teacher who can carry-off this look is one who is comfortable in his profession. JSM, by contrast, appeared to enjoy the wearing of the classic teacher's gown. This black cloak hung in a casual slant off the shoulder and the wings were often twirled as mock whips which flailed the air.

Mrs Edna Stanley was from 1958 - 1969 the Third Person on the music staff. Primarily an experienced piano tutor, with a list of students who acquitted themselves well in exams and performances, she also undertook some part-time classroom teaching and participated in rehearsals and concerts. Tall, slim and cheery, she was a valuable asset to the work of the Department. In a very large boys' school, Edna had the ability to cope with the rowdier end of the classroom arena and encourage the more musically sensitive with a no-nonsense, let's-get-on-with-it attitude.

JSM was an accomplished piano player and frequently performed quotations and snippets from musical classics as classes ebbed and flowed one period after another. JR was a capable trumpet player and on occasion would deliver the odd Blues tune or Jazz riff to his classes. The very first time I ever heard the Haydn Trumpet Concerto was one day in class when he stuck the record on the turntable and played along with the performance... it was dazzling. His main talent was as a very agile Tenor. He served for decades in leading roles with the Belfast Operatic Company with their many performances of Gilbert & Sullivan. Invariably, his forte would be as one of the comic characters, those who deliver the witty patter songs such as... *I am the very model of a modern Major General* or... *I am the ruler of the Queen's Navy*. His stage presence and humorous delivery always made him a firm favourite with audiences and actors alike. He was also for many, many years one of the leading tenors in the St Anne's Cathedral choir. He had a great love for church music and served there with distinction.

JSM and JR worked well as a double-act ... if we were to learn some songs, JR would take the lead as the vocal demonstrator and coach, whilst JSM supplied the piano accompaniment and any additional invective as appropriate. Classic songs such as *The Vagabond* by Vaughan Williams and *The Plough-boy* by Benjamin Britten are still fresh in the memory along with the then novel 'Pop Cantatas' like *Joseph and His Amazing Technicolor Dreamcoat* or *Captain Noah and His Floating Zoo*. These items proved to be great fun to learn and of immense worth for use at concerts.

Band at Whinlands Opening, Observer Vol 10, No 2, 1967.

JR ran a great Brass Band. This played the standards and repertoire that one associated with that kind of ensemble. However, JR also had a flair for arranging jazz or pop-songs for the group and these always generated great responses from audiences at any functions or events. I remember particularly his *James Bond Suite* and *Ragtime Count-down*. For Brass players, this was a very satisfying outfit to be part of and many have continued their participation as active members of local bands, and some have pursued a career in the music profession.

JSM had a flair for composition and produced many gems for the Orchestral Group in a suitably modern but tonal idiom. He valued Benjamin Britten, Poulenc, Prokofiev and other similar figures, people who still wrote in a key but who explored the exotic shores of unusual harmony, irregular metres and stimulating rhythms.

Between the two Music Rooms was a store to where JSM and JR would often repair. This long, narrow cell was a place of mystery to us as Junior School pupils but a veritable Tardis with two Doctors when we became Seniors. A shabby, gloomy den, housing a real working desk, a kettle and all the necessary accessories for a brew-up, copious piles of music and a cupboard that was our wardrobe entrance to a musical Narnia.

Behind its doors was a real treasure-trove of music scores and records which we could borrow. A meticulously detailed, 14-page typed catalogue was a further bonus given to music students. This was a sweetie shop without a charge. To go home on a Friday afternoon with the score and record of a Tchaikovsky symphony and a Beethoven piano concerto was just fabulous. In the Sixties this was a facility that helped us to explore the rich heritage of Classical music. We could not afford to buy LP records and in the days long, long before the Internet, this was a wonderful opportunity which laid the foundation for our musical knowledge and appreciation.

The Orchestral Group

Wednesday afternoons were Senior Games but for the musically artistic it was a splendid chance to rehearse with JSM in Music Room 1. This became a hot-house for the talented players and a stimulating studio for the creation of high quality music. By good fortune we had the skeleton staff of an orchestra... flute, clarinet, oboe, trumpet, horn, trombone, tuba, violin, double bass, timpani and percussion and this allowed us to play and create some fascinating music. The 'A' Level students were often given the task of arranging a movement from some masterpiece for performance by our particular ensemble... items such as the slow movement from *Concerto for Two Pianos* by Poulenc and pieces from *L'Arlesienne* by Bizet.

MUSICAL EVENING

An audience of about two hundred people turned up to watch the musical evening, presented under the auspices of Mr. Mercer, Mr. Ritchie and Mrs. Stanley. The first item was a recital by the brass band which was excellent.

They were joined by the choir in choruses in "When the Saints come Marching in" for instance. The next five or six items consisted of solos, and small group items including a trio sonato with Mr. Mercer (piano) Ashley Rodway (violin) and Mademoiselle Niclause (violin).

The "piece de resistance" of the first half was a musical drama called "The Midnight Thief". It was a "play", acted accompanied by a small section of the orchestra. After a short interval the orchestra played the slow movement of Haydn's "Surprise Symphony". After a few more solos the orchestra played "Two Scottish Fragments" written by Mr. Mercer for the musical evening and finished with the National Anthem.

After the National Anthem Mr. Leonard Pugh, (musical Adviser to the School of Music) said thanks to Mr. Mercer, Mr. Ritchie and Mrs. Stanley and the boys for the evening's entertainment.

He said he knew how much work had gone before it in copying out music and rehearsing. The function of the Musical Evening was to give to the boys experience in public playing and I think it has done this very well.

Robert McNair, 5a/JP

Rehearsal, Observer, Vol 9, No 3, 1966

Review, Observer, Vol 9, No 7, 1967

It should be mentioned that there was valuable specialist help from the City of Belfast School of Music in the form of tutors who coached pupils in small groups in school or as individuals in the main CBSM building in Donegall Pass during evening sessions. Their assistance was an essential part of the process of developing and improving the range and quality of musical life at Orangefield.

JSM was an Organist and Choirmaster and held a number of important positions in various churches through the years. We took part in some very creative services in Cliftonville Presbyterian. To be able to work with the organ, a choir and an instrumental group was immensely stimulating and rewarding. At one particular service Irene Sandford, the famous Belfast soprano, was the guest soloist. We were enthralled by the power and beauty of her voice, dazzled by her personal glamour and highly impressed by her convertible sports car.

When JSM moved to Rosemary Presbyterian Church, we played a major role in a Winter Concert in January 1972 which, along with various solos and ensembles included a performance of the Victorian masterpiece *Hiawatha's Wedding Feast* by Samuel Coleridge-Taylor. This was a setting of the famous poem by Longfellow and was in effect a secular oratorio featuring a choir, soloists and orchestra. A special service for Palm Sunday in March 1972 featured items by Purcell, Vivaldi and Handel.

Belfast Operatic Company

This organisation holds a special relationship with Orangefield. It began around 1960 in First Ballymacarret Presbyterian Church where John Mercer was the Organist & Choirmaster. Located within the catchment area of the school and having the Two Johns as major components it was only natural that over the

Belfast Operatic Company: Dido & Aeneas – Orangefield Participants
Back Row: John Dallas, Ross Hart, Tom Brown, Robert McNair, John Ritchie, Fred Donnan.
Front Row: Brian Miller Percussion, Roger Farlow Clarinet, John Hamilton Bassoon, Denis Totton Oboe, Alex Magee Trumpet, Roger Doherty Cornet, Robert Tate Horn, Ronnie Bryans Trombone, Gordon Myers Timpani, Garry Rodway Cello, John Mercer Conductor.

years a significant number of pupils and teachers found their way into its ranks. Ashleigh Rodway was a capable violinist and a handy cricketer but developed especially as a lyrical Tenor. He first appeared with the Company in the mid-sixties and then as principal tenor for two seasons in the early seventies while attending Stranmillis College. He gained a place at the London Guildhall and went on to sing professionally appearing with companis such as Kent Opera and D'Oyly Carte, that bastion of Gilbert & Sullivan.

In 1968 JSM made a major innovation to the usual repertoire of Operettas by staging the amazing Baroque Opera of *Dido & Aeneas* by Purcell. He also introduced instruments into the production that year using some of the senior players from school. Previously the accompaniment had always been in the form of two pianos, a very popular, functional and cost-effective solution for operatic companies across the globe but now additional colours were available. Parts had to be invented and copied by hand, practices undertaken on Wednesday afternoons.

There was a surge of excitement at the Dress Rehearsal when hearing the vocal parts for the first time and there was the thrill of performing to a knowledgeable audience on a 'run' in the King George VI Hall in May Street. This may have been the first time that each of us wore a bow-tie, that badge of office for real musicians and we were proud when we got an honourable mention in the review by Rathcol in the *Belfast Telegraph*.

The Lord Dunleith had been persuaded to lend his beautiful harpsichord for the opera. This elegant green and gold instrument with a florid painted scene in the lid was a treasure to behold and to hear. The authentic sound of the plucked strings brought a new dimension to ears used to the piano. Not to let an opportunity pass, an old upright piano in Music Room 1 was doctored by sticking drawing pins into the felt hammers and produced a remarkably effective imitation of a harpsichord. Baroque sonatas and descriptive pieces were discovered and rattled-off at Breaks and Lunchtimes. Couperin and Scarlatti had landed in East Belfast!

Combined Concerts

The first combined **Musical Evening** joining the musicians from the Boys' and Girls' schools was in **March 1968** for two nights in the Assembly Hall. In this venture we had the keen support and enthusiasm of Anne Williams the Head of Music in the Girls' School who was doing wonderful things in her own domain. The amalgamation instantly gave great satisfaction to all concerned. We now had the makings of a real orchestra in terms of size, variety and expertise. The Girls had lots of String players and lovely voices and we had good Woodwind and Brass so the impact was strong and rewarding for all participants. At that concert there was a group of 6 Mimers with make-up and costumes, 16 Speakers, 12 in the Percussion Group, 30 in the Band, a Choir of 50, 38 Recorders of various sizes and an Orchestra of almost 50 performers. Allowing for overlaps and multi-tasking there was the active involvement of a colossal number of pupils. The Mimers acted out the story of a little musical play set in Japan by Malcolm Arnold called *The Turtle Drum*. Singers and musicians provided the soundtrack.

The 1969 concert featured a similar item in *Ahmet the Woodseller* (a story set in the Turkish Empire) as well as an amazing variety of items showcasing the different groups and soloists. 1970 did not have one single big choral piece but instead had a wealth of contributions from a very diverse range of ensembles. The Choir had songs from *Oliver,*

Orchestra 1971

Flute	Alan Collins	**Percussion**	Gordon Myers
	Donard Collins		John Anderson
	Desmond Spiers		Margaret Watson
	A. Magill		Florence Caldwell
	Lynne Corry		Pamela Shields
Oboe	Denis Totton	**Violin I**	Sandra Bell
	Jim McNair		Sandra Thompson
	Helen Lyttle		Janetha Matchett
	Hazel McKnight		Lynne Matier
			Jane Galashen
Clarinet	Rodger Farlow		Janette Tate
	K. Henderson		Sandra Jones
	David Barr		T. Maginnis
	R. McCrea		
	Elizabeth McCougherty	**Violin II**	Lorraine Lavery
			Naomi McCall
Bassoon	D. Neill		Diane Bell
	Marion Johnston		Eileen Spratt
	C. Gray		
Horns	Lynn Diamond	**Violin III**	Julie Edgar
	Janice Turkington		Linda Geddis
	Karen Wynne		Valerie Payton
	Paul Harkness		
		Viola	Sandra Lowry
Trumpet	Tom Mercer		
	Alex Magee	**Cello**	Garry Rodway
	Phyllis Carlisle		Alan Revell
			Lilian Ball
			Heather Keary
			Deborah McMichael
		Double Bass	G. McKeown
Trombone	David Catherwood		
	Harry Kerr	**Recorders**	Margaret Burrell
	Iris Burrows		Sheila Pennington
			Jennifer Thomas
Tuba	David Irvine		June Montgomery
			Joy McFarlane
			Sharon Scarlett
			Lynn Arbuthnot

the Orchestral Group amused with *The Hippopotamus Polka* and *The Sound of Music*. The Brass players ranged from a 17th century motet to *Dixieland Blues* and joined with the Orchestra in the *Gendarmes' Duet* by Offenbach for the finale of the evening.

In 1971 the Dining Centre was commissioned as a suitable venue for the concerts in order to accommodate the large forces and larger audiences. The main item in the programme was *Joseph's Dreamcoat* which was a tremendous hit. Around this time there was even a little joint committee of girls and boys set-up to help develop cordial relationships. It helped generate an evening party for the orchestra ... this was heady stuff for segregated pupils in those days! 1972 had *Captain Noah and his Floating Zoo* as the big item and this proved to be another success with the audience.

John Mercer left Orangefield in June 1972 and went as Head of Music to Rainey Endowed, Magherafelt. John Ritchie became Head of Music and David Rutherford the replacement music teacher.

Denis Totton [1965-1972], *performer on the oboe and piano, organist & choirmaster, accompanist, music tutor, conductor and adjudicator. He taught Music in Laurelhill High School Lisburn and Methodist College Belfast. Denis lives in Ballyhackamore with his wife Ruth and Molly the cocker-spaniel.*

The Belfast Operatic Company

The Mikado in rehearsal with John Mercer and John Ritchie

John Mercer came to Orangefield in September 1959. He replaced Jimmy McAvoy who had gone to teach music in Methodist College Belfast. John was also the organist and choirmaster in Ballymacarrett Presbyterian Church at that time. He founded a musical society from within the ranks of his choir and augmented it with staff and pupils from Orangefield Boys'.

The first production of the Ballymacarrett Musical Society was staged in February 1961 at the Church Lecture Hall, Paulett Avenue. John Mercer was the Producer and Musical Director, Ronnie Horner was the Assistant Producer as well as playing a principal role. Fred Davidson and John Ritchie, teaching colleagues, along with Sam Young, a pupil, were also in the cast. Over the years the name of the Society was changed to *Belfast Operatic Company*. Remarkably, over fifty individuals, thirty pupils and twenty staff with connections to Orangefield have been involved with the Company. Former pupils Ashleigh Rodway, Tom Brown, Fred Donnan, Frank Truesdale, Andrew Neagle and Wilfie Pyper at various times starred in lead roles.

Other former pupils, for example, John Grayden, David Robinson and Peter Lockard have been Chairmen of the Company. John Grayden also served as secretary and then treasurer for a number of years. Thompson Steele is a past Chairman and was treasurer of the Company for twenty years. He is presently President of the Company.

One former pupil Wilfie Pyper first became involved with the Company in 1979 when he directed and took a lead in *Iolanthe.* He has been the Belfast Operatic's Director since 2010 and in 2012 Wilfie had the unique distinction of winning Best Director in Gilbert Class and Best Director in Sullivan Class in the Association of Irish Musical Societies Awards [AIMS]. Other Orangefield personnel, including Ross Hart and David Rutherford, Garry Rodway, Denis Totton, Mervyn Watson, Robert McNair, Walter Rader, Sam Lamont, John Dallas, David Craig, Ronnie Barr, Ronnie Bryans, Roger Doherty, Alex Magee, Robert Freeburn, Alan Kirker, Gordon Myers, Clifford Gilmore, Alan Patterson, and Moore Sinnerton, have assisted the Company both on and off the stage.

Serendipity

John Anderson [1968–1975], *returning from rugby on a games afternoon, has a chance encounter with the school orchestra and John Mercer ...*

I became a student at the school in 1968. I suppose I should have ended up at Ashfield Boys' Secondary School as I lived in BT4, but I somehow managed to pass my 11 plus exam and had the choice of Grosvenor High School or Orangefield Boys' Secondary. I chose the secondary school because I had three cousins who were already pupils there and they had told me how good the school was. I also thought that they might protect me against any bullying, but they emigrated to Australia in December 1968, and that put paid to that!

My first real contact with the Music Department was when I was about 13. I was on my way back to the changing rooms after playing rugby one wet Wednesday afternoon and heard the school orchestra rehearsing. My mate and I poked our heads round the door to the music room and Mr. Mercer, who was conducting the group, spotted us and made us come in to the room. He was quite a formidable character and he asked what we thought we were doing. I said that I thought the music sounded good and wanted to see what was going on. He said that as we were there we could stay and play in the group! I told him that I didn't play an instrument, so he sat me behind a pair of kettledrums and said that I should hit them when he pointed at me. He put my mate on the bass drum. At the end of the rehearsal he asked me if I would like to join the orchestra and, as I really hated playing rugby, I agreed. Little did I know then how important this would be for my future career. My mate refused the offer of playing the bass drum!

Mr. Mercer taught me to read music and showed me the basics of playing the timpani. There was a lot of music going on in the school at that time. We had a small orchestra, a concert band, and I think there was a brass band, or certainly a brass group. Mr. Mercer was an inspirational teacher and he encouraged me to start having piano lessons; I also started to learn to play the clarinet. I took 'O' level Music in a small class of around 5-6 students and music soon became my favourite subject.

Mr. Mercer encouraged me to audition for the City of Belfast School of Music, which I did and ended up being placed in the Concert Band,

John Anderson, Clarinet, School Orchestra.

which was conducted by Alfie Burch. After a few weeks of playing in the band I was moved to play percussion/timpani in the Youth Orchestra. It was good timing for me because there were hardly any percussionists around at that time and I ended up playing in quite a few of the ensembles.

I remember watching a television series which was set in wartime Germany. The theme music for the programme really excited me. I asked Mr Mercer what it was and he told me that it was the opening of Beethoven's 5th Symphony. He then gave me a boxed set of the Beethoven symphonies and told me that I could borrow it for a while. I started listening to the 5th symphony and then gradually to the others — what a revelation! I think I returned the set about two years later. Mr Mercer never once asked me to return the set. When he left the school at the end of my 'O' Level year I thought the world had come to an end! Then Mr. Ritchie took over.

Mr. Ritchie was a completely different character to Mr. Mercer, but he was equally as passionate about music and he was also a very gifted musician and teacher. I wanted to take 'A' level Music, but I was the only student who wanted to do this. Mr. Ritchie managed to persuade the headmaster Mr. Weston to allow me to take music and I was very lucky to be able to have one-to-one tuition. Mr. Ritchie gave me the run of the Music Department and I was able to stay after school to practise the piano and listen to recordings. I didn't have a piano at home and no one else in the family liked listening to classical music.

Looking back, I don't think I could have had better tuition anywhere else. Mr. Mercer and Mr. Ritchie really inspired and encouraged me to take up a career in music and I am very grateful to them both and to the school for everything they did for me. I was watching some rugby on television the other day (briefly) and was thinking how pleased I am not to have enjoyed playing it at school — things might have turned out very differently!

John Anderson, conductor

John studied at the Royal Academy of Music, later gaining a Masters' degree from the University of Leeds. He moved to Leeds in 1980 to take up the position of principal timpanist with the Orchestra of Opera North. In 1989 John left Opera North to become music director of the Grimethorpe Colliery Band. In 1990 he became associate conductor of the world famous Black Dyke Band and toured with them to New York, performing in Carnegie Hall and giving a master class at the Juilliard School of Music.

In 1995 John was the music director of the successful British-made feature film *Brassed Off*, recording the soundtrack with the Grimethorpe Colliery Band. He worked closely with the actors Pete Postlethwaite, Tara Fitzgerald and Ewan McGregor.

In 2004, John was awarded a Gold Disc for sales of the soundtrack album. *Brassed Off* is shown frequently on Channel Four and Film Four.

As a freelance conductor John has worked with the Hallé Orchestra, Kazakh State Zambul Philharmonic Orchestra, Uralsk Philharmonic Orchestra, Bohuslav Martinu Philharmonic Orchestra, Yorkshire Chamber Orchestra, Sinfonia of Leeds, Huddersfield and Slaithwaite Philharmonic Orchestras, Stephen Hill Singers, Chorus of Opera North, Bradford Festival Chorus and Leeds Philharmonic Chorus. He has worked with many eminent soloists including Paul Lewis, Raphael Wallfisch, Kathryn Stott, Lynne Dawson, Mary Plazas and Paul Nilon.

John was invited back to Kazakhstan in May 2013 to conduct the State Philharmonic Orchestra and Chorus. He has been principal conductor and music director of the Airedale Symphony Orchestra.

Born to Sing

'No guru, no method, no teacher,
Just you and I and nature and the Father
In the garden'

GERALD DAWE IN his autobiographical memoir, *'My Mother-City'*, Lagan Press, 2008, page 46, quotes Van Morrison describing his years at Orangefield from 1957 to 1960:

"There was no school for people like me. I mean, we were freaks in the full sense of the word because either we didn't have the bread to go to the sort of school where we could sit down and do our sort of thing, or that type of school didn't exist. Most of what was fed me really didn't help me that much later."

For *'Orangefield Remembered: A School in Belfast 1957 to 1990'*, Van Morrison has recalled of this time and place:

" 'Think of the smell of an orange' ... Mr Preston was the art teacher when I was at Orangefield and this is the kind of thing he would say, but I didn't really get it until many years later when I picked up a book on meditation in California and, right there, on the page at which I opened the book, were those very same words.

Sir Van Morrison, Cyprus Avenue, 31 August 2015 (Photo: Bradley Quinn)

I also liked Mr Weston who was a decent man, as we used to say then. There was Mr Fleck who sat on top of the desk at the front of the class and talked philosophically. I connected with his way of thinking outside the box. Mr Hammond whose guitar playing we should have had more of. Bunter Campbell and his mad rage that had us all 'afeared' of him. And Mr Scott who said I was going to be a singer even before I could see it as a reality myself.

I had some good mates in school and, all in all, I look upon it as having been a bit hard but mostly happy times and memories."

Orangefield 2014 (Photo: Bradley Quinn)

Orangefield 2014 (Photo: Bradley Quinn)

Friday 22nd August

Van Morrison at Orangefield

8.00-10.00pm (Doors 7.30pm / Seating unallocated)
For ex-Orangefield pupils and teachers only.
Venue: Orangefield High School

Tickets: £25 SOLD OUT

International musical legend Van Morrison performs in the Assembly Hall for ex-pupils and teachers of his old school. It was well over fifty years ago that a teenage Van Morrison walked out of the gates of Orangefield Boys' School for the last time. Since then he has become one of the most respected and successful musicians and songwriters of his generation, with a huge international fan base and a myriad of fellow musicians who cite him as both an influence and an inspiration.

Before he left Orangefield, a 14 year old Van and a couple of his Hyndford Street friends performed at the school concert as Midnight Special. This summer he returns for the first time to his former school to play three intimate concerts in the school assembly hall. While the Saturday night show will be open to the public, Friday & Sunday will be special nights with the audience consisting of former pupils and teachers of the school, including many who themselves have forged careers as artists on the international stage. This will be a truly unique occasion, never to be repeated.

> When I was a young boy
> Back in Orangefield
> I used to gaze out
> My classroom window and dream
> And then go home and listen to Ray sing
> "I believe to my soul" after school,
> Oh that love that was within me
> You know it carried me through
> Well it lifted me up and it filled me
> Meditation contemplation too
>
> Got To Go Back
> by Van Morrison

Eastside Arts Festival Programme, 2014

Faber & Faber in *Lit Up Inside: Selected Lyrics*, edited by Eamonn Hughes, 2014, describe Sir Van Morrison as the Grammy Award-winning singer, songwriter, author, poet and multi-instrumentalist who is widely considered one of the most important songwriters of the past century. His extraordinary achievements have been recognised with honorary doctorates from both the University of Ulster and Queen's University Belfast and the Ordre des Arts et des Lettres.

— 16. —

A SOUTHERNER IN ORANGEFIELD

Jonathan Bardon from Dublin, newly-qualified as a secondary school teacher finds himself in a different city, learning a new language, going fishing, and being queried by the School's Headmaster, "What's the use of History?"

'*WHAT IS YOUR opinion of the teaching of the Irish language in schools?*' It was the late spring of 1964, and I was being interviewed by a panel for a teaching job at Orangefield. As I spoke, with some warmth about the merits of the language and of the cultural benefits it was certain to bring to young minds, I could see the faces of my interviewers lose their initial welcoming smiles and begin to harden. '*But I think the Irish government is wrong to make Irish a compulsory subject*', I added in flustered haste. The expressions began to soften. '*Do you know my son Andrew?*' the chairman asked – he was a Church of Ireland clergyman with a comforting southern brogue. Indeed, I did: very well, in fact. '*You're all right, so,*" he declared with a grin. I got the job. There was only one other candidate.

I was made form master of a third form, 3P2 – to this day I have no idea what the P2 indicated, other than that it was evidence of John Malone's determination to avoid élitism and any impression of rigid stratification by perceived ability.* It was an uphill struggle attempting to manage a thirty-plus-strong class of lively fourteen-year-olds. To them, I was an exotic specimen of a rarely-encountered genus and, amongst other names, they called me the 'Irish teacher'. In turn, as a middle-class Dubliner, I became fascinated by their colourful way of speaking with dialect words unfamiliar to me. '*Sir, Jonty is a scardy ba*'. Totally perplexed, I found out with difficulty that '*scardy ba*' is the equivalent of my '*cowardy custard*'. And why was Stephen McFarland nicknamed '*Tatie*'? It took me time to work that one out. But it was not long before I knew the meaning of '*cowp*', '*curnaptious*', '*sleekit*', '*well happed up*' and other words and phrases, mainly of Lowland Scots origin.

It has to be admitted that my capacity to maintain control of several classes assigned to me was well below what was required to ensure a steady advance in the boys' learning. In one school (now closed) where I began my teaching practice, as I had attempted a history lesson, the usual teacher twice burst out of a store behind the classroom and beat up the entire back row with his big fists. That was not what I considered helpful guidance. John Malone's approach was rather different. He once glided into my tempestuously noisy mobile classroom and, as he advanced to the front, the boys meekly sank into silence. His gently-spoken advice on how to restore control began with this sentence: '*Jonathan, if I were you, I would begin by getting them all to sit down*'. Oh dear. Before he left, he turned to me to ask, '*By the way, Jonathan, what's the use of History?*' I was completely stumped.

I was expected to teach a range of subjects which, as well as History, included Religious

Instruction, Geography and English. In time, I began to devise tactics to engage pupils in what I hoped would be constructive learning. Even first formers in an English class were liable to become unruly on a Friday afternoon, so I would spend the entire period reading to them from a book of their own choosing – *Stig of the Dump* was a particular favourite. Olivier-like voice projection and Garrick-like gestures, with dramatic pauses and meaningful glances, worked a treat ... and they did have the merit of suggesting to them that books might, on occasion, be of interest. This was the best training I ever got in public speaking.

Once a week, I had to take a class of sixth-formers for General Studies. From the outset, these very bright and entertaining young men took control and decided what were the important issues of the day worth discussing. On reflection, I am surprised that more time was not devoted to analysis of the fractured nature of Northern Ireland's society. Was this because very few of them had actually conversed with Catholics? (At least that is until Gerry Dawe and his mates were playing their part in making central Belfast the capital of the show band scene and the dance hall craze).

After all, the region's discontents had been given a brief but dramatic staging during the autumn of 1964. The republican candidate in the West Belfast constituency had placed a small tricolour in the window of a shop in Divis Street. Ian Paisley, the founder of the Free Presbyterian Church, demanded the implementation of the Flags and Emblems Act and when the police duly removed the flag, rioting erupted. Eamonn McCann, with whom I had recently shared a house in University Street, suggested we go and take a look. Not having bothered to find out what was the cause of the trouble, merely out of idle curiosity, I walked with Eamonn and Austin Currie on a Friday evening close to where rioters – barely deterred by water cannon – were engaged in intense conflict with the police. *'Where are you from?'* a Reserve RUC constable asked me, having heard me say something to Eamonn. 'From *Dublin*', I responded with a smile. He swung his baton. For the first and only time in my life I was knocked unconscious. *'Get up! Get up!'*, a sergeant almost screamed as I came to and then advised me to get home as quickly as I could.

When I appeared at Orangefield next Monday, with a large bandage dressing on my skull, naturally members of staff and pupils alike were anxious to know the cause of my injury. When told, most of the boys and some of the staff, regarded the whole episode as a hoot. It was clear, however, that several of my colleagues thought my venturing into the Divis Street maelstrom a grave error of judgement, an indication of my ignorance of local conditions.

Indeed, I was woefully ignorant of the origins of tensions which manifested themselves that autumn. A History graduate though I was, who thought himself well-versed in Irish History, I was only dimly aware that memories of previous massacres and dispossessions had become etched deeply into the folk consciousness, passing down from one generation to the other, reverberating destructively down the centuries. I was impelled to find out more, to delve much deeper. From my principal mentor, Douglas Carson, I felt I learned more about History and its value than I had in four, much-enjoyed years at Trinity College Dublin. His skill was to bring the past to life, to make that past seem relevant and important, using detail based on rigorous and dispassionate attention to the sources. His special 'A' Level subject was Roman Britain. His handouts, written in beautiful script on wax paper for the Roneo machine, have to be collectors' items. From him, I learned not to talk down to the boys, regardless of previous academic achievement: he knew how to engage, to excite, to encourage dispassionate and informed investigation, to bring contemporary sources to life.

Another mentor of crucial importance to me was Thompson Steele. His interest in local history was insatiable. A great many of the boys' parents worked in the shipyard, the Sirocco works, surviving linen mills, and other enterprises which had made Belfast a great industrial city. Local history was not anywhere on the curriculum agenda, but 'Thompy' managed to slip it into his classroom, often with a song and his guitar. Indeed, I learned a great deal from him, most notably when he asked me to accompany him and a party of boys to the Mournes for a school week – we found out how granite was split, how the slopes were farmed, and how the Belfast Water Commissioners engaged hundreds to construct the great wall there. My classes seemed to know very little about the history of their own immediate localities and that got me engaged in a search so that I could tell them more. And that is a search I have continued.

Rodney Usher recruited me to do my bit with the under-12 rugby players. This was a mistake. In spite of having been compelled to play the game for years, I lacked the physical courage to be any good at it and my knowledge of the rules was woefully vague. Eventually, and inevitably, my ignorance was exposed. After I had refereed a Saturday match and allowed Orangefield to win, a justifiably outraged games master, in charge of the losing side, seethed down the phone to Rodney. With concealed delight, I agreed to take responsibility for a completely different extra-curricular Saturday activity – fishing.

Though I could demonstrate to them the rudiments of fly casting, I was usually the learner in the Fishing Club. Kevin Balmer taught me how to catch pike and rudd, and those like Denis Quinn with angling fathers, decided each week where we should go, bringing me to parts of Ulster I had never visited. They knew where we could fish without payment. *'You're not Sunday fishers, I hope?'* one farmer asked as we filed in through his gate. Assured we were not, he made us welcome. Some new recruits to the club were wide-eyed: they had barely ventured beyond the confines of east Belfast and now they were seeing the countryside for the first time. And that, of course, was why John Malone regarded *Whinlands* as a vital part of the educational programme he managed.

One summer, I arranged to take half a dozen of them in my Vauxhall Viva van to camp by the River Nore in Co. Kilkenny. During the last week of term, there was a sharp knock on the door of my mobile classroom. It was a father, a Unionist councillor, I think. What was I doing enticing his son over the Border to pitch his tent under the dark grey clouds of the Free State? When I pointed out that the owner of the farm was well known in evangelical circles, which he was, the father relented and gave his consent.

We fished in all weathers. One Saturday we arrived at our lough, near Ballynahinch, to find that it was completely frozen over. Undaunted, the boys smashed holes in the ice with great rocks and began to fish like Eskimos. Later that afternoon, a terrified stag, pursued by a pack of hounds, leaped over the boys' heads. The dogs (I thought they were intent on eating me) were now being patted enthusiastically by the boys. Members of the North Down hunt, including Brian Faulkner, cantered up to the ice and quickly dispersed, leaving a man in a boat poking the ice, moving slowly forward to reach the stag. It took two hours to dislodge and free the unfortunate animal.

Health and Safety? On occasion we took the bus, particularly to pike loughs in the heart of Co. Down. More often I packed them into my Vauxhall Viva van. On one occasion, thirteen boys were crammed in, including one not far short of thirteen stone (who was allotted the single passenger seat). After a particularly successful trip to the River Quoile, John Malone rang me around 10.30 that Saturday night. *'Mrs McElroy has just been on the phone, Jonathan – Alan hasn't returned yet from fishing with you'*. I froze. My van was full enough on the return journey, but now I had the horrifying realisation that, yes, I *had* left Alan behind. Fortunately, John rang twenty minutes later: Alan had arrived home, having hitch-hiked home from Downpatrick. He was *only* thirteen years old.

When in 1966, Douglas Carson moved on to the BBC, along with Don McBride I took over as joint editor of the *Orangefield Observer*. This involved regular contact with the Girls' School and led, in turn, to the formation of a Youth Club for senior pupils of both schools, the Action Society. Since I possessed a First Aid certificate – expired though it was – John asked me to take classes in first Aid. The course was to conclude with demonstrations of bandaging by boys and talks by uniformed members of St John's Ambulance. I chaired the proceedings and, on stage throughout, I was one of those due to be bandaged. The Assembly Hall was full and I think girls were there as well. 'Sir! Sir!', a little boy at the front kept saying to me as proceedings began. I shushed him. At the end as the hall was emptying, I asked the boy what he wanted. *'Sir! Your spare is open!'* I had only recently learned what a 'spare' was.

Throughout my four years teaching in Orangefield, my stomach muscles were like iron. This had nothing to do with fitness: it simply reflected the energy which had to be expended to do the job. Tension just had to be released by all in the staffroom. A mad cacophony prevailed: chanting, wise-cracking, farmyard animal noises, yelping, good-humoured taunting, practical joking ... spying a Union Jack on a chair, Sam McCready once leapt on a table, wrapped the flag round himself, and sang *'Land of Hope and Glory'* all the way through in falsetto. None of these antics deflected a cluster of sandwich eaters – usually led by Duncan Scarlett – from debating with intense seriousness the issues of the day. I liked to sit with Barney Megarry to discuss the best way to grow large carrots, and then to join with other war veterans, to listen to their memories of the most terrible conflict of all time.

I still, on occasion, am stopped in supermarkets by middle-aged men who declare, *'Mr Bardon! Remember me? You taught me'*. Some I don't remember. *'You taught me when I was in first form'*, one said. I didn't remember. When he told me who he was, David Ervine, I lamely responded that he had more hair then. He laughed warmly. I vividly remember frenetic discussions with Ronnie Bunting, Walter Ellis and Bruce Cardwell and less frenetic ones with Robert Crone and Trevor Magee. Trevor would bring me in little items passed on to him by his grandfather and insist that I keep them. They included a cut-throat razor, which I still have. From Trevor I learned the value of producing artefacts in the classroom and tutorial room – particularly as an icebreaker at the beginning of an academic year. John Hewitt, who went on to be an actor, asked me to stay behind after school to teach him how to do different accents. At the end of one class, the last one of the day, Sam Mateer remained in his seat. *'Sir, I've something for you'*. He then produced a large brown paper bag containing a dozen bottles of beer which he had brewed himself. I was so moved, I'm pretty sure I shed a tear – it was just about the most appreciated present

I have ever received. He went on to be what I – and many others – consider to be one of the very finest painters Belfast has produced. *[See Eds. Notes]*.

My sojourn in Orangefield, between 1964 and 1968, was during the last years of peace. Like most of my friends and colleagues, I was convinced that the bitterness of the past was slowly but inexorably being dissolved. How wrong I was. David Ervine was not the only former Orangefield pupil to become embroiled in what was to become the most protracted violent conflict in Western Europe since the Second World War. Ronnie Bunting, one of only two or three Protestants to be interned in 1971, later joined the irreconcilables and paid for it with his life.

Though I was there only for four years, my memories of Orangefield are still extraordinarily vivid. They are very warm memories.

Eds. Note: *the Class title P2 meant the boys were following a public examination course leading to a qualification awarded by the College of Preceptors.*

Jonathan Bardon *is the author of several landmark works of Irish historiography, including A History of Ulster (2001), The Plantation of Ulster (2011), and A History of Ireland in 250 Episodes (2008). In 2015, he published Hallelujah, the story of a musical genius, G.F. Handel, and the city of Dublin that brought his masterpiece, 'Messiah', to life. In 2002, Jonathan was awarded an OBE for his services to community life in Northern Ireland.*

Cut-Over Bog Pastel 50 x 50 cm

Maas Bog – Donegal Pastel 40 x 40 cm

Sam Mateer [1963-1969] *graduated from the Ulster Polytechnic at Jordanstown with a teaching diploma and a degree in Fine Art. He exhibited with the Royal Ulster Academy [RUA] from 1985 and went on to found the Pastel Society of Ireland in 1988. Sam is best known as a landscape painter but also turned his attention to political developments. In 1998 he received the RUA's Silver Medal for Shankill, Greysteel and Enniskillen Poppies. Sam Mateer died in 2010.*

— 17. —
MEMOIRS: SET 4

History in Room 7

And still they gazed and still the wonder grew,
That one small head could carry all he knew.

Oliver Goldsmith, "The Deserted Village" [1770]

HISTORY WAS FUN. I can't remember which side I was supposed to be on as thirty first formers charged up and down the ditch and mound of Navan fort just outside Armagh. But I was definitely part of a battle between Cuchulain's Red Branch Knights and East Belfast cattle raiders. It was June 1963 and this was a field study finale devised by Douglas Carson and his rival general, the geographer, Duncan Scarlett. The resulting mêlée was a perfect example of Douglas's determination to make history come alive for us.

Douglas had fallen into teaching almost by accident. When John Malone had been short a history teacher, the legendary JC Beckett, Professor of Irish History at Queen's University Belfast had told John Malone that Douglas Carson was worth a look. JMM arrived at the family farm to find Douglas cheerily at work in a field at Ballyutoag. It must have been obvious to John that this man might not be a natural fit — but then he had already hired an art teacher, Sam Preston, who was a practising hypnotist!

So, in September 1962, this was the teacher assigned to teach History to the new boys of 1G. We trooped past the cloakroom to the end of the corridor and the back staircase and into his domain, Room 7. Douglas always strode into the classroom swinging a weighty leather briefcase — and lessons quickly evolved a pattern. Those at the front were asked to keep their desktops raised so that he might pause to lean on them as he traversed the room from blackboard to desks with his long, loping ploughman's stride, unfolding the latest instalment in his story.

And this was a story with pictures. Some lessons consisted solely of reproducing a highly detailed drawing executed in coloured chalk of a Roman legionary, a mediaeval knight, or a map of Anglo Saxon Britain from Wessex to Dalriada. What was sketched casually in a few minutes took us an hour to emulate. The blackboard masterpieces were augmented with cyclostyled notes handwritten in Carsonian minuscule. Those notes were our textbooks: history according to Carson. In another age Douglas would have made a very happy monk, copying texts in his cell while adding lavish illustrations in the margins.

He believed in beginning at the beginning. We began with Paleolithic man and after three years had progressed to George III talking to the trees in Windsor Park. Along the way, I remember the Celts bringing the plough to Britain, Offa's Dyke, Harold swearing on the relics, the privateers beaching their ships to careen the barnacles from their hulls, Drake and his fire-ships at Cadiz, Monmouth's cavalry tumbling into the ditches of Sedgemoor, Walpole and the War, "Now they are ringing their bells, soon they will be wringing their hands", and even how the word "cabal" emerged from the allegiances of Restoration politics.

Interspersed with the History was the constant rivalry between Room 7 and Duncan Scarlett's Geography room which had to get by with the vague label, 'Social Studies', rather than a proper number. This frequently erupted into end-of-year conflict with each classroom raiding the other and boys being kidnapped and carried off to be held as hostages. During one assault the enemy's "colours" (a captured jacket) was run up the school flagpole.

End-of-term exams were one giant memory test of the kind that would be outlawed in any school today, with the results announced in reverse order. Even classroom discipline was highly stylised. Punishment was elevated to event status and the build-up to its dispensation was milked mercilessly. The victim was first shown the instrument of torture, "the block". This was an offcut of 2X1 timber filched from the woodwork room on which a mirror image of a swastika would be heavily chalked in white. Next the boy would bend over the desk and the resounding thwack and puff of chalk dust would be greeted with whoops of delight from his baying classmates as a white swastika was imprinted on his charcoal grey trousers.

The love of a good story meant it was no surprise that, when GCE 'O' Levels came around, Douglas decided that we would study Roman Britain. The lure of Julius Caesar, Caligula and Nero coupled with the promise of intricate illustrations of villa plans and Roman road systems proved irresistible.

The thrill of the rolling narrative with its hairpin turns and eccentric characters underlay everything. From today's vantage point of bite-sized history — Henry VIII and the Pope, the rise of Hitler and (if you're really lucky) the Norman Conquest — it all seems a very long time ago. For although it wasn't obvious to me then, the lesson implicit in all of this was that with the broader the sweep of history you cover then the more things begin to make sense. History was not a guide to the future or an infallible means of understanding the present — but it was a highly effective way of understanding the past.

Much as he enjoyed teaching, I think Douglas found the canvas constricting. In particular, there was limited opportunity to indulge his love of Irish history. He left us in fourth year before GCE 'O' Levels were complete and, trailing clouds of Park Drive, went to work as a producer at the BBC. He was a marvellous communicator and broadcasting was a natural next step.

Would someone like Douglas be able to teach with the same freedom in a state secondary school today? Probably not, but then none of this could have happened without the unique freedoms that Orangefield provided for all of us, for so short a time, all those years ago.

Flashbacks

Mr Lannie the metalwork teacher, one of the kindest of men but with a volcanic temper; Bob Ashe, 'Ernie' to the boys, whose late discovery of literature transformed a basketball coach into one of the most passionate teachers I have ever met. Nick "less noise boys" Watson, an inspiring English teacher, who would regale us with chilling tales of growing up in working class Glasgow. The one that sticks was how a friendly neighbour took time each week to coach him cricket. One week he didn't arrive and the young Nicholas went off to look for him, only to find that he had fallen into a vat of acid at the factory where he worked. No happy endings guaranteed in a Nick Watson anecdote.

Ronnie Horner and Sam McCready, drama production values that soared high above anything expected of schools' drama, let alone drama in a secondary modern school; Alec Cunningham's immense patience with struggling mathematicians; Don McBride breaking off from Art to analyse the latest episode of, the then, brand new Dr Who; Jim Holland exasperated by Glenn Dickson's Marxist take on Wordsworth's Lucy poems.

The Chemistry double period with Bert Caldwell as the American and Russian fleets met during the Cuban missile crisis in 1962. Robert Crone's live commentary during fierce playground football matches; Jackie Redpath and his encyclopaedic knowledge of the Bible; Big Gordon Copeland organising darts tournaments in the smoke-filled "common room"; John Hewitt, fag in mouth, calling for silence, "It's WD lads", as Billy Flackes reported on Ulster in 1969.

The field trips to Whinlands with Duncan Scarlett and Matt Maginnis that gave a boy from East Belfast, with a lifelong love of mountains and wide-open spaces, new experiences. And springing from that, something that has always stuck in my memory – a group of us sitting high in the Mournes on an absolutely still, silent day when someone, I think it was Paul Gardiner, produced a transistor radio and out crackled Paul McCartney singing 'Yesterday'.

Trevor Poots [1962-69] became a television producer, working mainly in news and current affairs. Among other things, he was a founding member of the BBC Spotlight programme, and produced many of Sir David Frost's interviews with international politicians and celebrities. He still returns with his son to walk in the Mournes.

Time flies!

Ferran (Fernie) Glenfield [1965-1972] is a graduate of Queen's University Belfast, Trinity College Dublin and the University of Oxford. He is currently the Bishop of Kilmore, Elphin and Ardagh and lives with his wife Jean in Kilmore, County Cavan.

A HALF-CENTURY has passed since I walked into the red-bricked school that was Orangefield Boys'. I did not realise it then but my time at Orangefield was an education for life.

I was taught by superb teachers, among them: Dessie Taylor for Maths, Alan Hunter in English, Duncan Scarlett for Geography and Ken Stanley in History. I was given an appreciation in French by the Sinnerton brothers, a grounding in Geology with Stead Black and the rudiments of Science by Bert Caldwell. During my time at Orangefield, I was spared the "holy terrors"! The likes of Wee Bart McClelland, Matt Maginnis and Jake Gallagher passed me by. I did, however, have Dutchie Holland for French and survived to tell the tale!

Learning in Orangefield was not confined to the classroom, it pervaded the pores of the school. Trips to *Whinlands* in Annalong and the input of staff like Allan Kilgore gave me a taste of the great outdoors. The Mournes became part of my life. When living in Dublin, I thrilled to see the whale-backed mountains in the distance, on a clear day from Dun Laoghaire pier. Then there was the theatre. I got a taste of it in stunning school productions: George Bernard Shaw's *St. Joan* and Brian Friel's *The Enemy Within*. I was captivated by the footlights and still am. Sport, too, featured prominently, lunch-time football, cricket in the summer, but above all, rugby became an abiding passion.

I was coached and encouraged by real rugby men, of whom Rodney Usher was the tallest tree in the wood. I played rugby throughout school and was privileged to be part of a successful Medallion side that had a great Cup run, only to be beaten by the eventual winners, Methody. After school, I played rugby for Queen's, Malone, Trinity and Cork Constitution and watch it avidly today.

Orangefield during my time was an oasis in the wilderness of Ulster's Troubles. We were not only sheltered from the storms battering the Province, we were given a pathway through the mayhem and murder. The staff and boys were an eclectic mix: socialists, loyalists, nationalists, boys from all corners of East Belfast and beyond. Boys from the back streets, lads from council estates, young men from the leafy lanes, all gathered together, all taught to respect one another.

I shall never forget hearing Bernadette Devlin, the nemesis of Unionism, speak about the inequalities alive in Northern Ireland among Catholics and Protestants. Her presence in our third form class was electric! As barriers were erected all over Belfast we crossed boundaries playing rugby in Dublin, making trips to Lansdowne Road for internationals, and debating in schools like St Malachy's on the Antrim Road. As a result, I have never been one for the narrow ground, preferring the pleasant places and the rich inheritance of the island and peoples of Ireland.

Friends from school days have largely faded from view as I have spent most of my working life in Cork and Dublin. However, I still see some familiar faces on rare forays to the Oval or Ravenhill. Denis Totton still keeps in touch and when I was elected as bishop in the Church of Ireland, I got a welter of emails from school pals: Billy McKee, Roger Bradley and Steven Simms to name a few.

Two men had a profound impact on my life: David Francis and John Malone. It was the wonderfully Welsh Mr. Francis who put me on my way to Queen's to study Geography rather than Law in Trinity. He advised, "lawyers and accountants are some of the most boring people I know. I don't want you boring people for a lifetime! No, you are an outdoor type who has no need to escape to Dublin. Geography at Queen's is best." I took him at his word, never became a wealthy lawyer but always knew where I was going!

I remember John Malone as an austere figure, with a fringe of white hair on a noble head framed with horn-rimmed glasses. He would appear on Saturday mornings, walking a West Highland terrier around the playing fields, taking in the games, pausing and chatting to spectators and players alike.

He looked a most unassuming, avuncular man.

Later I discovered that, as principal, he was the fulcrum of the school. It was John Malone who gave the school its outlook and reputation. It was he who gathered an incredible collection of staff. In many ways he personified Orangefield Boys'; it was his creation. I am indebted to him for his vision and leadership which transformed the lives of countless boys like me and educated us for life.

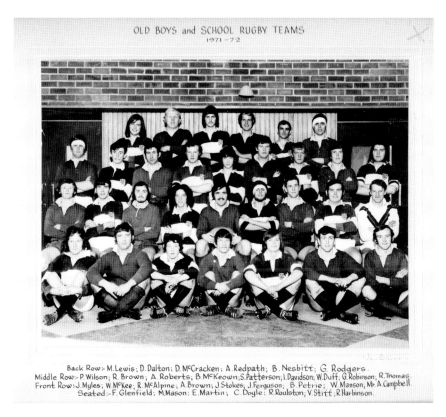

OLD BOYS and SCHOOL RUGBY TEAMS 1971-72

Back Row:- M.Lewis; D.Dalton; D.McCracken; A.Redpath; B.Nesbitt; G.Rodgers.
Middle Row:- P.Wilson; R.Brown; A.Roberts; B.McKeown; S.Patterson; I.Davidson; W.Duff; G.Robinson; R.Thomas.
Front Row:- J.Myles; W.McKee; R.McAlpine; A.Brown; J.Stokes; J.Ferguson; B.Petrie; W.Manson; Mr.A.Campbell.
Seated:- F.Glenfield; M.Mason; E.Martin; C.Doyle; R.Roulston; V.Stitt; R.Harbinson.

Sport and other things ...

Philip Monks *[1972-1979] is Principal of Lisnasharragh Primary School.*

I TRANSFERRED FROM Strandtown Primary to Orangefield Boys' School in 1972. That year the school magazine, *The Observer*, had a photograph of all 220 'firsties' on the front cover! During my first four years, I was in Alan Campbell's class. (Pupils and teachers alike called him 'Soupy' for obvious reasons.) I was elected to be the 'AC' class monitor and can still recite most of the boys' surnames in alphabetical order! 1972 through to 1979, were some of the worst years of 'The Troubles', and I particularly remember the challenge of walking to school during the Ulster Workers' Council (UWC) Strike in 1974.

At Orangefield, there was a wide range of different sports on offer. I was much more interested in games than in lessons, and had the opportunity to represent the school on its football, hockey, rugby and cricket teams. In those days, most inter-school matches were played on Saturday mornings, and the Orangefield pitches at the Laburnum were always a 'hive of activity'. Paul Acheson was our hockey coach who himself played for East Antrim Hockey Club. One Monday morning, I enjoyed informing him that I had read about his 'sending off' during a weekend club match in *The Ireland Saturday Night* (or *'The Ulster'* as it was affectionately known) for 'voluble dissent!' In later years, I had the honour of being the House Captain for Davidson House. Orangefield was where I first played squash, which turned out to be the game that I would spend countless hours trying to master.

Our PE teacher, Mr Usher, took us to the Templemore Avenue Pool for swimming lessons, after which we had to get changed in the 'Ice Box' which, as the nickname suggests, was a very cold, communal changing-room located behind the seated area at one end of the pool. Most boys were good swimmers, and many of us achieved our 'One Mile Badge'. The annual Inter-House Gala was also held at Templemore Avenue. The practical subjects were a particular challenge for me. After a failed attempt at making a miniature table for a pot plant, I remember Mr Megarry, my Woodwork teacher, writing on my report "last job not so good!" I also recall long-term hostage, Brian Keenan, being my English teacher for a short spell.

The school's outdoor activity centre, *Whinlands*, played a big part in ensuring that I enjoyed my time at Orangefield. I visited the house in Annalong no less than sixteen times — is that a record? Soupy's Christmas dinners at *Whinlands* were legendary, and I know that some members of staff were very aggrieved if they were not invited down for this very special evening. Some of the more unusual trips included a GCE Maths 'O' Level revision weekend, and a visit to help paint the new extension. When in Sixth Form, and at Stranmillis College, 'Soupy' asked me to help out with subsequent 'AC' classes that also had the opportunity to go to *Whinlands*.

Another notable school trip was our week in London in 1975. Most boys travelled by minibus. However, I think I am correct in saying that a few of us completed the journey in Soupy's yellow Volkswagen Beetle, or 'the custard car', as we called it! When we were there, we were shown round the House of Commons by Bill Craig MP, saw the West End show *Sleuth*, went to London Zoo, and saw England draw with Wales in the 'Home Internationals' at Wembley Stadium. On that occasion, it seemed we were miles away from the pitch, and I remember only being able to identify the English captain, Alan Ball, due to his distinctive red hair! On the final day, we were allowed to travel from Chigwell in Essex to the centre of London on 'the Tube' — I still have the board game, 'Escape from Colditz', that I bought in Hamley's! At the end of the week, we returned to Wembley to witness stunt motor-cyclist, Evel Knievel, do himself some serious damage as he attempted to leap over 13 London buses! They don't make them like that anymore!

At the end of my fifth year, I managed to scrape together nine GCE 'O' Levels and moved across to the Sixth Form Centre in the 'New Building' to begin 'A' Level courses in English, Economics and Biology — an eclectic mix of subjects that would not have been facilitated in too many grammar schools! There was close collaboration between the Boys' and the Girls' Schools for Sixth Form classes. My 'A' Level teachers included Mr Thomson and Mr McClelland in the Boys' School, and Mr McCambley and Miss Rainey in the Girls' School. I was a member of the Sixth Form Committee, and remember helping to organise discos in some very dodgy locations including at 'The Stables' in the long-gone Glenmachan Hotel. A Sixth Form highlight was a charity bed-push where six of us pushed a hospital bed from school to the centre of Belfast. (I am sure that a thorough risk assessment for this fundraiser had been completed beforehand!)

One of Orangefield's most enterprising projects was 'Factory Week'. I spent many lunchtimes with Mr Douglas making 'shoe and lace' templates aimed at assisting young children to learn how to tie their laces. We even had the opportunity to invest in our own company. No doubt, the profits were quickly squandered in the Tuck Shop — there were no 'healthy eating schools' in those days! 'Factory Week' was just one of many pioneering projects at Orangefield, many of which had been introduced in the forward-thinking John Malone's time as Principal.

My abiding memory of Orangefield is of the highly talented and dedicated teaching staff. The teachers were genuinely committed to providing as wide a range of learning experiences for us 'working class Protestant boys' as possible. For teachers like Alan Campbell and Philip Hewitt, nothing was too much trouble — should it have been taking us to the artificial ski slope in Craigavon for lessons prior to the ski trip at Aviemore (three boys with broken limbs on that visit), driving us to Lansdowne Road to watch Ireland play the 'All Blacks', or inter-schools camping holidays at Magilligan Strand during the summer holidays. It is no surprise that so many of the teachers who taught at Orangefield during the 1970s progressed to important posts within the Northern Ireland education system — Gordon Topping, Philip Hewitt, Graeme Thomson, Tom McMullan, Martin Graham, John Patterson, and Stanton Sloan to name a few.

The student body at Orangefield certainly had its fair share of characters and, undoubtedly, a few who were to be avoided at all cost! It was a school where you were encouraged 'to stand on your own two feet' and become an independent learner — there was certainly no 'spoon feeding'. I found this to be a distinct advantage when I reached higher education.

After graduating from Stranmillis College, I entered the teaching profession. Since 1982, I have held a number of different posts, including Vice-Principal of Grange Park Primary School, Vice-Principal of Ballymagee Primary School (both in Bangor) and Assistant Adviser with the South Eastern Education and Library Board. Since 2006, I have been Principal of Lisnasharragh Primary School, which is only ten minutes from the old Orangefield campus.

Staff 1973/4

Seated: Chris Acheson, Margaret Chambers, Eileen Quiery, John McLaughlin, Ken Stanley, Brian Weston, David Francis, Larry Lannie, Thompson Steele, Edward McClelland.
2nd Row: Eileen Gardner, Maurice Popplestone, John Reaney, Henry Sinnerton, Anne Preston, John Gowen, David McBride, Ronnie Moore, Raymond Scott, Philip Hewitt, John Allen, Jack Eaton, Michael Floyd.
3rd Row: Desmond Taylor, Colin Kinney, Brian Moffett, Jim Morrow, David Park, Carl Weathers, Billy Murdoch, Tony Sherlock, Rowland Davidson, Jack Cranston, Drew McFall, Graeme Thomson, Eric Trevorrow.
4th Row: Tom McMullan, Bruce Comfort, David Rutherford, Douglas Ferguson, John Ritchie, Bill Comyns, Nathan Todd, Norman Johnston, Ross Ewart, Gavin Robinson, Henry Blakely, Paul Gibson.
5th Row: Randal Atkins, Jim Chambers, Jim Mullan, Ross McQuarrie, Paul Acheson, Desmond Walsh, Stead Black, Robert Caldwell, Rodney Usher, Ken Smyth, David Clarke, Randal Drury, Jeff Turkington.

– 18. –
REFLECTIONS ON OBSS

Gordon Topping OBE, DL, former Chief Officer of the North East Education and Library Board, reflects on his time at the School, 1972-1975.

IT WAS EARLY 1972 and I had come home from Cardiff for the Easter holidays. I was studying there at Cardiff University. Later that year I was intending to take up a job in Devon, but I was persuaded to apply for a post in Orangefield as a Geography teacher and that was to change my life. Some weeks later I got the good news, so in September 1972 I, along with a number of other new teachers (such as Philip Hewitt and Bob McKinley) joined the staff of Orangefield Boys'. After 40 years, I can still recall the journey to school by train and bus and the trepidation of walking through the front door with over 1000 boys milling around. I didn't need to worry though, the staff were welcoming and the boys were, well, enquiring. It wasn't long before I was 'Dream' Topping, so called after an advertisement on television for a sweet dish! I think.

The Troubles were at their height, the Bay City Rollers were the pop group of choice, and tartan gangs were beginning to roam the streets. However within the walls of Orangefield normal work continued in relative peace and tranquillity with the most committed, dedicated eclectic group of staff I have ever met, giving the young people a sense of stability and continuity.

The Geography Department reflected the ethos I was to come to recognize as Orangefield's – creative, innovative, highly professional but above all fun-loving. My colleagues included Stead Black who had just taken over as Head of Department, Harry Adams an outstanding sportsman, and Davy McBride a motorcycle 'buff'. Stead led us on the principle of *'primus inter pares'* (first among equals) giving us the room to float ideas, make suggestions, and the independence to deliver the curriculum as professionals. As a new teacher he was massively supportive, assisting if there were any class management issues and sending the alarm if an inspector was arriving.

Orangefield Boys', a school with a wide ability range, was always at the forefront of educational development ensuring that all the pupils achieved their potential. This attitude was especially dominant in the Geography Department. In the 1970s geography teaching and learning were undergoing significant change and during this period, amongst other things, we introduced topic work, field trips, worksheets to assist learning and the mode 3 CSE (Certificate of Secondary Education) - an external examination internally devised. All this was assisted by the new Resource Centre which the school had developed and was managed by Tom McMullan. Our aim was to develop in the boys an awareness, understanding and appreciation of the world around them.

In line with these developments, during my first year Stead Black asked me to organize a field trip for the 'A' level class. So in 1973 off we travelled to South Wales where we stayed in a youth hostel in Brecon. There we completed a town study, investigated the National Park, and examined heavy industry by visiting a simulated coal mine and a steel works. For some of the young people it was their first time away from home. The trip gave them an insight into a different environment and one which would rapidly disappear in the next decade. From then on field trips were to become an integral part of the Geography syllabus at Orangefield.

Some years before I arrived, the school had the vision and foresight to develop outdoor and social education with the purchase of *Whinlands* in Annalong. Often I would spend up to 8 weeks there each year. The Mourne Mountains became familiar to many of the boys, because we studied the granites, examined the effects of glaciation, followed river courses and discussed the effects of human intervention on the landscape. That first day climb up the Mournes was essential if any of us were to get a good night's sleep.

I can still vividly recall a field trip in 1974 with an outstanding 'O' level class. My colleague David 'Gusty' Spence, who joined the staff in 1973, and I had planned a particularly busy schedule for the group. They were up early and worked all day until late in the evening. On the last evening however we went out for a snack and on returning a huge water fight took place only ending when everyone was exhausted and absolutely soaked. This sort of fun together with stories of the exploits of 'Herman the German' ensured there was a good balance between work and play and developed the relationship between the teachers and the boys.

Classwork could be both entertaining and challenging. I remember spending ages with a boy trying to convince him that the blue bits on the map were the sea. The challenge though was to make the learning relevant and meaningful as well as enjoyable. The satisfaction for any teacher is to see the glint of understanding in a boy's eye and the delight on his face when he realizes he understands.

Whilst the classroom was challenging and demanding, the staff room was a place of relaxation and recuperation. The banter and craic brought the staff together. The fish and chips on a Friday and the bun runs made sure everyone was well fed. Perhaps now is the time to disclose that I was responsible for cancelling the fish and chip order one Friday in May 1975. Apologies to the staff who went home hungry but we were stuck in *Whinlands* and intensely jealous!!

As I look back over 40 years I am so grateful to have had the 'Orangefield experience' – I made many friends, and learned so much in such a short time. My experience was to shape the remainder of my working life. I will always look back on that time with fond memories of an outstanding school, great staff and terrific pupils.

Stead Black's A Whinlands Tale: "Herman the German"

At night in Whinlands it was usual to entertain the class in outside games like 'hunt' and 'tig' or inside with 'black spot', 'I went to the seaside', or ghost stories. The class sat round the open fire with the lights turned out to create a suitable atmosphere. For many years I refrained from telling 'Ghoststories', but the first and only time I told one was about 'Herman the German'.

The class involved was my first GCSE Geography class doing Fieldwork at Whinlands. I started by taking them outside and showed them where Herman's plane had crashed. We returned to the house and sat in the darkened front room. I told them that when the Moon was full, 'Herman' roamed the grounds and that during the crash his hands had been severed, and they often rapped on the windows and rumour had it he had been turned into a blood-sucking creature.

There was a great deal of scepticism, particularly from Murray, Holland and Evans. However, some of the class appeared slightly apprehensive, so after a short time, Murray reluctantly persuaded me to set up a 'Ouija Board'. So we all sat round the table, and the first letter that came up was 'H'. I of course was reluctant to go on, but there were no dissenters amongst the class, so the board eventually produced 'HERMAN'. I of course was very frightened, so words like 'chicken' were used.

Eventually the class went to bed, some rather timidly. I got them settled in the front dorm, except for the two girl cooks from Orangefield Girls' School who were sleeping in the back staff dorm.

I listened until they had settled down, and went downstairs and turned the lights off at the junction box. I then placed spare mattresses from the other dorms outside the front dorm. I then found a large pole, tied a glove on it and lightened it with some ash from the fire. I rapped on the front window, and started to suck like a blood beast. Of course when the curtains were pulled back there was absolute horror, shrieking and screeching, 'pandemonium' could not describe what was taking place. They all ran to get out of the dorm, as they couldn't get the lights to work, and into the landing where they tripped and fell on to the mattresses and on top of one another. The screeching got even worse. I then turned the lights back on, but it was a 'nightmare'. Nobody would go back to sleep. So they all sat up in their beds throughout the night.

Eventually, they all fell asleep on the journey back to school in the Minibus. That was the only time I ever told the story of 'Herman the German'.

— 19. —
THE SCHOOL CERTIFICATE COURSE AND SOME MORE …

Billy Burnison *was a member of staff from 1966 to 1979. He left Orangefield at Christmas 1979 to take up an appointment as a School Inspector with the Department of Education. Billy writes:*

Preparation Time in Avoniel Primary School

I WAS APPOINTED to be a religious education teacher in Orangefield Boys' Secondary Intermediate School in the spring of 1966. Prior to that, I taught for five years in Avoniel, a feeder primary school for Orangefield. The children in my classes were a joy to teach. I was kept busy as there were 44-46 of them to look after. One amusing incident comes to mind: I asked a boy (let's call him John) on one occasion to go to the nearby post office for me (Yes, we did that sort of thing in those days!). I gave him what I thought were very clear instructions: *"John,"* I said, *"I want you to go to the post office for me. Buy a stamp, post this letter and bring me back the change".*

I handed John some money and the letter and off he went with a smile on his face. No doubt, he was more than pleased to get out of sums and spellings, even for a short period. When he returned some 20 minutes later, he proudly came up to me and said, *"Sir, I bought you a stamp* (which he handed to me), *posted your letter* (without a stamp!) *and here's your change"*. Yes, they were good days. The experience I gained teaching in primary school would, unknown to me at the time, prove to be a great preparation for my teaching in Orangefield.

After five very happy years teaching in Avoniel, I decided to return to Stranmillis Teacher Training College to take a one-year, full-time study course in Religious Education (RE). Following my appointment to Orangefield, I was very excited about the prospects of teaching Religious Education to teenagers. During that summer, I spent much time thinking about what I would teach and how I would teach it. I also thought much about how I would get on teaching post-primary pupils: the challenges they would present, the problems I might face. I was really up for all this.

One day, not long after my appointment, John Malone contacted me and asked me to call with him as soon as possible as he had a matter he wished to discuss with me. I couldn't imagine what that could be. Being a bit concerned as to what the matter might be, I went to see him without delay. It was a bit of a shock to discover that instead of teaching RE on a full-time basis, as per my appointment, he was asking me if I would consider teaching the class of first form pupils with special learning needs. This would entail teaching them English, Maths, History, Geography and, of course, RE. I would also be teaching RE to other classes. He thought that I would be very suited to teaching this special needs class as I had years of experience in teaching primary children all aspects of the curriculum, all day and every day.

To say I was surprised at this suggestion, is putting it mildly! I had left primary teaching because I wanted to teach RE to older pupils, and here was John Malone asking me to continue a primary-style of teaching, albeit with older pupils. He filled me in on some of the details of what the job entailed and what would be required of me (e.g. I would be teaching the same class of boys for the four years of their secondary school lives in Orangefield). He also mentioned that I would have a number of "other duty" periods which would give me time to draw my breath from classroom duties. When I later asked a teacher what I would be doing in my "other duty" periods, he smiled and informed me that I had got that wrong – they were actually "free" periods.

Having been a primary school teacher, I couldn't imagine what it would be like having "free" periods. My entire time in Avoniel had been spent in the classroom, apart from break and lunch times. Indeed, it was nearly impossible for me to go to the loo unless it was at break or lunch times! John Malone then sent me on my way to consider his proposal. I went home and thought much about what I should do. At first, I was very uncertain. It seemed to me, however, that I hadn't much option as he was the principal and I was a mere beginner secondary school teacher. The more I thought about it, however, the more it appealed to me. I had really enjoyed teaching primary school style – all elements of the curriculum to the same children throughout each school day. Furthermore, I would still be teaching RE to pupils in different year groups.

Consequently, I contacted my new principal to let him know that I would be happy to do what he had proposed. And so I started on a very exciting period in my professional career. I should say that the special needs class in each of the other year groups was also taught on a similar basis by three other teachers. I would be joining a team of teachers with an interest in children with special needs and with my primary-teaching background, I felt I was well equipped to handle whatever lay ahead in secondary teaching. I would also get to meet some of the pupils I had taught in Avoniel!

Early Years in Orangefield

By the time my special needs class arrived in 4th year, I knew them pretty well. During the previous three years, in addition to covering the school-based curriculum, we went each year to *Whinlands*, the school's Field Centre in Annalong, for a week's residential; we also had Christmas parties in my home. Many years later, while reminiscing about these parties with one of the boys who had been in this class I reminded him that my mother provided the food and drinks, *"Yer mother!"* he exclaimed, "*I thought she was yer wife."* I was in my late twenties then and my mother was in her late sixties! My wife indeed!).

We went to a local circus; we visited Belfast zoo; and, on one occasion, we enjoyed youth hostelling in County Donegal. During that trip to Donegal, a pupil literally nearly died when he took an asthmatic attack and discovered he had lost his inhaler. As his breathing became more laboured, I sent for a doctor who arrived accompanied by the local priest who offered to administer the Last Rites, should that be necessary. I think I remember that, on hearing this, the pupil was miraculously cured – or maybe it was just the injection administered by the doctor doing its magic – there was no way he was going back to East Belfast, dead or alive, having been given the last rites by a Catholic priest!

I really enjoyed my fourth year with these boys of mine. As this was their final year in full-time education, time was given to what they might do after they left school. This took the form of them going on work experience placements in local firms and businesses; attending link classes in the Belfast College of Technology, as it was then known; and on practical elements of careers education such as visits to factories, and hearing what visitors to the classroom had to say about the world of work. The curriculum for this year group owed much to earlier developments undertaken by Sam Preston and Thompie Steele in an effort to make it as interesting and relevant to the pupils' needs as possible. So much did I enjoy it, that I offered to continue teaching fourth-year pupils instead of going back to teaching another class of first year pupils for a 4-year period. John Malone agreed to this, and so was born what came to be known as the "non-exam" class. I also stopped teaching RE to pupils other than my own, so that I could concentrate my efforts on my 4th year boys.

Raising of the School Leaving Age (ROSLA)

At this time, the pupils could leave school officially at 15 years of age, although most remained for a further year to take their formal GCE and CSE Examinations. According to when their birthday was, they could leave school at the end of the spring term i.e. at Easter. However, during my second year of teaching a 4th year class, the government announced that the school leaving age was to be raised to 16 years and the Easter leaving date was to be abolished in 1972. This was met with dismay by many pupils who looked at having to stay on at school with horror. Some teachers were not enamoured with this development either as they already found it difficult to keep reluctant teenage learners interested and motivated, without having to do it for a further year! What was the government thinking of, inflicting this on pupils and teachers!

In response to this announcement, the BBC made a series of programmes with the specific aim of supporting teachers and helping them to implement this additional year of formal education. During the year prior to the raising of the school leaving age (ROSLA as it became known), the Belfast Education and Library Board, over a period of some eight weeks, organised a series of weekly evening sessions in our school for teachers from surrounding schools to get together to watch these programmes. These were interesting and, on the whole, helpful sessions. The teachers were able to explore and share ideas and suggestions in relation to curricular, behavioural, school and classroom management and other such relevant issues. Some imaginative and creative ideas were presented for discussion and possible implementation. They also discussed matters relating to, for example, motivation, links with parents, working co-operatively with other schools and colleges of education, and matters concerning what might constitute personal and social education.

In the early stages, the pupils in my fourth year class were not overly concerned about this development. However, when they realised the full implications for them, they were not amused, to say the least. The reality for them was that, depending on the date of their birthday, some would be able to leave at Easter and some in June as usual. For others, however, it was a different and unwelcome story. Not only could they not leave in the June of their 4th year, but they would have to remain at school for a further year, with none being able to leave at the Easter of their 5th year. Disaster for some!! One pupil's birthday was such that he missed the current leaving date by one day. ONE DAY! Can you believe it? He spoke to me with some consternation as, prior to new compulsory leaving date, he would have been able to leave at the coming Easter but now he could not leave until the end of the next school year ie his 5th year. The conversation went something like this:

"Mr Burnison, when can I leave school?"

"In June of next year," I replied.

"What! Surely you mean June this year, sir."

"No, I mean June next year."

"I don't believe this. Why do I have to stay on here for another year and a bit instead of leaving this Easter?"

"Because you were born a day too late. If your birthday had been a day earlier, you would have been able to leave this Easter."

"Hold on," said he, "are you telling me that if my ma and da had got their act together to have me a day earlier, I would have been able to leave this Easter instead of June next year?"

"Exactly! You got it in one." I replied.

We ended this conversation with him saying to me, "*This is terrible. I already have a job to go to as I thought I was leaving at Easter. I'll call in to see you from time-to-time next year*". And he was true to his word: he did call to see me from time-to-time! When he was not working.

Evolution of the School Certificate Course

And so began the next stage of my professional experience: the development of a two-year non-examination curriculum alongside Sam Preston, Thompie Steele, other interested members of staff and the school management team. The pupils in the two 4th year classes (who would move on to 5th form the following year) were those who had been in the special needs 3rd year class; those who, although capable of passing, chose not to take the CSE / GCE formal examination route, for whatever reason; and some who had behavioural problems. They were a real mixture, some presenting us with real challenges. At the commencement of the first year of the new leaving dates being introduced, Sam Preston and I each had a 4th year class of 20 pupils. Although the BBC and Belfast Education and Library Board initiative in preparation for this new venture had been helpful, much still had to be done in our school to devise a curriculum and school experience tailored to the needs and interests of our pupils. During the course of that first year, Sam Preston and I worked very hard to devise the beginnings, at least, of such a curriculum and related activities.

The following year, these 4th year pupils moved into the new 5th year and were taught by Austin Hewitt, newly appointed for this purpose, and myself. Sam Preston was joined by Thompie Steele to teach the "non-exam" 4th year classes. The four of us formed a great team: we got on very well together, worked co-operatively and were mutually supportive. We engaged in year-based team teaching to maximise the particular skills of each teacher for the benefit of the pupils. We, as a team, made strenuous efforts to develop the curriculum and devise behavioural strategies. This involved us in much experimentation in relation to curriculum activities, teaching methods and disciplinary matters.

The final outcome of all of this activity was "The School Certificate Course". This programme was, subsequently, disseminated to other schools. In due course, its worth was acknowledged by the Department of Education who appointed a schools' inspector with particular responsibility developing educational programmes such as the School Certificate Course, for dissemination to secondary schools throughout the province.

The curriculum of the "School Certificate Course" included the following:

- *Core subjects:* mathematics, English, history, geography, religious education and personal and social education, all taught by the core team of teachers;

- *Additional subjects:* art, science, woodwork and metalwork, each taught by the school's specialist teachers in these subjects;

- *Community service:* this involved the boys being placed, for example, in NSPCC playgroups and community centres for a half-day each week;

- *Link courses:* these were provided by the Belfast College of Technology. Pupils in 4th year attended the college for a half day each week and in 5th year it was for a full day. These were mainly job sampling courses which introduced the boys, for example, to electronics, bricklaying and plumbing;

- *Work experience:* this took place during the course of a week for each year group. The boys were placed with local employers, most of whom endeavoured to give them the best possible experience of the world of work;

- *Residential activities:* these took place during an annual week-long residential in *Whinlands*. This was a special feature of each year and was hugely enjoyed by all. A week away from home and, more importantly, a week away from school! You couldn't beat that! During the week the boys visited places of local interest, engaged in practical outdoor activities such as canoeing and bouldering and walked in the Mournes. They also developed their personal and social skills as they learned to work together when their team was helping to prepare meals, set the tables at meal times and wash dishes. Yes, it was great fun.

The curriculum was enriched and enlivened, for example, by:

- having occasional guest speakers to the classroom to give careers' talks;

- organising educational and leisure outings to places of local interest;

- using local youth clubs for youth-based activities;

- linking up for joint activities with pupils and teachers from local maintained secondary schools;

- occasional camping activities; and

- providing table tennis, snooker, darts, chess and other small games equipment in the pupils' base classrooms. They engaged in these activities before school started, at break and lunchtimes as well as after school had finished. In addition to the pupils developing skills and becoming more socially integrated, they were in a relatively safe place and away from possible trouble.

The course was designed to interest and motivate pupils who often struggled with school. It was always hoped that this would lead to improved attendance and improved behaviour from some of the more challenging pupils. A further intention of the course was that, in the course of its two-year duration, the pupils would develop a range of personal and social skills that would equip them for life beyond school.

In implementing this course, we were supported as follows:

- the school's senior management members encouraged us to be imaginative and creative in what pupils did, and were willing for us to improvise and take risks;

- Dessie Taylor, who was in charge of the school's timetable, arranged our timetable before planning the timetable for the rest of the school;

- the school's pastoral care and careers teams were always on hand to provide help and support as requested; and

- we had time to visit the homes of the pupils to discuss matters with parents and to gain their confidence and co-operation.

We could not have operated without such staunch support from colleagues.

On completion of the course, the pupils were awarded a School Certificate which acknowledged what they had done and achieved during the final two years of their formal education.

Personal Reflections

Developing this course proved to be a challenging and sometimes difficult professional exercise. Most of the pupils bought in to what we were trying to achieve. There were, however, a few who remained anti-school and unmotivated despite our best efforts to combat this. There were also those who retained aggressive tendencies that sometimes made it difficult for both their peers and their teachers. It should be remembered that these developments took place at a time of serious political, social and community unrest, at a time when there were malign influences at work in the lives of some of our pupils. In spite of all of this, there were many areas of success. The following give a flavour of some of those areas:

- *School Attendance*

Many of the boys in the School Certificate classes had a poor attendance record. By the end of the two-year course, in most cases, their attendance had improved, sometimes significantly. Overall, the average attendance for these classes was in the region of 90%. We regarded this as pretty good. Having timetabled time for home visits and developing close links with the Educational Welfare Officer, made helpful contributions to improving individual and overall class attendance.

- *Behaviour*

Promoting and encouraging good behaviour and dealing with unacceptable behaviour was part and parcel of the teachers' daily experience. Efforts to improve pupils' behaviour included building good classroom relationships; treating one another with respect; valuing the pupils as individuals; visiting homes to talk to parents; and having the support of the school's pastoral staff. The behaviour of many of the pupils improved, in some cases by a significant degree.

- *Relationships*

We made strenuous efforts to create good classroom relationships. This was done by treating one another with respect; valuing and listening to what the pupils had to say; endeavouring to trust them and creating opportunities through the curriculum and the classroom-based games activities, for the pupils to succeed. This was hard work but, in many cases, good (and sometimes excellent) pupil/pupil and pupil/teacher relationships were established. The good relationships established with parents contributed to improved classroom relationships. Boys often asked me when I was going to visit their parents.

- *Personal and Social Development*

Personal and social development was regarded as a central element of what we were attempting to achieve. Many of the boys entering the School Certificate programme were seriously lacking in personal and social skills. They often found it difficult, for example, to communicate effectively, control their tempers or talk to strangers and interact with adults. Involvement in activities such as community service, college link courses, residential activities and meeting with teachers and pupils from other schools, all helped many of them to improve their personal and social skills substantially.

- *Preparation for Life after School*

Preparing the pupils for life after school became a central theme during the final year. This was done via the more academic parts of the curriculum and, to a significant degree, via work experience, Further Education College link courses, visitors from the world of work to the classroom, careers advice provided by the school's careers personnel. As a result some, at least, of the pupils left the school with a sound basis for seeking employment. It was not unusual for work experience to lead to permanent employment in the placement firms.

It would be remiss of me if I failed to emphasise that, although this is my personal story, whatever was achieved through the School Certificate Course was the result of a highly committed and professional team of teachers. Sam Preston, Thompie Steele and I did much of the ground work in the early days. This was added to by Austin Hewitt, John Allen, Davy McBride and John McLaughlin who became involved later, making their various contributions. All gave unstintingly of their time, effort and skills to provide their young people, often with a learning or behavioural disability, with a rich school experience and a range of opportunities to become more confident, self-assured and caring. It should also be said that the teachers outside the core team made strenuous efforts to make their subjects as interesting and practical as possible for these boys, taking account of their learning and other needs. We didn't always succeed, but at least we tried!

Amusing Incidents and Happenings

During my years teaching the School Certificate classes, there were fraught times, difficult situations and belligerent pupils. There was, however, much more than this. There was much fun and lots of friendly banter. Good humoured interactions were often present in the classroom and in the other venues we visited …

1. *The Promise of a Windsor Chair*

I arrived home one winter's night to discover that one of my pupils, "Blackie" by name, had been up to see me at my house earlier that evening. He had been released from Rathgael, the local establishment for bad boys, where he had been placed by the court following some relatively minor indiscretion. I decided to go to see him in his house right away as I was interested as to why he wanted to see me. So off I went in my car to Blackie's house. When I arrived there, I knocked the door and was invited in by his father.

"Blackie, Mr Burnison's here to see you," he shouted up the stairs to let him know that I had arrived. He appeared downstairs eventually and said,

"Hello sir, I was at your house tonight, but you weren't in."

"Yes, I know that," I said, "that's why I'm here."

"Sir, I brought you a Mars bar, but I got hungry on the way home and ate it. Sorry about that."

"*Never mind about that. Maybe on another occasion,*" I replied. He chatted about what life was like in Rathgael. He then turned suddenly and dashed upstairs to get something he wanted to show me. He came downstairs grasping a lovely, 3-legged Windsor chair that he had made while in Rathgael. He went on to tell me that this was the only thing that he had ever completed in all his woodwork classes. I was fascinated to see what he had made – a thing of beauty. "*Blackie, I wish you'd made one of these lovely chairs for me.*"

"*I was going to, sir*" he replied, "*but they went and let me out before I could do it. But the next time I'm in, I'll make you one.*"

Yes, "Blackie" was a real character.

2. The Smokin' Chimp

It was a lovely day and the boys were really excited. Why all the excitement at another day in school? No, this would not be another day in school; we were going to the "azoo" (as the boys called it) for a day's outing. Most, if not all, of them had never been to the "azoo". They had arrived in school attired wearing a variety of clothes: jeans, flares and Dr Martens boots, to mention just a few. When the school attendance register was marked and the boys were told to be careful about their language and behaviour, we all piled into the school minibus and off we went to the "azoo". This was a great venture to some of the boys who had never been across the River Lagan and on to the north side of the city where the "azoo" was.

We finally arrived at the "azoo" and, as they had piled into the minibus earlier, so they piled out of it – shouting, pulling and scrambling over one another. I took their entrance money and made sure the minibus was looking tidy and locked. By the time I had purchased the tickets, most of the boys were well on their way into the "azoo". Most of them had raced passed the lions, leopards and tigers and were some distance ahead of me. The few who waited for me wanted to have a good look at the ferocious-looking big cats, which they did. As we progressed through the "azoo", I got a real shock when I turned a corner and saw the "azoo" keeper (I knew it was the "azoo" keeper as he was wearing a smart uniform and a shiny peaked hat) surrounded by the boys who had raced ahead. I can tell you, the keeper looked anything but happy. I was somewhat uncertain as to what awaited me as I went over to see what was going on with the boys and the "azoo" keeper. As I approached, he asked in a rather unpleasant and aggressive tone,

"*Are these your boys? Do they belong to you?*"

"*Yes they are.*" I replied with some pride. My boys. Yes, I liked that.

"*Well, get them out of my zoo,*" he demanded in a nasty, still aggressive voice.

"*I beg your pardon? What do you mean by "Get them out of my zoo." We've just arrived, just paid our money to get in?*"

"*I don't care when you arrived or what you've done. Just get this lot out of my zoo, NOW!*"

By this stage the boys were getting somewhat unsettled and noisy, no doubt itching to see the rest of the "azoo". There was also some sniggering and low laughter going on which I didn't quite understand.

"*Settle down lads. I need to get this sorted or we'll be out on our ears and on our way home.*"

"*Excuse me*" I said to the keeper, "*what is your problem? We've just arrived and you want us out. We're going nowhere until you tell me your problem.*"

"*There's my problem!*" At this point he pointed over to a cage. I couldn't believe my eyes!

There, sitting in this cage was the largest chimp I'd ever seen. It was sitting looking at us, as if it were listening to what we were saying and understanding what was going on! It was holding on to a bar of the cage with its left hand and smoking a lit cigarette (or "feg" as the boys called it) with its right hand. As I stared at it, it brought the "feg" slowly to its mouth, inhaled deeply with its huge lips and the "feg" disappeared visibly before my very eyes.

This was unbelievable! There before me was a real, live smokin' chimp. And the boys loved it, giving it a cheer of sorts when it dropped the butt, picked it up between its middle finger and thumb and finished it off with a final draw of its huge lips. Outwardly I had to sympathise with the zoo keeper, but secretly, I thought it was hilarious. I agreed with the zoo keeper that he had a point when he asked us to leave, but pleaded with him as I emptied the pockets of the boys of their "fegs" and matches (I went around for the rest of the day feeling like a walking Gallagher's cigarette factory!).

"I'm really sorry about this. I'll make sure it doesn't happen again. Please let us stay. Some of these boys have never been to a zoo before."

After I had further reprimanded the boys on their atrocious, unacceptable behaviour (imagine, giving a chimp a "feg", a lit "feg" to boot), telling them that this could lead to the poor chimp getting cancer, the zoo keeper relented and let us stay, much to my relief. The rest of the day went swimmingly. Yes we had a "never-to-be-forgotten day at the 'azoo'". By the way, I never did find out who fed the "feg" to the chimp!

Let me finish, however, on a more sombre note. John Harris, a boy in my class, was a very pleasant and likeable young person. He was well-liked and popular among his peers. He was good-humoured and never gave me any problems. Yes, it was a pleasure to have John in my class. One day, following a careers talk, John rushed out of the room with a number of his mates when the bell went for lunch. They were in a mad rush to get to their classroom to be first on the small snooker table. They scampered across the car park, pushed through the front door of the school and ran down the corridor and into their classroom. I followed as quickly as I could. As I was striding into the front entrance hall, I was met by a boy who was clearly upset. *"Come quickly, sir"* he said, *"there's something wrong with John."*

"What do you mean: something wrong with John?" I asked.

"Sir, he was lifting the snooker table when he suddenly dropped it and fell on the floor. He isn't moving."

I took off down the corridor and rushed into the room where John was lying where he had fallen: he was absolutely still. I knew at once that there was something seriously wrong with him. As I stood there, one of the boys told me that John was lifting the snooker table, when he suddenly collapsed where he was now lying. David Francis, a senior teacher called for the ambulance and informed Brian Weston, the school principal, of the situation. The ambulance crew arrived and worked with John but were unable to do anything for him. They informed us that, sadly, John was dead, probably from a massive heart attack. This was a sad, sad day in the life of my class and, indeed, the whole school. The rest of the boys were shocked and had very little to say in class that afternoon, nor for the next few days. Three days later, many teachers and pupils from the school joined John's family and friends at his funeral.

This was the saddest experience in the whole of my professional career. To lose a pupil like that is so unexpected that it is truly shocking.

Since then, I have thought of John and his family on many occasions. What a loss for them! I'm sure, like me, they have many happy memories of their son, a pleasant and friendly young person who did them proud.

Conclusion

What can I say by way of conclusion? I look back on my years in teaching with a great deal of affection. The years in Orangefield were particularly challenging and interesting. Being involved in the ROSLA initiative was exciting and both personally and professionally demanding. I worked with a great team of teachers who shared my interest in doing what I did in the best interests of my pupils. And the boys we taught, in most cases, were terrific. Undoubtedly, a small number of them were difficult to interest and motivate. Most of them, however, were great: they were often amusing, fun to be with, well-mannered and appreciative of what I was attempting to do for them. They have given me many very happy memories and amusing stories to tell others. I wouldn't have missed my years in Orangefield for anything, nor would I have missed teaching the boys who passed through my classes. Many sincere thanks to my former pupils and colleagues for all that they gave me.

Ken Hamilton's 'Model Sleeping', Oil on canvas. 18"x14"

— 20. —
SPORT AT ORANGEFIELD: PART 2

Rugby

Jim Stokes, Philip Hewitt, Stuart Duncan, Alex Redpath, Gordon McConnell and Raymond Thomas recall the history of Rugby as a team game played at the School over three decades.

SENIOR RUGBY 1957-58

BACK ROW MR. MALONE J. FOSTER N. LINTON R. HOGG MR. USHER J. GALBRAITH J. MACKIE C. FRANCEY T. BLAIR MR. HAWTHORNE
MIDDLE ROW R. McELREA G. SMITH D. NEILL H. MORROW W. SPENCE (Captain) M. LYONS D. MARRIOTT T. KAVANAGH R. HEANEY
FRONT ROW J. VINT D. BOTHWELL G. ROBINSON J. WELSH V. BRADLEY

WHEN THAT WONDERFUL educationalist, John Malone, was preparing to become Principal of a spanking new school in east Belfast, he wanted the best teachers available, in every sphere. Well, he got them, and whether they were involved in music, sports, sciences, arts or the spoken word, his undercover work in sussing out his staff proved spot on.

That was never more emphasised than in games, and particularly football, rugby and basketball. But attempting to bring a sport into a new school from an area saturated with football folklore, was going to take a phenomenal effort. In Rodney Usher that task was made to look easy.

John Malone had plucked this wiry, sharp-featured student straight from Stranmillis College graduation and gave him his brief. It was no easy task for this rugged wing forward, who had starred for old Kings' Scholars outfit, when they won every trophy in Ulster Branch's junior rugby sideboard. Rodney Usher then progressed to play senior rugby for CIYMS and Ulster, so the rugby pedigree was there, but more to the point, the teaching pedigree was on an even higher plane and on a par with any school in the country.

Rodney garnered the help of keen advocates of sport to help put those leather boots with hammer-in studs onto the famous old pitches at Laburnum from which the smell of mud from the previous day would often linger at the next morning's Assembly!

It was with great satisfaction that Rodney saw his charges progress in the game both as players and administrators. If, in the 1960s, two out of three boys at Orangefield fulfilled their sporting dreams in pursuit of football success, rugby's oval ball had its very dedicated followers. The initial exponents of the game transplanted from the playing fields of Rugby included Jim Stokes, Adrian Roberts, Jackie Gordon, Michael McBride, Richard McAlpine, Harry Williams, Davy Bothwell, Jim Barr, Victor Bradley, Bill Duff and George Robinson. These boys were the explorers, educated in a game which was foreign to their upbringing.

But while Orangefield Boys' Secondary may not have been to the forefront of Schools' rugby in the province, those involved left an indelible mark on the sport, and never more so than at Malone Rugby Club, and to a lesser degree, at CIYMS and Civil Service.

The groundwork of Orangefield was finally to shine through with the first Ireland international in flanker Willie Duncan, who stepped into the shoes of the famous Fergus Slattery to win two caps, against Wales at Lansdowne Road, and England at Twickenham. He also played for the Barbarians.

Back in those amateur days, there were Ireland 'A' internationals and wing three-quarter Joey Miles, lock forward Dermot "Dinky" Dalton and flanker Stuart Duncan who wore green on a couple of occasions. In 1972, Miles played against the All Blacks at Ravenhill. Unfortunately, he picked up an ankle injury soon after, and missed a chance to play for the full Ireland team in the then Five Nations.

There were other former Orangefield boys who played for Ulster, notably Stuart Duncan, Willie's younger brother, who made his debut as a flanker against Rob Andrew's Yorkshire side and became a regular member of the provincial set-up. Stuart received International honours at age-group rugby as well as playing in several Ireland XV friendly matches.

The Duncan brothers in action at Gibson Park

One of the most talented and assured players to come out of Orangefield was fly-half Gordon McConnell who broke the club mould and went to Rodney Usher's club CIYMS. A player with pace and flair, McConnell made one appearance for Ulster against Yorkshire in 1972, but unfortunately was injured and missed the glorious chance of playing against the touring All Blacks.

In the early years, it was Jim Stokes who caught the eye and in 1962, barely a year out of school, he was the youngest player to play for the Malone 1st XV in the then Senior League.

Coach Rodney Usher expressed his view on Jim Stokes's many all-round sporting talents: *"A superb rugby and soccer player who as a wicket-keeper/batsman, played First XI cricket for Cregagh when they were a thriving Senior team in Division One of the NCU, and was also a useful basketball exponent playing for Belfast Dodgers.*

Jim played for Malone 1st XV for 11 years before a knee injury curtailed his career. He started as a fly-half before moving to number 8, an extremely rare feat in the days when during club rugby you would be playing against British and Ireland Lions on a regular basis. "Stoker" was also a goalkeeper for the Northern Ireland Youth soccer squad in the 1962 European Championships as an under-study to the great Pat Jennings. He made his Home Nations debut against England alongside a certain George Best. He stopped playing rugby for a season when he joined Glentoran before returning to Malone."

Following his playing career, "Stoker" became a respected sports journalist and was Rugby Correspondent for the *Belfast Telegraph* for 15 years.

On Joey Miles, Rodney Usher said he was a special winger: "*An excellent rugby player,*" said Rodney. "*A sprinter of note who ran for Northern Ireland, Joey was a speedy wing three-quarter with good hands and feet. Played for Malone 1st XV for many years and Ulster.*"

During a playing career 1969-1982, Joey also played for London Irish and Irish Wolfhounds. He was capped for the Ireland A side in 1977. In a sporting biography [1977] of the great New Zealand winger, Grant Batty, can be found the following passage: "*[Grant] suffered only one setback before winning selection in the team to play Wales. That was against Ulster in war-torn Belfast. Batts marked a fellow called Joe Miles, a winger of no special distinction. Until that particular game, that is ... 'He's the*

Malone captain Jim Stokes (with moustache) in action against CIYMS in the Ulster Senior League in 1972

Ulster versus New Zealand "All Blacks" at Ravenhill, November 1972. Ulster lost 9 points to 13 against the New Zealand Test team which played Ireland the following Saturday. Orangefield "Old Boys" playing – Right wing Joe Miles and Second Row Dermot "Dinky" Dalton.

only bloke who completely outplayed me on the wing throughout my career. He ran round me and over me and tackled me when I tried to do anything.'"

In a distinguished post-playing career, Joey has held numerous senior positions in Ulster and Ireland rugby circles as a selector, chairman and manager of touring sides to Europe including France, Romania, Georgia, as well as to Australia, New Zealand and Japan.

Cecil Shaw, who played mostly for Malone 2nd XV, is the only player from Orangefield to play in the Varsity game at Twickenham. Cecil, who is also a double World Champion drum major like his father before him, won a Trade Union Scholarship to Ruskin College, Oxford, and captained the university side in 1974 against Cambridge, a game they narrowly lost 16-15.

An outstanding Medallion team in 1964/65 was coached by Jim Stevenson (Instonians, Ulster, Ireland) assisted by Duncan Scarlett. In the first round of the Shield, Orangefield beat neighbours Grosvenor High School at Gibson Park, and then were victorious away to Omagh Academy in the second round of the competition. The Medallion side's entry to the quarter finals saw the team face Dungannon Royal at Bladon Drive, Belfast. After a closely-contested game, Orangefield won 6-3.

Gordon McConnell continues the story of the side's best run in the Shield competition: *"The semi-final beckoned and our opponents were Ballymena Academy who travelled to play at the Laburnum. We lost that game by two penalties and a late try to nil. I can still recall the disappointment of that loss, but we were grateful to Mr. Stevenson and Mr. Scarlett who each gave us a half-crown in appreciation of what we had achieved that season. Orangefield was starting to be known on the schools' rugby scene having defeated three rugby-playing grammar schools, and losing narrowly to another."*

The Medallion's success was due in no small measure to the rugby skills of Dermot "Dinky" Dalton, later of Malone, Ulster and Ireland 'A' fame, and Gordon McConnell himself, who later was to play for Queen's University and CIYMS. Rodney Usher described Gordie as "*An excellent out half with great feet and hands*" and hailed the unstoppable "Dinkie" as "*A big forward in all respects.*" These individual talents were ably supported by boys like Glen Rodgers. Glen joined Civil Service, where he played until his late fifties, and was President of the Club for many years. Peter Wilson also played Senior League rugby with Civil Service. Alec Redpath turned out for Instonians and Portadown, while Alan *"Killer"* Kennedy and Kevin Balmer played for CIYMS.

The Medallion side moved on to be a great 1st XV team, coached by Mr Usher, and captained by Sam Young, who also happened to be an outstanding tennis player. Gordon McConnell remembers: "*The next season we entered the Schools' Cup for the first time. This was, I believe, brought about by two factors. Firstly, our success in the Medallion Shield the previous year, and secondly, most of the Medallion team coming back to school. This was because, with the foresight of John Malone our headmaster, we had, as a secondary school, both grammar and technical streams which facilitated pupils taking GCE 'O' and 'A' Levels through to sixth form. The teachers who looked after the team for the next three years were Rodney Usher and David Francis.*"

Gordon was at the forefront of Orangefield's move into the big league, the Ulster Schools' Cup competition, the Holy Grail in rugby in colleges, secondary, and, particular grammar schools throughout the province. Orangefield's initial game in 1964 was against Regent House in Newtownards which ended in a brave defeat. The following year they faced Coleraine Academical Institution, one of the big guns of schools' rugby. Stubbornly, they held the Northwest side to a scoreless draw on their home ground, but in another low-scoring game, narrowly went down 3-0 at Gibson Park. The following year they picked up their first-ever victory in the Schools' Cup when they defeated Portora Royal 3-0 in Enniskillen with Gordon himself scoring the only try of the game.

The following season rugby at Orangefield made the headlines, but for different reasons. The School made a visit to the Model Boys' ground at Whitewell where conditions were Arctic! It's now part of Orangefield rugby lore, as the game made local and national headlines, in the *Belfast Newsletter*, *Belfast Telegraph* and the *Daily Express*.

Gordon, who missed the match because of a bad influenza, recalls: '*The conditions were wet and icy with a bitterly cold wind, as a result of which some players on both sides, suffering from exposure, started to collapse, or give up and leave the field. At one point, an ambulance attended and drove on to the ground in order*

Cup-tie boys collapse

FIVE GO TO HOSPITAL AFTER RUGBY MATCH PLAYED IN DOWNPOUR

Express Staff Reporter

FIVE boys were taken to hospital suffering from exposure after playing in a schools' Cup Rugby match yesterday. The game, a second round tie between Belfast Model School and Orangefield School, Belfast, was played in heavy rain.

At half time, Stewart Gamble, Orangefield's 18-year-old out-half, and Derek Douglas, 16, the Orangefield full back, collapsed. Gamble, who was kicked on the head, was suffering from concussion as well as exposure.

Daily Express Report, 9th March, 1966

1965-66 1st XV team
Back row L to R: R. Dunlop, A. Redpath, G. Rodgers, P. Wilson,
Centre Row L to R: Mr. R. Usher, N. Campbell, S. Gamble, R. Barr, I.Davidson, J. McCambley,
Front Row L to R: D.Douglas, A. Kirker, S. Reilly, S. Young [Capt.], G. McConnell, M.Watson, M. Adamson.

to remove a player to hospital. The game ended with each team having about ten or eleven players, and the ball was fly-kicked on the ground because it was virtually impossible to handle it. The referee was asked to abandon the game, but refused to do so, and the Model went on to win.

The Model went on to reach the semi-finals that year where, at Ravenhill, they lost to Coleraine Inst."

In the heyday of rugby at the School, no fewer than nine teams were fielded at U12, U13, U14, Medallion and Ist XV levels. Over the decades, the close connections established between Malone Rugby Football Club, founded in 1892, and Orangefield, owed much to R.B. Fleming. Bryce Fleming was a Senior Youth Employment Officer in Belfast during the 1960s.

The popular Malone Club fielded as many as fifteen rugby teams and, in 1972, Bryce became President of the Ulster Branch (IRFU). Coincidentally, that was also the year in which Jim Stokes was Malone club captain and he enthuses on the work put in by Bryce in helping boys to play rugby at every level:

"Nobody enhanced Orangefield's rugby credentials more than R.B. Fleming, or Bryce, 'Mr Malone' to everybody associated with the game. Bryce had joined Malone as a player back in 1949, but it was as an administrator that he made a remarkable contribution to the

game, and in turn, enhanced the lives of many, with Orangefield Old Boys getting a fair whack of his many attributes. Bryce had this wonderful knack that enabled him to help young people reach their goal, and obviously rugby was high on his personal agenda. He introduced people to the game at an impressionable age, youngsters who would not normally have had rugby on their particular radar.

He found Orangefield a very rich seam of vibrant talent. When Malone became the first club in Ireland to introduce Colts or Under-16 rugby, the team was flooded with players who had been initially coached on the rudiments of the game by Rodney Usher, Eric Greene, Stead Black, and later Jim Stevenson. East Belfast had seen the light! The first captain of Malone Colts back in 1962 was the then Orangefield head boy Adrian Roberts, and in their first game against a now-defunct Newcastle Pirates side, contained no fewer than 12 former Orangefield pupils."

No fewer than four former pupils have held office as President of the Club: Adrian Brown [1998-99], Dinky Dalton [2000-1], Raymond Thomas [2004-5], and Bill Duff [2007-8]. Captains of the Club have included Jim Stokes [1972-73], Joe Miles [1975-76], Harry Williamson [1983-84], Willie Duncan [1984-85] and, on three occasions, Stuart Duncan [1996-97, 1997-98, and 2000-01]. William Coulter became Honorary Secretary, a position also held for many years by Raymond Thomas.

Many more former pupils played for the Malone Club and helped keep the 15 or so teams afloat in the days when the province was going through troubled times. They include Robin Bell, Stevie Brown, Stephen Burrowes, Robin Cairns, Angus Cairns, Ken Campbell, Fred Cartlidge, Tommy Cartlidge, Brian Copeland, Willie Coulter, Paul Davidson, Adam Earl, Mark Gamble, Noel Gilmore, Jackie Gordon, Jim Kennedy, Eddie King, Eric King, Fred King, Sammy Moore, Phil Murray, John McKee, George Martin, John Newberry, William

Malone Colts 1962
Back Row: *George Robinson, Louis Keery, Jim Rainey, Brian Murdoch, Jim Stokes, Clifford Lyons, Charlie Montgomery.* **Middle Row:** *Billy Davidson, Adrian Roberts (captain), Fred Isdell (Malone President), unknown, Jim Barr.* **Front Row:** *Clifford Quinn, Jim Schofield, Cecil Shaw, unknown, David Bothwell.*

Norwood, Ian Patterson, Mark Pengelly, Brian Petrie, Sam Reilly, Brian Young, Jack Young.

George Martin became a Manager of the Malone First XV. Jack Young became President of the Ulster Society of Referees affiliated to the Irish Ruby Union. David McCracken played for Malone as well as the British Army.

Throughout the 1970s and 1980s, Orangefield continued, valiantly, to field a number of teams in different age groups. Rugby retained its place as a sporting activity, despite a gradual decline in the numbers of pupils staying on at school to complete GCE "A" Levels in Sixth Form.

During this time, it was always a dilemma for rugby master, Philip Hewitt, whether to enter a team for the Schools' Cup competition with a squad of 17 to 19 players, who mainly comprised fifth formers, and found themselves playing against opponents one or two years older than them.

Under Coach Hewitt, Orangefield didn't enter the Schools' Cup competition but instead opted for participation in the Ulster Schools' 7-a-side tournament, in a year when Orangefield was at its strongest in this format of the game. In fact, the team drew Methodist College, just after they had won the Schools' Cup: *"Our boys weren't phased"*, remembers a proud coach, *"and we took them to extra time after being ahead most of the game. Unfortunately, they scored first in the sudden death stage to end our dreams."* A couple of years later, in the

UNDER 13 XV RUGBY 1971-72

Back Row - C McCarter, J Stevenson, J Templeton, B Evans, M Tuff, G Fee, T Tate, R Armstrong.
Middle Row - J Simms, K Anderson, C Burns, E King, S Porter, S Boyd, P Scott, P Waddell, Mr A Campbell
Front Row - G Martin, S Moore, G Ellison, E McClure, H Foreman, R McCrea, A Stevens, B Robinson, G Thompson

same competition, an Orangefield victory over Royal School Dungannon gave Coach Hewitt bragging rights over his brother who just happenedto be principal of the beaten grammar school!

Other stand-out rugby moments of this time included an Under 13 XV side winning the Secondary Schools' Under 13 competition thanks to star performances from Tommy Kincaid, Brian Copeland, Alan Earl and Stephen Brown. Tommy Kincaid would later play in Irish League football and go into football management. Later, Coach Hewitt's Medallion side entered the Shield competition and drew RBAI in the first round. 'Inst' went on to win the Medallion Shield that year, but Orangefield was the only team to score a try against them, with Brian Copeland earning that honour.

Against all odds, coach and players continued the uphill battle of keeping going a team game dominated by grammar schools in Ulster. The following annual report from the early 1980s provides evidence of the determination and commitment of coaches and boys to maintain rugby as a competitive sporting activity at Orangefield.

Coach Hewitt noted, *"The victories against Bangor and Grosvenor were the two highlights of the year. Throughout the year several players suffered injury – R. Gorman broke a collar bone; I. Montgomery sacrificed one of his teeth; M. Graham broke a bone in his hand; and R. Cooke broke a leg. In order to 'fill out' the side, there were one or two 'phantom' players drafted in – John Newberry and Ian 'Doughnut' Patterson."* John Newberry went on to play rugby at senior level with North of Ireland while 'Doughnut' made it for Malone Tornados.

Keep Trying: The Oval Ball

1st XV					
Armagh 1st XV	L	0-24	C.I.Y.M.S. Colts	L	4-24
Wallace 1st XV	L	0-47	B.H.S. 2nd XV	L	0-4
Banbridge Ist XV	L	0-32	Malone Colts 'B'	L	3-28
B.R.A. 3rd XV	L	6-11	**Bangor G.S. 2nd XV**	**W**	**6-0**
Friends' 1st/2nd XV	L	0-40	**Sullivan 2nd XV**	**W**	**14-9**
Malone Colts C	**W**	**32-13**	**Cooke Colts**	**W**	**32-0**
C.I.Y.M.S. Colts	L	12-29	**Grosvenor 2nd XV**	**W**	**16-0**
Antrim Grammar G.S. 1st XV	L	6-24	Y.M.C.A. Colts	L	14-16
Y.M.C.A. Colts	**W**	**14-0**			

MEDALLION XV				UNDER 13 RUGBY TEAM			
Armagh	18-6	W	H	Friends' School Lisburn	10-4	L	A
Wallace	20-4	W	H	Grosvenor High School	16-0	W	H
Omagh	4-26	W	A	Armagh Royal School	4-16	L	H
Dundalk	7-4	W	H	Down High School	8-8	D	H
Model	6-24	L	A	Wallace High School	18-6	L	A
Antrim	24-8	W	A	Annadale Grammar	8-8	D	H
Rainey (Med.Shield)	3-0	W	A	Omagh Academy	14-4	L	A
Down H.S.	24-0	W	H	Foyle & Londonderry College	4-4	D	H
Annadale (Med.Shield)	4-4	D	H	Model	24-0	L	A
Replay (Med.Shield)	4-8	L	A	Antrim Grammar	24-4	L	A
Inst	4-12	L	H				

Eds. Note: We are grateful to the following contributors to *Rugby at Orangefield* –

Jim Stokes [1957-1961], *who was rugby correspondent for the* Belfast Telegraph, *provided much of the detail about the game in its early years as well as the sporting careers of a number of his contemporaries at Orangefield.*

Philip Hewitt *joined the staff at Orangefield in 1972 as a teacher of Religious Education and Maths. In addition to his contribution to team games, Rugby and Cricket, he served as a Housemaster and Senior Housemaster. Philip became Head of Religious Education before leaving Orangefield in 1990 to become an RE Adviser with the North Eastern Education and Library Board.*

Stuart Duncan [1981-86] *won Junior and Senior Sportsperson Awards at Orangefield. After leaving school at 16, He joined the firm Beggs & Partners (Belfast) where he is now the Group Operations Manager. A member of Malone Rugby Club since 1980, Stuart served for three terms as President and is an Honorary Life Member of the Club. Stuart is married to Andrea and they have two children.*

Raymond Thomas [1966-72], *Chairman of the School Council at Orangefield, joined the Civil Service where he worked for the NHS (Finance Department). He joined Malone Rugby Club in 1970, served as President in 2004-5, and currently is Honorary Secretary of the Club.*

Gordon McConnell [1959-1966] *after taking a degree in Law at Queen's University Belfast became a solicitor and played rugby at a Senior Level with CIYMS and Ulster.*

UNDER 13 "A" RUGBY XV
1963-64

Back Row:- K.Munro; J.Henderson; R.Goodwin; G.Copeland; I.Wilson; G.Rowson; J.Miles
Middle Row:- Mr.Sinnerton; K.Lowry; P.Gardiner; M.Ellison; G.McNally; G.Haile; T.Coffey; Mr.Douglas
Front Row:- S.Mateer; D.Haggan; K.Balmer; V.Stitt; C.Doyle

MEDALLION RUGBY XV
1963-64.

Back Row:- R.Brendan; A.Kirker; W.Turner; R.Harbinson; M.Watson.
Middle Row:- Mr.E.Twaddell; D.Lindsay; W.McClintock; J.Johnston; D.Boyd; T.Brown; N.Campbell; Mr.D.Scarlett
Front Row:- N.Pickles; R.Barr; M.Adamson; S.Reilly (Capt); D.Hassard; R.McAlpine.

UNDER 13 XV 9-A-SIDE RUGBY. 1975-76
WINNERS - SECONDARY SCHOOLS 9-A-SIDE RUGBY.

Back Row:- Mr. P. Hewitt; D. Packenham; T. Algie; A. Earl; J. Newberry; A. Orwin; Mr. K. Balmer.
Front Row:- S. Walsh; T. Kincaid; G. Clarke (Capt.); C. Greer; T. McClure.

UNDER 12 XV RUGBY
1976-77

Back Row:- Mr. G.B. Weston; S. Cardwell; I. Lemon; S. Thompson; J. Gardiner; N. Reaney; W. McDonald; L. Ruddick; A. McVicker; Mr. P. Evans.
Middle Row:- M. Eadie; I. Anderson; W. Patterson; M. Graham; E. Gray; L. Johnston.
Front Row:- M. Millar; S. McCrory.

1st XV RUGBY
1978-79.

Back Row:- C. Martin; B. Copeland; J. Smith.
Middle Row:- Mr. P. Hewitt; A. Earle; M. Pengelly; I. Houston; Mr. J. Mullen.
Front Row:- M. McBride; A. McConkey; S. Brown; J. Newberry; P. Evans.

MEDALLION XV RUGBY
1979-1980

Back Row: S. Hedley; S. Black; C. Girvan; W. Allen.
Middle Row: Mr. B. Comfort; R. McCambley; J. Weir; J. Gardner; L. Ruddock; R. Keynes; Mr. P. Gibson
Front Row: G. Watson; M. McQueen; J. Purdy; N. Reaney; M. Taggart

UNDER 14 XV RUGBY
1984-85

Back Row:- C. Brown; G. Collins; J. Hill; A. Bagwell; A. McCullough
Middle Row:- P. Stanfield; G. Martin; G. McShane; M. Nelis; N. Hutton; A. Perry; Mr. P. Hewitt
Front Row:- B. Fulton; L. Dillon; R. Reid; J. Hynds; S. Warke.

MEDALLION RUGBY TEAM.
1987-88.

Back Row:- P. Martin B. Campbell A. Corry D. Scott N. Graham
Middle Row:- N. McWilliams D. Lee A. Hodge P. Floyd W. Thompson P. Anderson Mr. P. Hewitt.
Front Row:- W. Bennett P. Ferguson M. Patterson M. Burston M. Ross

Hockey

UNDER 14 XI HOCKEY
1966-67

Back Row:- N. Darbyshire; P. McMillan; B. Allen
Middle Row:- Mr. J.T. Scott; B. Campbell; M. Coulson; T. McIlwaine; Mr. J.M. Malone
Front Row:- T. Sterling; K. Gamble; D. Foster (Capt.); W. Elliot; R. McLean.

A SURVIVING, THOUGH incomplete, hockey archive comprises more than thirty team photographs at all age levels, and provides ample evidence of the popularity of the sport among boys at Orangefield. As a choice on games days, and at its peak during the 1970s, there would have been a hockey team in each year group, practising after school and playing matches on Saturday mornings at different venues from Lisburn to Ballycastle.

Trevor Scott, who had been appointed as an Art teacher and spent seven years at the School, introduced Hockey as a team sport in 1966. Trevor Scott's memories of players include Gary Coulson who was one of the first names on the team sheet because of the consistency of his keeping as was Paul Gray who clearly loved his hockey. Brian Nixon could always be relied upon to score goals and Jim Hodgen showed skill and leadership qualities throughout his school playing career: 'A. Treacy, K. Hamilton and M. Johnston were proficient hockey players and gave of their best week in and week out.'

Trevor was ably followed by such notable names in Orangefield as Marty Graham, Bob Hamilton, Paul Acheson, Jeff Turkington, Norman Johnston, Ivan Armstrong and

Granville Hall. In addition, Marty Graham arranged fixtures for the various teams and co-ordinated the sport throughout the School. At the time, there were very few competitions for secondary schools in this sport. Nonetheless, the photographic archive shows Orangefield Under-15 X1 competing successfully in the Taylor Cup winning the trophy for the fourth time under coach Jeff Turkington in 1976-77.

Games afternoons, lunchtime tactics sessions, Saturday morning matches and regular competitive matches gave the players the necessary skills, but most of all, the sport of hockey taught boys about working as a team. Hockey was also part of the School's House system and as a team sport was every bit as competitive as football and rugby.

Many boys in the school benefited from the opportunity to participate in the sport of hockey during their Orangefield career and a number of players kept up their interest after leaving school.

One of the highlights of the year Orangefield boys looked forward to was the match against the staff, especially when some of the lady members could be persuaded to take part. A rowdy audience was readily available for this fixture!

In addition, Hockey matches between former pupils and the School's 1st XI teams formed part of the sporting activities organised by the Orangefield Old Boys' Association as part of their wide-ranging programme of events.

1st XI HOCKEY.
1970-71
WINNERS OF TAYLOR CUP.

Back Row: Mr J.T. Scott, R. Nixon, J. Hogden, R. Brown, K. Gamble, A. Tracey, K. Hamilton, P. Gray
Front Row: M. Johnston, R. McCrory, B. Nixon (Capt), G. Coulson, T. Sterling

UNDER 13 XI HOCKEY
1971-72

Back Row:- Mr. P. Acheson, J. Galbraith, W. Cousins, W. Morgan, Mr. M. Graham
Middle Row:- D. Smith, L. Russell, R. Stanex
Front Row:- C. Boyd, G. Leahy, G. Barrett, G. Heathwood, T. Galway

1st XI HOCKEY
1972-73

Back Row:- M. Mayne, K. Hamilton, M. Ewing
Middle Row:- Mr. J.T. Scott, B. McConkey, B. Rasool, W. Bownes, A. Kennedy
Front Row:- M. Hill, P. Martin, M. Johnston, G. Coulson, M. Herron

UNDER 13 XI HOCKEY
1976 - 77.

Back Row:- Mr. I.B. Armstrong; R. Spratt; B. McCune; F. Brady; M. McElveen; T. Deuchars; S. Bell; Mr. G. Hall.
Front Row:- S. Martin; S. West; S. Whiteside; I. Ferguson; K. Surgenor; J. Davidson.

UNDER 15 XI HOCKEY,
1976 - 77
WINNERS - TAYLOR CUP.

Back Row:- Mr. J. Turkington; S. Hughes; A. Coulter; B. Thompson; R. Hanna; A. Magilton; B. Payne; D. Moore.
Front Row:- G. Smith; K. Andrews; T. Fyfie; P. Robinson; B. Blair; G. Patterson.

UNDER 14 XI HOCKEY
1979-1980

Back Row: P. Jones; N. Florence; C. Crocket; R. Murdy; A. Barron; Mr. N. Johnston.
Front Row: M. Elwood; D. Johnston; H. Myles; A. Coulter; D. Coulter.

UNDER 14 XI HOCKEY
1980-1981

Back Row:- I. Coulter; D. Pinder; I. Carson.
Middle Row:- Mr. I. Armstrong; G. Wilson; R. Patterson; P. Ennis; H. Mullan; Mr. N. Johnston
Front Row:- D. Morgan; S. Hastings; A. Quiery; G. Burton; M. McCrea.

Athletics

1962-1963 Cross Country Team
Pictured in the centre of the front row, Johnny Moreland, wearing the distinctive Ulster vest having won the N.Ireland Schools' Under 15 Championships at Belfast Castle, Cave Hill. Teachers pictured include David Craig, [Left] and Don McBride, [Right], coach and sprinter who represented Northern Ireland at International Level.

THE O.B.S.S. ATHLETICS archive from 1958 to 1985 provides evidence of boys participating in an extensive range of track and field events: 100 metres, 200 metres, 400 metres, 800 metres, mile, hurdles and relay; long jump, high jump, shot, discus, javelin, and the 'hop, step and jump'. The throwing of a cricket ball was added into the mix.

In addition to competitive team and individual sports undertaken as part of the annual Inter-House competitions, the Athletics archive also provides details of Inter-Schools Athletics events in which Orangefield was involved. From 1958 to 1963, for example, the School took part in Inter-Schools competitions involving young athletes from across Belfast and beyond: Model, Ashfield, Ballygomartin, Linfield, Everton, Dunlambert, Mountcollyer, Clounagh, Killicomaine, Dundonald, St Patrick's and Larkfield. Reports from the *Orangefield Observer* of the time highlight in particular competitive rivalries Orangefield had with the Belfast Model and Ashfield.

Athletic success was achieved by the following boys who became Ulster Champions: Trevor Adair (High Jump), Ken Wray (100 metres), and Sam Lewis (Long Jump). Sam Lewis also won the Irish Schools' Long Jump, and is the only Orangefield boy to have won an Irish Schools' Championship.

Don McBride recalls during his third year as 'An Assistant Master of Art and Craft with General Studies' at Orangefield, he had built up a cross country and road-running group of third year boys helped by the 'Around the School Relay' on a Thursday after the end of classes at 3.30 pm. Every class entered a team of six boys to compete in the one-lap race. From this pool of boys, Don McBride took a team of six to compete in 'The Round The Houses Relay' race in Ballyclare. The Orangefield team won against stiff competition from twenty other schools from across the province.

This event gave Don McBride the idea to promote a Northern Ireland Junior Cross Country relay-type race around the grounds of Orangefield:

"As we had little or no funds for a Winners' Cup, I noticed Paddy Hopkirk, who had recently won the 1964 Monte Carlo Rally in a Monte Mini Cooper S, in a television interview had mentioned that his house was coming down with cups and trophies. I contacted Paddy Hopkirk with the idea of obtaining one of his trophies for our cross country competition. Mr Malone was full of enthusiasm for the race and, even in those pre-Education for Mutual Understanding days, made sure I contacted across Northern Ireland as many Protestant and Catholic secondary and grammar schools as possible."

In 1964, the Cross country team won the Under 14 Paddy Hopkirk Cross Country Cup. In 1965, Orangefield Boys' also won the East Antrim Shield. For the School's newspaper *The Observer*, Vol 7, No 6, April 1965 [Price 4d], R. Hurst, a pupil and member of class 5H wrote the following article titled *"The Big Race"*:

CROSS-COUNTRY CLUB.
WINNERS, PADDY HOPKIRK UNDER 14 CROSS-COUNTRY CUP
1964-1965.

Back Row:- B.Brown; N.Hamilton; J.Crone; A.Henderson; A.Redpath; C.McConnell; D.Hibbert; T.Linton
Middle Row:- J.Cree; P.Balloch; R.Holmes; B.Petrie; H.Ross; E.Frizzell.
Front Row:- B.McBurney; R.O'Neill; P.Woods; W.Murray; L.Lacey; Sitting on ground - T.Roberts, P.Millar, J.Ferguson
O.Clarke.

"On Wednesday, 31st March, an unusually clear and sunny day, one hundred and eighty boys arrived at Orangefield to participate in the first junior cross-country championship. Thirty teams of all denominations ran the course of eight hundred yards across jumps and hills. Each team of six runners had to run twice around the course. When all had finished, they would have covered a distance of five miles. Orangefield 'A' team of Kelly 3B, Flood 3P1, Turner 3P1, Brown 3T1, Cree 3G, Wood 2T1 won by a convincing margin and the School 'B' and 'C' teams finished in eighth and eighteenth places respectively.

After changing, the boys had some tea and buns, and the trophy Paddy Hopkirk so generously donated as a prize for the winner was presented by Miss Mary Peters who had captained Great Britain against the U.S.A. recently. Miss Peters commented the only way to the top is through hard training. It is hoped to hold this event here again next year. By then changing rooms will have been extended for an even greater number of entries, as there were one hundred and eighty pegs for the same number of entrants.

Mr McBride, the organiser of this sporting event, would like to thank the parents who prepared the tea, the Room 14 boys, Mr Malone, and in fact all concerned for their tremendous support which made the championship such a success. He also looks forward to recruiting more members into the cross-country club from first and second form to keep up the winning standard and maybe keep the Championship trophy in Orangefield next year."

SENIOR ATHLETIC TEAM
1963 - 64.
WINNERS' INTERMEDIATE CUP AT INTER-SCHOOLS ATHLETIC CHAMPIONSHIPS

Back Row:- H. Moneypenny; J. Crone; R. McGookin; R. Stewart.
Middle Row - Mr. Usher; T. Brown; L. Hanna; B. Nesbitt; C. Morrison; R. Hurst; D. Wylie
Front Row:- A. Harrison; R. McAlpine; W. Bleakley (Capt.); S. Bracken; D. Hassard

ATHLETIC TEAM
1976-77

Back Row:- S. Patterson; J. McNeice; N. Beattie; D. Packenham; C. Greer; P. Burton; Mr. K. Balmer
Front Row:- S. Thompson; T. Hunter; J. Rutherford; S. Lewis; W. McDonald
S. Lewis won The All Ireland Junior Long Jump Title *

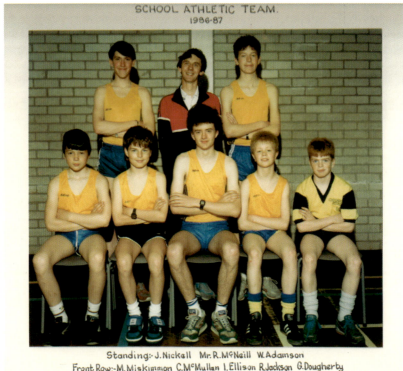

SCHOOL ATHLETIC TEAM.
1986-87

Standing:- J. Nickell Mr. R. McNeill W. Adamson
Front Row:- M. Miskimmon C. McMullan I. Ellison R. Jackson G. Dougherty

Mary Peters.

Q. When did you first take athletics really seriously?
A. In 1956 around the period of the Melbourne Olympics at Portadown College.
Q. Why did you choose to be a Domestic Science teacher when your interests were in Athletics?
A. Ever since I was twelve I wanted to teach Domestic Science. I was always keen on sewing and knitting and I felt that if I was a P.E. Teacher I wouldn't want athletics as a hobby.
Q. Did you find it mentally hard to work your way to the top?
A. I was surprised at gaining a British Team place in 1961 which came about through a shot-putt of just over 40 feet. I then became dedicated which made it easier for me to maintain my place.

Q. What are some of your most outstanding experiences as an athelete?
A. The Opening Ceremony of the Olympic Games in Tokyo. It was overwhelming to know how hard you have worked for something and achieved it. Winning the Silver Medal in the Empire Games. Being chosen as Captain of the British Team.
Q. How many medals are you going to win?
A. I hope to win a medal in the Pentathlon.
Q. Do you prefer Pentathlon to individual events?
A. Yes, I prefer pentathlon because you have more friendship with the other athletes.
Q. How do you direct your training towards the Pentathlon and how often do you train?
A. I train every day, three days in the gym and four days in the open.
Sometimes I do some weight lifting as well as track work. I like to practise the high jump at least five times a week, the long jump three times per week and the shot-putt three times a week. I do some sprinting every training session and exercises for strength and mobility.
Q. Do you think the lack of facilities in Belfast has an effect on the standard of the athletes?
A. Yes I do, because in Russia they have indoor facilities and their standard is very high. I think that if we were given equal facilities and weather conditions we could equal Russia and America. Also, there are not enough tracks in Belfast and there is not enough co-ordination between schools and clubs.
Q. If you go to Mexico do you think the altitude will have any effect on you?

P.T.O.

A. No, I don't think so because some people have been doing research on this and they have found that in a higher altitude their performances have improved.

Q. What advice would you give to a young person who wanted to take up athletics?

A. Join a club. There you can train with other people. If you didn't you would become lazy and isolated. Company is very important.
Take it seriously — you'll get as much out as you put into it.

Q. Do you hope to compete in any competitions in the future?

A. Well, I hope to compete in indoor championships in Madrid and also I hope to go to Mexico. There are other trips too, but only five or six athletes will be going, so I can't say anything definite.

<u>Iris James, Phyllis Ramsey and John McDowell.</u>

Interview from the Orangefield Observer, Volume 10, Number 4, January 1968.

John McLaughlin represented Northern Ireland in the marathon at the Commonwealth Games, Christchurch, NZ, 1974, and Edmonton, CA, 1978.

Don McBride, International sprinter, with Mary Peters.

Badminton

Back Row:- Mr.R.King; R.Archibald; R.Cole; D.Harvey; C.Mitchell; A.Stevenson; Mr.J.M.Malone
Front Row:- D.Vance; J.Crone (Vice-Captain); I.Millar (Captain); J.Russell.

A FEW YEARS after the School opened in 1957, Jim Parker, Head of the Science Department, formed a Badminton Club which met regularly in the School Assembly Hall and proved popular with the boys.

When Jim Parker left there was a gap of two years until Raymond King arrived and revived the Club. Before long, the Club enjoyed a membership of about forty boys. As well as taking part in regular games in school, some boys played for their Houses while others represented Orangefield in inter-school competitions. The *Observer*, Vol 9, No 5, February 1967 reports on a three-day trip to Dublin of a combined team of senior pupils from the Boys' and Girls' School with Grosvenor High to play a series a matches: 'The accompanying teachers were Mr. King and Miss McMurry. We were very glad to have Mr. Glendinning, who was a student at the Boys' School, with his Mercedes with us; he proved very helpful on more than a few occasions, including two breakdowns."

After Raymond King left in 1967, Raymond McNeill, a member of the Physical Education Department, and like Raymond a keen badminton player, took over the Club. By this time the Games Hall had been built in the Science playground and more courts were available for match games. While playing singles and doubles matches as part of Club activities and annual Inter-House sports activities, some boys also participated in Inter-school tournaments.

Of course the most interesting matches were those matches played against the staff, especially if the boys won!

Bob McKinley worked alongside Raymond McNeill and remained in charge until the merger of the Boys' and Girls' Schools. Bob's review of the year in the magazine, '33 Orangefield High School' ['33 OBHS], reported:

"The 1989-90 season finished triumphantly with a friendly match against Cairnmartin. This gave a chance for the younger boys of talent to emerge. Among those successfully seizing this opportunity were Stuart McKenzie (4HB) who dazzled his opponents with a fluorescent track suit, and Darren and Paul Quate (4CN) who proved themselves as a 'quate' successful double combination.

It is apparent that there is a good depth of badminton talent, with the emergence of Jonathan Cowan (4CN) and Jason McCreight (4MR) – he stretched Mr Lawther to the limit in a recent match at Avoniel. In matches in the Junior Boys' League and Cup the School has relied heavily on the abilities of Simon Davies (4HB), Michael Bennett (4PH), David Speers (4CN) and our Number 1, Colin Gallagher (5FE).

The team finished second in most matches in the League, and we gained maximum points against Methodist College Belfast. Farooq Ghafoor (5MY) showed glimpses of dazzling artistry against Sullivan Upper, but alas the coaching skills of Mr. R. McNeill (ex-Orangefield) helped Sullivan to a victory.

Despite the unavailability of the huge talents of S. McMichael and I. Thompson (5MY), the Junior Boys' Badminton team managed to draw in a Cup match against Cairnmartin early in the season."

Overall, the outlook for next season is very bright.

BADMINTON CLUB.
1979 - 1980

Back Row: C. Fawcett; R. Gorman; D. Dalton; Mr. R. McNeill.
Front Row: D. McCleland; S. Watson; G. Martin; A. McVicker; S. Ferguson

BADMINTON CLUB.
1980-1981.

Back Row:- S. Ferguson; A. McVicker; A. Stitt; Mr R. McNeill;
Front Row:- A. Crone; M. Johnston; D. McClelland; P. Coulter.

BADMINTON TEAMS
1982 - 1983.

Back Row:- J. Stewart; M. Johnston; A. Doyle; P. Elder.
Middle Row: F. Grant; D. McCleland; A. Graham; Mr. R. McNeill.
Front Row:- M. Magill; I. Wilkinson; C. Gourley; E. Mack; G. Thompson.

BADMINTON TEAM
1984-85

Back Row:- Mr. R. McKinley; M. Crockett; G. Joseph; R. Lowey; Mr. G.B. Weston
Front Row:- J. Elder; P. Boyce; C. Gourley; S. Dornan.

MINOR BOYS' BADMINTON TEAM
1986-87

Back Row:- Mr. R. McNeill; B. Stafford; P. Ritchie; I. Thompson; S. McMichael; S. Johnston; Mr. R. McKinley
Front Row:- D. Majury; M. Bennett; C. Boyd; A. Perry; C. Gallagher.

— 21. —
ROOM 14 AND OTHER MATTERS ...

Walter Rader [1961-1965] remembers being introduced to the concept of "moderation in all things", "sportsmanship", and the need "to make judgements" on the facts presented to you ...

MY EXPERIENCES AT Orangefield Boys' School gave me the opportunity to learn in an environment where I was encouraged to develop my strengths, which at that time certainly were not particularly academic. In these few reflections, I recall aspects of my time at Orangefield which stand out for me and were to make a contribution to my personal development and future career.

Room 14 Duty

It might have been the location, at the top of the science corridor, close to the central hall, just round the corner from the PE Department, which made Room 14 such an interesting learning environment. The learning that I want to reflect upon took place after school hours and on Saturdays when a rota of pupils undertook Room 14 Duty.

There were always a significant number of sporting teams training or playing matches after school and at the weekend. The limited changing room space meant that leaving school bags and clothes hung up in changing rooms was impractical. That's where Room 14 came into its own. I can't remember who invented Room 14 Duty, and it may not have been solely to address the clothes and bags issue, but it was a great learning opportunity. For me it introduced systems and processes, customer service, efficiency, deadlines and being in face-to-face contact with your 'clients'.

I recall that there were always at least two pupils on duty in Room 14, with a desk across the door — our reception. We received and logged the school bags and clothes of the sports team members, and watched over their items until they returned from practice or playing their match.

This was all long before technology might have offered a solution, so one of the Room 14ers received the clothes and bags at the door and called out the owner's name to the other 14er who wrote it on the Black Board alongside a number. The 'receptionist' then had the awesome responsibility of writing the correct number in chalk on the main items — School Bag and Blazer — and telling the owner that number. Then there followed the process of stock control, laying each customer's items on the desks in numerical order.

During week days, the main rush was in the first 15 minutes when things tended to be hectic. This was also when mistakes could be made — the wrong number on the wrong blazer, the wrong blazer with the wrong school bag, would equal mayhem later at collection time. And that is to say nothing about the customers who swore that they gave you a particular item and wanted it back NOW, only to discover it had been lying in the changing room all the time.

The opening rush having passed, there was some breathing space in which to sort out the items, and to make sure that some semblance of numerical order had been achieved. There also tended to be a discussion about the spelling of names on the board and did we understand what we had written. Who's that at 47?

There tended to be between 40 and 60 customers, but on really busy days, particularly when there were visiting teams, numbers could exceed 100. Whatever the number, you were always guaranteed impatience when everyone returned, all at once, demanding their items Now!

For me, it introduced the concept of systems and processes, although I had little idea that's what I was doing at the time. Clarity of record-keeping was also important, as was keeping calm under pressure. I'm not sure that we always adopted the maxim – *the customer is always right!* However, I did learn that people become angry, quite quickly, if they don't get the service they want, or if their items go missing. A very useful lesson for later life.

Moderation in reporting

Room 14 duty also took place on Saturday mornings when there was an extensive range of both home and visiting teams' items to look after. The opening and closing rush was elongated as not everything started at the same time, thankfully. There always seemed to be more people on Saturday so the volume of customers was greater. As if the volume of work on a Saturday was not sufficient, an extra duty was added on. Again, I'm not quite sure who invented the additional duty but I do recall that the English teacher, Mr. Watson, had something to do with it.

The additional requirement was that a Room 14er made contact with either the referee, the team captain or the host teacher, of each match, to find out the score which was then recorded on a sheet which had been ruled out by hand earlier in the day. The really exciting bit was that we were allowed access to a telephone so that the results could be rung through to the *Belfast Telegraph* Sports Desk for the *Ireland Saturday Night* publication.

There was, what might now be described as 'in-service training' provided. Mr Watson (he of the English Department) had a telephone in a cupboard in his room which was linked to his store room down the corridor. A couple of Room 14ers were put through the training – making the call to the Tele Sports Desk, speaking to the correct person, speaking clearly and communicating the correct information; the latter was very important. I quite enjoyed this and seemed to end up collecting the information and making the telephone calls most Saturdays. It also meant that I got to wander around with a clipboard – well actually it was a piece of hardboard from the woodwork room and a large bulldog clip.

One Saturday, when there were a lot of teams playing, it proved difficult to contact the right people and get the scores. Eventually, as the deadline for making the call to the 'Tele' was getting close, I managed to track down the Captain of one of our football teams. Orangefield had been playing a team from outside Belfast and the very excited Captain gave me the score.

Remembering the training – *communicate the correct information* – I wanted to make sure I had indeed got it right and the jubilant Captain confirmed the numbers which I wrote down 'Orangefield 17, the other team 3', and in due course I reported this to the sports desk.

On Monday I was invited to see Mr Watson and Mr Weston (Vice Principal). During that conversation I was introduced to the concept of 'moderation in all things', 'sportsmanship' and the need to 'make judgements' on the facts presented to you. In short, given the score in question, *"Orangefield had indeed won but perhaps it would be sufficient to report a score of 7 – 3, or better still 5 – 3?"* I had been introduced to several new concepts: the figures may be factually correct but we should not be seen to gloat in victory; being seen to rub people's noses in it is not good for future relations; win and lose graciously; and on many occasions, you will be required to make a judgement about the facts.

NRW

Nicholas Robert Watson was an English teacher with whom our class seemed to have quite a lot of contact in the first couple of years. In what might now be regarded as neither an acceptable nor PC statement, Mr Watson described himself as a Scotsman who taught English to Irish children. When a new pupil joined our class, Mr. Watson would invite one of the existing pupils to set about this 'statement of purpose'. I don't recall anyone ever raising any issues with it.

Not only did Mr. Watson seek to broaden our horizons through English as a school subject but during Second Form he organised a day trip to Dublin. There we were, in full Orangefield School uniform, on the morning Enterprise (steam) train for the 100 mile journey to the capital of Ireland. As far as I can remember, no one in the group of 25 pupils had ever been to Dublin before. We had a CIE bus to take us around, complete with a tour guide. We visited Trinity College and saw the Book of Kells; we visited the Crusaders in the crypt of a church; went to Dublin Castle and, perhaps the highlight of the whole day, had lunch in Cleary's restaurant. We even had some free-time in the afternoon – Orangefield pupils loose in Dublin – with the strict instruction to be back outside the Post Office building at 5.00pm.

It was also Mr. Watson who organised a trip to the synagogue in North Belfast and to Saint Anne's Cathedral. The impact of what I was seeing, hearing and experiencing on these unique visits was not fully apparent to me at the time. However, I still remember those visits today, and have applied the concept of 'seeing and doing' in many of the appointments which I have held over the years since leaving Orangefield.

Technical theatre

I was never on stage in a school play. For me, the most interesting part was what happened front of house interacting with the audience, and backstage with the set, sound and lights. Long before schools owned their own stage lighting equipment, there were great black boxes of equipment which could be borrowed from the Belfast Education Authority in Academy Street. It was like a treasure trove of experiences when these boxes arrived for each school play. Those of us who showed an interest were encouraged to get involved in matters technical. After Orangefield, a friend and I started a part-time business providing stage lighting and sound equipment to church and community groups across Northern Ireland. This enterprise ran for more than 18 years. It also involved providing the sound system for the annual Orangefield Sports Day with Rodney Usher telephoning to ask if I could help out again this year.

Through John Mercer, Head of Music at the School, I also got involved with what was then the Ballymacarrett Operatic Society which later became the Belfast Operatic Company. Most of the stage crew seemed to be former Orangefield boys.

Careers Interview

Mr. McClelland was the careers teacher as I was leaving school in 1965. He had also been my housemaster – Bryson House – so I thought I knew him quite well. My careers interview did not go quite as planned, from either side I suspect. The opening question was ... *"Well Rader, and what do you want to do?"*. I got the impression that my answer wasn't quite what was required. I said ... *"I want to work with people"*. Now Mr McClelland, it would seem, had not been quite prepared for this option. There was, what seemed to me, to be a long silence. He then said that there were plenty of jobs out there so I might need to give a bit more thought to what I wanted to do. That was my career interview.

It never occurred to me, at the time, that teachers talked to each other about pupils but a couple of days later the Art teacher, Mr. Preston, said that he understood I was interested in working with people and he made arrangements for me to have an interview in a Wholesale Warehouse, and so I embarked upon a career in sales; selling things to people.

The sales field proved to be another marvellous learning experience because as a salesman, and later a manufacturers' agent, I spent most of my time on other people's turf trying to persuade them to purchase the products that the firm I worked for wanted them to buy.

Youth Work

I was always interested in other aspects of working with people and became involved in my local youth club, first as a member, then as a helper and later as a volunteer leader. My sales rep days were a wonderful training ground for working with people in different situations. In the early 1970s, I had the opportunity to give up selling and to train as a Professional Youth Worker. This led to a wonderful and challenging 26 year career in Youth Work, during which I had many contacts with schools and communities. Even though I did not fully appreciate what was happening at the time, my Orangefield learning journey laid the foundations for my aspiration to work with people. The experience, skills and knowledge I acquired, whilst at Orangefield, have stood me in good stead over a 40 year period.

Walter Rader has worked in a variety of roles within the Public, Voluntary and Community sectors: NI Representative of the Queen's Award for Voluntary Service; Deputy Chief Charity Commissioner; Director of the Big Lottery Fund; Lay-member of the House of Commons Standards Committee. In 2010, Walter was awarded an OBE for his services to the community in Northern Ireland.

— 22. —
THE ORANGEFIELD OBSERVER

After long discussion these words have been chosen as the school motto. While they were first used by Lord Cecil in a speech to the League of Nations they seem to meet the need of the school for a single straightforward statement of duty. A boy in his first year, a fifth former, a monitor, a prefect, a member of staff—everybody—can set this before him as an aim in life. It is valid in all situations in school, at games, in work and at home.

Our motto will appear on the Honours pocket which Mr. Douglas has designed and which boys who gained honours last year in any sphere of activity may soon be able to purchase. Adrian Roberts, Head boy, and Victor Bradley, Deputy Head Boy, will be first to have pockets. They hope to wear them at the prize distribution.

J.M. Malone

THE *OBSERVER* MADE its first appearance within a year of the School's opening. Mr. Hammond, who had been working on a Youth Hostel Association news-sheet, suggested the idea of a school paper. Mr Malone welcomed the idea warmly, later explaining he considered a paper preferable to a magazine *"which cast an eye over a year some months after it had gone."*

Mr Hammond became its first editor and gathered about him a team of boys to fulfil the various roles of reporters, photographers, typesetters, sales and so on over time. This model was followed for the various manifestations of the paper which varied in size, frequency of publication and reflected the influence of successive editors who included Messrs. Stevenson, Carson, Bardon, McKinley, Acheson, H. Sinnerton, Burnison and Ms Gardner. Several other teachers including Mrs Harbinson, Messrs. Craig, Douglas, McBride, Preston, and others supported various aspects of the task.

The purpose of this account — based on an examination of some 49 editions available from 1958 to 1968 — is to indicate some of *Observer's* main features. A further aim is to suggest that in its content, style and tone it was an active and potent collective effort — of teacher and taught — in helping to forge the character of the new school.

Long before "mission statements" became commonplace, the *Observer* recorded the actual life of a school *with* — or *on* — a mission. Its mantra, put simply — *"get involved in the wider life of the School (i.e. games, clubs, societies) – and you will enjoy it more and your schoolwork will improve."*

The Front Cover

This was the paper's "honey pot", - as with most publications. An attractive, well-executed, interesting cover – a piece of pupil (or teacher) art work (as in the Christmas card competition), photograph of a school trip, sporting activity, important visitor or arresting headline promised an interesting content. That the paper was valued may be demonstrated by a 1968 monthly circulation of 1,000+ copies (OBSS and OGSS); a tripling of its cost from 2D (1958) to 6D (1968); and that copies were available to the author from former pupils and staff – obviously prized by them, even fifty years on.

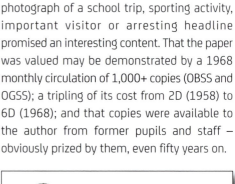

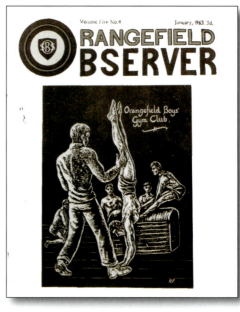

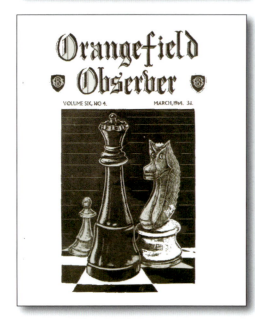

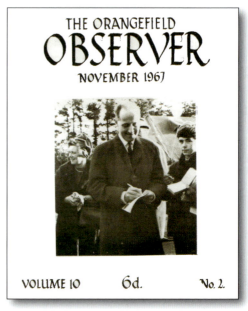

The Back Cover

(a) This was usually given over to tabulated sports results as below, *Vol 9, No 2, November 1966*. The 'Scoreboard' was often accompanied by short accounts of a match or two of particular interest, photographs and profile(s) of particularly talented sportsmen. Naturally this part of the paper was eagerly seized upon, scrutinised, argued about and, where appropriate, shown to parents and pupils in other schools. From 1960, when the Girls' School provided more copy, their sports news was also published.

SPORTS RESULTS

SOCCER

Under 12 'A'	V. St. Patrick's	L 4 - 6
	V. Ashfield	W 4 - 0
	V. Ashfield	L 0 - 4
Under 12 'B'	V. Ashfield	W 5 - 1
Under 13 'A'	V. St. Thomas	W 3 - 1
	V. Dunlambert	D 2 - 2
	V. Ashfield	W 1 - 0
Under 13 'B'	V. Dunlambert	W 2 - 1
	V. Park Parade	L 1 - 2
	V. St. Augustine's	W 2 - 1
Under 14 'A'	V. Ashfield	L 1 - 3
	V. St. Augustine's	D 0 - 0
Under 14 'B'	V. Ballygomartin	W 2 - 1
	V. Park Parade	D 1 - 1
	V. Park Parade	W 5 - 0
Under 15 'A'	V. St. Augustine's	W 8 - 1
	V. Dunlambert	W 9 - 0
	V. Ashfield	W 3 - 1
Under 15 'B'	V. Dunlambert	L 0 - 8
	V. St. Augustine's	W 3 - 0
2nd XI	V. Dunlambert	L 1 - 4
	V. Lisnasharragh	D 3 - 3
	V. Barnagheega	L 0 - 2
1st XI	V. Ballygomartin	W 2 - 1
	V. Ashfield	W 6 - 1
	V. Ashfield	W 2 - 1

SOCCER WIN

The 1st XI had a convincing, if not competent, win over Ballygomartin 1st XI in the first round of the Sir Robin Kinahan cup. A goal early in the first half by Robert Megaghy and a spectacular back-heeler by Alex McCune proved good enough for the First XI, to keep their unbeaten run. It was not until three minutes from time that Ballygomartin could penetrate the hard-tackling defence of Orangefield and our First XI were never troubled for the remaining short time.
                                                                L. Walker.

HOUSE SOCCER RESULTS (1966-67)

U 13	winners	-	Davidson
	runners-up		Hughes
U 15	winners	-	Musgrave
	runners-up		Davidson
Over 15	winners	-	Davidson
	runners-up		Bryson

over-all result:
1st Davidson
2nd Musgrave
3rd Hughes
4th Bryson

RUGBY

Under 12	V. Ballygomartin	L 0 - 15
	V. Ashfield	L 3 - 6
Under 13	V. Ashfield	W. 21 - 0
	V. Rainey	L 3 - 8
	V. Bangor Grammar	D 6 - 6
Under 14 'A'	V. Ballygomartin	W 14 - 0
	V. Rainey	L 0 - 14
	V. Bangor Grammar	W 10 - 8
Under 14 'B'	V. Wallace H.S.	D 6 - 6
Medallion	V. Ballygomartin	W 17 - 0
	V. Model	W 6 - 3
	V. Rainey	W 14 - 11
	V. Bangor Grammar	W 6 - 3
2nd XV	V. Ballygomartin	L 0 - 9
	V. Malone Colts (B)	L 0 - 9
	V. Rainey	L 0 - 19
	V. Down H.S.	L 0 - 9
	V. Bangor Grammar	L 0 - 42
	V. M.C.B. 3rds	L 8 - 19
1st XV	V. B.R.A.	L 0 - 3
	V. Malone Colts 'A'	W 6 - 3
	V. Down H.S.	W 6 - 0
	V. Portora Royal	L 0 - 15

BASKETBALL

U.14 V. St. Augustine's		W 35 - 23
U.15 V. St. Augustine's		W 52 - 39
U.19 V. Model		W 56 - 35

BADMINTON

Senior (friendly) V. Grosvenor   L 2 - 4

CROSS COUNTRY RESULTS

U14 v Coleraine	lost
U16 v Coleraine	lost
U18 v Coleraine	lost
U18-16 Down High	won
U18-16 Grosvenor	won
U16 v Regent House	lost
(1st T. Roberts)	
U18 v Regent House	lost
U14 v Boys Model	won
(1st B. Steenson)	
U14 Wilson Shield - 3rd out of 13 teams	
U14 v Dunlambert	lost
U14 v Boys Model	lost
(1st B. Steenson)	

U14: Great running has been turned in by B. Steenson and G. Clarke. The former has been first in quite a few races. G. Clarke broke the record at the Ballyclare relays with a time of 3.15 against 72 boys.

U16: T. Roberts has returned to cross country with marked success.

U18: G. Mahood and E. Frizzell have been running very well and are nearing 50 miles in training.

The Orangefield Observer

(b) By way of contrast, but emphasising their importance by positioning on the back page, were the full results of the Summer 1965 public examinations. In brief: Advanced Level GCE 26 passes; Ordinary Level GCE 243 passes; Junior Technical examination 21 passes with distinction, 117 passes with credit; College of Preceptors + Externally Moderated Certificates 27 boys were successful in one subject or more.

And, by the way, whatever happened to the prediction of the Ministry of Education's MacBeath Report [1955] that only a small proportion of non-qualified pupils would be capable of an exam of any worth...

Between the Covers

What were the ingredients of this printed offering?

Information: effective communication is greatly prized, particularly by those who are going to be affected by it ... coming events, opportunities, new procedures fell into this category. But also news of clubs and societies, trips at home and abroad, reports of important school events — Prize Distributions, House ceremonies — all contribute to being a part of, rather than apart from, the "system."

Cartoons and Jokes: satirical humour directed against those in authority, teachers, prefects and monitors.

Interviews with interesting people

Reviews: (a) of school plays, musical performances and the like; (b) of books, films, records and television.

Self-expression: *artwork, creative writing, public debate, current affairs and so on.*

Thanks and appreciation *to various individuals and bodies for their help with school events and activities.*

Letters to the Editor which allowed complaints to be aired, comment on possible improvements and so on.

Accounts of pupils' holidays and part-time jobs.

Exam and other successes.

Sports results and reports.

In its format and content the *Observer* was a cross between a club newsletter/magazine, a newspaper and a comic and thus contained elements of all, and more, of these means of communication in its first ten years.

School Clubs and Societies

Observer Vol 2, No 4, January 1960.

A survey of out-of-school/ extra-curricular activities, Vol 4, No 5, March 1962, demonstrated the high level of participation by pupils and teachers in a wide range of pursuits, 21 in all:

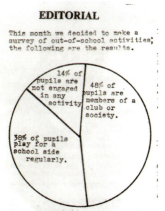

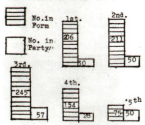

The editorial concludes: "*A spot check was made on all boys taking part in these activities during the week ending Saturday February 24th, and the total was found to be 367.*"

Each edition of the paper therefore contained several short accounts of some of these various activities. In some cases clubs and societies had a long life-span, as for example the bicycle/motorcycle and chess clubs, usually reflecting the length of service of the teachers involved. Others were short-lived because the original founding-teacher's interest was not taken up by his replacement.

However, it would be remiss not to acknowledge the role of some pupils in starting and running their own clubs — with little teacher involvement. Two such were the Orangefield Balloon Aviation Company founded by twelve pupils from forms 1, 2 and 3 who sent balloons — with messages requesting the finders to inform the members of their landing place. The second was the "Orangefield Aces Dance Band" which, starting with classical music, moved on to more advanced pieces like the "cha, cha cha ...".

Quite apart from the inherent interest and fun of such pursuits members would have benefitted from learning valuable inter-personal skills, group organisation and duties of office. Teachers of course also were "winners" – the fun of sharing the enthusiasm of younger "followers" whilst the School was enriched by the collegiate spirit this generated.

A count taken of the clubs and societies formed in the period 1957 – 68 resulted in the following list of 30+ interests:

Bicycle/motorcycle, Art + modelling, Nature Study (later becoming a Young Farmers' Club), believed to be the only city-based YFC in Ireland, Chess, Fishing, Judo, Photography, Film Society (in conjunction with Grosvenor HS), Mathematics Society (!), United Nations Organisation Group, Dramatic Society, Student Christian Movement, Record Club, Choir, Action Society, Cycling Proficiency, Badminton, Gymnastics Club, Oxfam Group, Printing and Italic Handwriting Club, Aircraft Recognition Club, Recorder Class, Savings Club, Scripture Union, Film-making, Radio Club, Model Yacht Club (later to develop into a Sailing Club), School band, Tennis Club, Bowling Club, Scalextric and Table Tennis Clubs.

The suggestion by a pupil of having a shooting range on the School's roof was not pursued...

Given this plethora of clubs, catering for a range of tastes, many of them formed within months of the School's opening (and some existing until the merger in 1990), Mr Malone could state in his December 1959 Annual Report – *"No boy in the School felt like a cog in a great machine because all types of clubs existed to suit his interest or ability."*

Other surveys followed in quick succession: Smoking Habits, Pocket Money, Television Viewing, Attitudes to Prefects. Such information on these topics would no doubt prove interesting and useful to the growing boy and his situation in relation to peers.

Staff Movements and "Personal"

Usually accompanied by their photo – taken of course by the *Observer* photographer – new teachers were asked about their own former secondary school, higher education, previous teaching experience, participation/interest in sports and hobbies. Teachers who were leaving were asked what they thought of the pupils, any interesting experiences, where they were going to etc. Some leavers took advantage of the opportunity to take "parting shots" at pupils and/or colleagues ...!

Ancillary staff were similarly welcomed on joining and thanked when leaving. Significant personal events including engagements, marriages and births were also often reported.

Cover: Young Farmers' Club

Do you know?

Some boys liked to share their interests, knowledge and skills, so a popular item allowed that: what is the oldest thing alive? how does a dynamo work? how do you make a radio receiver?

THINGS YOU SHOULD KNOW

Pro Tanto Quid Retribuamus

In the year 1888, Belfast was granted the right to have an official Coat of Arms and this motto:- Pro Tanto Quid Retribuamus. Until 1842 an unofficial seal had been used. Unfortunately no replica of this can be found.

The motto is taken from Psalm 116: V12. "What shall I render unto the Lord for all his benefits toward me?" Many a mariner has sung this praise and it is appropriate for Belfast which is a port, to have this motto.

The Red Hand of Ulster

The Red Hand has long been a symbol well-known in Ireland. It comes, it is said, from the legend of two brothers who raced over the sea, to search for a new land. They saw Ireland and sped towards it, each one striving to leave the other brother's boat behind. One of the brothers, perceiving that the other was winning, drew his sword, and severed his hand at the wrist and cast it on the shores of Ireland. He was the winner of this race, though it cost him his hand. He is said to have been the founder of the O Neill family. The O Neills have used the Red Hand for centuries, and it has always been the right hand. The left hand may sometimes be used, but an authority on heraldry has declared this a mistake. The badge of the O Neills, centuries ago, was the shape of an inverted shield, point uppermost, with a right hand severed at the wrist, and two lions supporting the hand. The O Neills' motto, which has gone with the hand since the first appearance of the hand (about A.D. 1015) is "Lamh Dearg Eirin":- "The Red Hand of Ireland".

Raymond Harrison (3T1)
David Atkinson (3T1)

How I spend my spare time ...

A-Hunting we will go

On Saturdays I go out hunting with my father at nine o'clock. We have to go early to get the wild pigeons. At ten o'clock we change to the hares and hunt them for the rest of the day.

When it is dark we go out after the ducks and geese till 12 o'clock at night. The dog sleeps with me in the tent and keeps me warm.

Other days we go hunting rabbits with a ferret and I have seen us getting ten or eleven rabbits. One day we got twenty-five rabbits in the one field.

Jim Keery (2D)

My Saturday Job

I go to the milk place in the morning at half past three to see if there are any jobs.

If you go up late, at eight or nine o'clock and go in to see Bob, the man that takes you on, he will say "But", he says, "you will have to be up here at half three or somebody else will take your place".

When I get a job I wait for the driver to come and then we go out for the milk to Dobson's Dairies. After I have finished the round my driver and I go up to Dobson's to throw off the load. If I have a shilling with me I will buy two tins of rice.

Then I go home and come up the next Saturday for my pay. I get ten shillings for the day so I try to get on every Saturday.

Fred Godden (2D)

My Job as a Knocker-out

Where I work they make cooked ham. When the hams come in they are raw and there are big bones in them. They are given to a boy called Junior. He takes the bones out of them with a curved knife in a room called the House.

They go into the boiler next and the temperature is a hundred and ninety degrees. After that they are set down in the yard to cool. Then they are brought into another house and set in water to stop them from sticking to the sides of the Shapes.

My job is to stack them along a big table and knock the hams out of the Shapes. Then we wash off the skin with hot water and cold before we roll them in the bread crumbs.

Then Walter, the Boss's father, comes in and takes them to the shops.

Derek Aitken (2D)

All this of course was a reinforcement – in the real terms of boys themselves – if you want interesting things you *"have to put yourself about"* ... *"nothing comes easy but it's worth it ..."*.

Interviews

No one was safe! Any visitor, distinguished or otherwise, was in danger of being accosted by an *Observer* reporter and subjected to questioning ... Often reporters acted on their own initiative, making arrangements to interview folk at their convenience – or just turning up! Over the ten-year period interviewees included: Belfast's Lord Mayor – pianist Russ Conway – swimmer Anita Lonsborough (Olympic Gold medallist), - a visiting marriage guidance counsellor (by a 2nd Form reporter) – Mary Peters – UTV star Tommy James – Belfast Director of Education, William Eakin – guitarist Bert Weedon – Santa at Robbs and the Co-op! [*Vol 9, No 3, December 1966*].

Orangefield Girls' Secondary School

The Boys' counterpart opened in September 1960 and from the start became involved in most aspects of the *Observer* to the advantage of all the pupils. Both "parties" could share interests, experiences, views and of course, complaints! – and learn how 'the other half' lives. The girls' involvement in sports, the Duke of Edinburgh Award, scheme, clubs and societies, outdoor pursuits, foreign travel and so on, together with a sense of humour and the ridiculous, struck common chords. In hard, practical terms co-operation equalled a larger readership and as the *Observer* did have financial pressures from the outset (never mind an added attraction in buying from the opposite sex....)!

Communication and co-operation between the two schools was obviously enhanced and valued – exemplified in the joint Prefect parties, boys helping girls with cycling proficiency (and girls tolerating boys' dancing). There were obvious advantages too when some school productions provided mutual support in staging the event and supporting them. Towards the end of the '60s, OBSS's population had outgrown its accommodation and was glad to make use of some of OGSS's. [*Vol 9, No 1, 1966*].

The Girls' School's emphasis on the importance of schoolwork and in taking part in out-of-school activities of value also served to reinforce OBSS's position.

Vol 5, No 7, June 1963, Selling Observer

Vol 4, No 8, June 1962, Girls' Sports

Correspondence: Vol 5, No 6, 1963 (above) and Vol 5, No 7, 1963 (below):

Vol 5, No 3, Dec' 1962, Dancing class

```
Dear Sir,
    We would be very grateful if
you would divulge the name,
address and telephone number of
the handsome bloke whose photo-
graph was in last months
'Observer' wearing a smashing
pyjama jacket. It would also be
a service if you would refrain
from publishing such appetising
photographs minus details.
    Thank you.           5B
The gentleman referred to was
Gerald Walker, fourth-form
casualty on the playing fields.
The other facts requested are
carefully-guarded secrets, but a
visit to the hospital would no
doubt elicit them. - Ed.
```

What about "flirting" (is that still a word?) The *Observer* provided a conduit through which "messages" might be passed.

OGSS enlisted the talents of four OBSS pupils for their production "The Heiress of Rosings" - described by a Stranmillis College lecturer as *"promising to be valuable members of the OGSS Theatre Club."*

Vol 9, No 5, Feb 1967

Vol 7, No 6, April 1965

Vol 7, No 6, April 1965

A subsequent letter to the editor from an OGSS pupil claimed that their school had been invaded by hordes of boys who weren't in their club anyway!

Letters from former pupils/those on courses

1. From Alec Duncan, OBSS's former Head Boy, writing from his new school in England where he had been made *their* Head Boy: "*I am proud of Orangefield – and my School football jersey has been envied by many pupils here … ".*

2. From Peter Aitken at Outward Bound School, Aberdovey: "… I am weathering this course not too badly. The day starts early at 6.30 am … then cold shower and PT; go bare-back riding along the beach. On an expedition … we did 60 miles in three days … the course is not as tough as I was led to believe – most enjoyable …".

3. From Barry K. Spence, the first OBSS pupil to attend an Outward Bound School [1960]: "I've had the time of my life and so will you if you stick to the two mottoes: 1 *Be just and Fear Not,* 2 *To serve and not to yield."* [Similar letters were received from boys who joined the Armed Forces].

– Lesson: Good outcomes require good inputs …

Last October, five Orangefield boys entered Stranmillis College in the hope of qualifying as Intermediate School teachers in four years time. Now, four months later, probably due to more good luck than anything else, we are still there. The boys, Billy McLaughlin, Victor Bradley, Adrian Roberts, my brother Ken and I, are enjoying ourselves and have already been out on three weeks teaching observation and are now on teaching practice one day per week.

Our usual day begins with the first lecture at 9.00 a.m. and ends at 4.15 p.m. We get two official breaks, 10.45 – 11.15. a.m. and 1.00 – 2.30 p.m. Each lecture lasts for fifty minutes with a gap of five minutes between each.

Our subjects range from Metalwork to Speech and include English, History, Maths, Education, R.E. and P.E. Four of us are specialising in Woodwork and Metalwork, and others doing P.E.

Each student has a personal tutor, ours being Mr. Fleck, late of Room 10, who has gone out of his way to help us and make us feel at home. Another ex-Orangefield member of staff, Mr. Hawthorne, is our Maths lecturer.

Jim Switzer, Vol 6, No 3, Feb, 1967

Congratulations...

Congratulations.

On Wednesday, 11th March, Brian Nesbitt, a seventeen-year-old prefect at Orangefield Boys' Secondary School, saved a life.

Brian, a holder of the Duke of Edinburgh Award at Silver Level, and awaiting presentation of the gold award, was on his way to school when he saw a boy lying on the footpath, his legs and arms twitching. Brian, who had done First Aid with the British R-d Cross Society as part of his Duke of Edinburgh's Award, immediately thought that the boy was having a fit.

But when he got off his bike and investigated more closely, Brian realized that the boy was not breathing - his face was blue and his eyes bulging. The only thing to do was to apply artificial respiration and Brian began to use the kiss-of-life method.

There was something lodged in the boy's throat, a piece of bread or apple, perhaps, that the gone the wrong way. As Brian persevered in his artificial respiration he sucked out this foreign body and the boy began to breathe normally again. Two minutes later his colour had returned and he regained consciousness.

A life had been saved. If you had been in Brian Nesbitt's place would you have known what to do?

GLENN RODGERS.

Vol 6, No 5, April 1964

Puzzles

Puzzles with or without a prize! – featured in many *Observers* – education and knowledge could be fun … …. Most were mathematical or geographical.

"Identify this country. Write your name and class and the answer in the spaces provided. First correct solution drawn at 3:35 wins a shilling."

Vol 7, No 2, Nov 1964

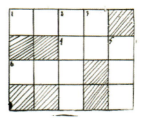

HORIZONTALEMENT
1. Animal qui attrape les souris
4. Partie du visage
6. Femenin du mot "un"

VERTICALEMENT
2. Animaux qui portent les enfants sur la plage
3. Tu – leve
5. Exclamation

PUZZLE CORNER

Good King Wenceslas wished to give his carol singers some payment. He found that if he gave them 5d. each he would have 7d. over. He therefore borrowed 6d. from the Queen and found he had just enough to give each person 6d. each.

How many carol singers were there?

First correct answer to Miss Corbett or Room 12 at the end of school wins 1/-

Cartoons

Mr Ashe in America.

Selected from Volumes in 1962 and 1964.

Stop Press 1:

FOURTH FORM MAKES HISTORY
Splendid start on 'The Road Ahead'

Orangefield has done it again! Not only are the Fourth Formers the first members of a school in Ireland to complete a twenty-mile all-night walk, but they are also the first boys to undertake the Duke of Edinburgh's Award as a school activity.

Vol. 1, No 5, February, 1959

Stop Press 2:

THE HOME FROM HOME. *"The school is at present considering a house outside Annalong, which seems to meet many of our requirements."*

Vol 7, No 6, April 1965

Stop Press 3:

"As we go to press, great news arrives. The Carnegie Trust, to whom we applied for a grant towards 'Whinlands' is contributing no less than £4,500 – the full purchase price of the house. We reproduce the Headmaster's telegram: **Word just received of Carnegie's unbelievable generosity. Heart-felt thanks from whole school.**"

Vol. 8 No 1, October 1965

Once *Whinlands* became "on stream" the *Observer* was the ideal way of recording progress and developments, thanking those who donated money, time and effort and publicising its facilities and opportunities to non-school groups. It also *"writ large"* the School's belief that school, learning and education could be fun – but also that effort, co-operation and a lot of other worthy individual and collective endeavour was essential.

The School Council

Again, once the School Council came into being, the *Observer* was probably the best possible medium to broadcast its activities. This was very important: the major problem of a Council is that it simply becomes a "talking shop" whereas, by publicising its activities it could be held to account (now that sounds a good idea ... wonder could that be applied on a larger scale....)

SCHOOL COUNCIL GAINS EARLY RESULTS

A committee was elected to draw up a Constitution.

There have been two further meetings of the Council since then and the following motions have been debated:- Prefects duties, School Meals, Bicycle Sheds, Homework Timetables and locks on Toilet Doors.

The Debates have been sometimes heated, and always long never adjourning until 5 p.m.

Mr. Malone came to the last Meeting to make his replies to the questions of Homework, and Doorlocks. On both these points the Council were more than satisfied with the results of their requests.

A small public gallery will be opened at the next meeting and any member of the school, or public, is at liberty to "sit in" on the Council's debates.

Letters to Editor

Dear Editor,

I would like to thank Mr. Weston for letting Orangefield Boys mingle with the girls at the dancing club. It is about time that we began to be sociable with the girls, when they are just over 100 yards away. I would like to see more clubs arranged between the boys and the girls as it would lead to a more friendly attitude.

THOMAS MARTIN 4T2.

Vol. 5, No 3, December 1962

FAVOURITISM?

Dear Sir,
I would like to complain about the way the House teams are picked. I have noticed that it is the old favourites who get picked each year. I have been at the school for 2½ years now and Davidson house has not picked me once. I think other people should get a chance too.

Terry McKeen 3P1

TAKE YOUR PICK

Dear Editor,
I think that instead of having only shilling dinner tickets we should be allowed to buy 6d ones: then you could have either dinner or pudding. Some people only take dinner and they are losing money. My parents and some of my friends are also interested in this idea.

T. McMinn 1A

BUST!

Dear Sir,
Why does the school not hire buses to take ALL the school teams to where they have to go? Why should we have to pay busfares?

Roy Rankin IC

Vol. 6, No 4, March 1964

"For Sale"

A charge of 6d per insertion was a valuable facility for pupils short of pocket money – and for parents having to replace endless uniform clothes and sports gear ...!

Mystery Master – Prize Competition...

```
FOR SALE
One Leon Paul Fencing Foil
– never been used. 25s. o.n.o.
                    R. POTTER 4T2
```

For Sale – Tank transporter with tank. Good as new. Cost 25s. but going to first good offer.   William Watt (3T3)

For Sale – Football boots, size 8, new studs. A give-away at six shillings o.n.o.   Brian Lamont (3T3)

```
         FOR SALE
```
Pair of Frogfeet (Surfmaster). Used once. Going at 18/6 o.n.o. T.Blair (4C)

Magnetic Football, new at Christmas. Magnets in perfect condition. Sacrifice at 12/-   D.Hobson (2B)

Roller Skates, fast machines, cost 45/-. Going for almost nothing. M.Dowds (2B)

```
         FOR SALE
Two Budgies (females) in excellent
health.            C. Ramsay 4B.
```

Guess who?

Prize: 2/6

Boys and Prefects

PREFECTS   S PATON 1B

I THINK
they adopt snooty attitudes –
    B. McAllister (5A)
they are a nuisance and have too many privileges –   H. Keery (5A)
some are too strict – big name hunters
    T. Kerr (5A)
they have the patience of Job –
    V. Bradley (5A)
they do a good job but some let power go to their heads –   B. Porter (5A)
they are unjust –   L. Lodge (5A)
they are obnoxious –   I. Kennedy (5A)
they are given too much responsibility and freedom –   B. Gillespie (5A)
they are power crazy –J. Wallace (5A)
they're hopeless: not too bright –
    J. Hagen (3T1)
they are alright –   D. Hanna (1D)
they're big mongrels (I don't like them)
    E. Lynn (1D)
they're far too strict and loyal to school
    D. Gillespie (3T2)

(Research by Michael McMullan 5A)

Vol 3, No 8, 1961

THOSE PREFECTS AGAIN

Last month the boys were able to express their views on the prefects. Now the prefects have a chance to get their own back.
"I think offenders should be locked up."   *Joe Norris.*
"Without late comers we would be without a job."   *Brian Stanley.*
"Gun law is the only alternative."
Adrian Roberts.
"Some pupils over-estimate my strength."   *Mike Dunsire.*
"I cannot comment on the grounds that I may incriminate myself."
Ronnie Bradford.
"Some have big chips on their shoulders."   *Tom Kerr.*
"Most boys obey school laws."
David McSarley.
"They are quite a good bunch of lads on occasions."   *Willy McLaughlin.*
    V. Bradley 5A.

Vol 3, No 9, June 1961

Reviews

An integral part of the earliest *Observers*, reviews of school musical, theatrical productions, books, films and television output provided opportunities for some pupils to exercise their critical faculties. In the school situation, these are often applied to "set texts", as for exam purpose: this was *real* life! I *chose* to read this book, *pay* to see this film or play – therefore I *have a right* – as have others – to express an opinion, all par for growing up.

As one may imagine, the choice(s) was/were eclectic, but all the more valuable for that. Short Stories by H.G. Wells; Glubb Pasha – A soldier with the Arabs; The Great Golden Book of Bible Stories; Spin bowling; Animal Facts and Fallacies; The Boy Electrician (Principles of electricity).

Film Reviews included *The Great Dictator; All Quiet On The Western Front; Twilight of the Gods; The Devil's Disciple.* A television review of a *St Patrick's Night Special* began …

T.V. REVIEW

Studio 8

On St. Patrick's Night (17th March) at 6.20 p.m. came a special T.V. programme "The Shamrock" from N. Ireland. This programme was full of Irish interest, Mattie McKane, Richard Hayward, Ann Maguire, Roy Johnson and Sean Maguire.

Roy Johnson introduced the performers and the first person that he introduced was a singer Mattie McKane who sang very sweetly. Her song was "I know where I am going".

After Mattie's song we saw a film about St. Patrick. We saw him walking around the hills of Downpatrick. Then they showed us where he had lived as a slave, the churches he had built and where he was buried.

First Impressions

The first thing that I thought was amazing was the trophies the school has. Most of them were won for soccer and basketball. I think this school is great for sports. I am on the under twelve's team. We were knocked out of the cup by the Model. We are not a bad team. Mr. Corry is a very good football teacher because he's not like any other teacher. He dosen't shout at you for getting knocked out of the cup.

David Patteron
Form 1LA

What impressed me most was the way there is a sort of law about the place. For example you are fined a penny for leaning against the goal posts of the five-a-side pitch when there is a match being played on it. Prefects are sort of Sergeants and monitors (class) are Constables who keep the peace.

Jackson Baile
Form 1MB

"They used to call me Big Jim in P.7"

FREEDOM FROM HUNGER

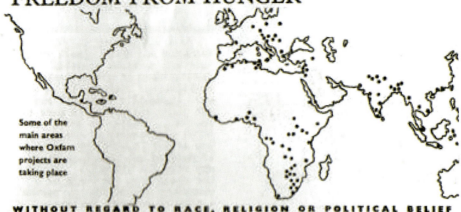

Some of the main areas where Oxfam projects are taking place

WITHOUT REGARD TO RACE, RELIGION OR POLITICAL BELIEF

Well! Well! Well!

As we go to print efforts are reaching fever pitch in connection with the Freedom From Hunger Campaign. We hope to collect £200 which is the amount needed to sink a well. All the classes here have entered into the spirit of this venture. The money-raising escapades have been very varied but we feel that at least one item per class should be mentioned in print.

1A Lucky Dip.
1B 'Lend-a-hand' at home.
1C Shoe-shining Service (badly needed?).
1D Beauty Bar – manufacture and sale of various preparations (have the boys noticed the vast improvement?).
2A Hat Competition (Hats made from vegetables and fruit).
2B Fancy Dress Party.
2C Dancing Competition.
2D Bring and Buy Sale.
3A Jewellry Sale.
3B Car washing.
3C Concerts at Lunch time.
3D Fortune Telling (Hair raising revelations!) and Treasure hunt.
3E Guessing name of a doll competition.
3F Hair-styling Salon.
4A Beauty Competition (How did Mr. Gallagher manage to attend?).
4B Candy Apples.
4C Place Names Competition.
4D Sale of Home-baked Biscuits.
5A "Magic Pool" and Coffee Party for monitors of Both Schools.
5B Chopping Sticks, cleaning cars and window-cleaning

OXFAM – COFFEE PROJECT

Most people in Britain today are aware that an organisation known as Oxfam exists. Perhaps less know what it does but still less again assist it in any way. You in this school can assist Oxfam, an organisation relieving poverty stricken human beings like you and I throughout the world. If you want to help these people then come to Lab. 4 every break and lunch time. There you can buy coffee and biscuits of the finest quality at a price well within the limits of every pupil in this school. However if you do not enjoy coffee or biscuits any donations will be gratefully accepted.

So far we are very satisfied with our progress having a profit of £45 at the time of writing (March 1st). We hope to raise at the very minimum £120 before the summer break. I hope that whoever reads this article will at the very least think about this great world problem.

Alex. Redpath.

OXFAM – Vol 5, No 7, 1963. Vol 9, No 6, 1967.

Conclusion

This survey of the *Observer* aimed to indicate some of the paper's main features and to suggest that its publication – and of course reading – by pupils, teachers and others – helped to forge the character, tone and spirit of the new school in its formative years.

Any summative, analytical approach at this stage would, I feel, do it a disservice. Yes, it was irreverent, cheeky, courageous, insightful, humorous, educative – all these and more. But the old saying "the whole is greater than the sum of its parts" applies. Thus I will – boldly – claim that the paper was essentially a *celebration,* with all the goodness and wholeness that word implies. John Malone, writing for the fiftieth edition, Vol 7, No 4, 1965, commented:

"The one quality of the Observer *I must choose to commend is its honesty. It prints articles whether they are critical of aspects of school or not. May it continue to develop as the mouthpiece of the School and its members."*

Translated into the life and work of the School, the *Observer* was much more than a record – rather a proclamation of an educational philosophy which impacted on many practices of the larger educational scene. In the words of Brian Weston, then Vice Principal, *"It was a trying time – and we tried everything!"* This was expanded upon in the confidential reports of staff committees set up in the School in the year 1965/66. Then members of the social education Sub-committee reported that *"breathlessness"* was the dominant impression of that year.

But creativity of all kinds *costs* and most teachers so involved would not have missed it for the world ... and, in their best moments, would agree with 16th century poet Thomas Tusser as quoted in *Observer*, Vol 1, No 5, February 1959:

> "The greatest preferment the childe
> We can give
> Is learning and nurture, to traine
> him to live."

Raymond King served in OBSS (1963-67) as a teacher of Geography and History. He moved to Newtownbreda Secondary School (now Breda Academy) as Head of Social Studies (1967-73) and then to Park Parade (1973-76) as Vice Principal. Appointed Headmaster of Monkstown Community School (now Abbey Community College) in 1976, he retired in 1999.

Eds. Notes:

John Malone, introducing the fiftieth edition of the *Observer*, Vol 7, No 4, January-February, 1965 paid tribute to David Hammond, who had left Orangefield to join the Schools Department of the BBC in Northern Ireland.

"Not the least of Mr Hammond's contributions to Orangefield and its traditions was the original idea for the Observer. When in 1959, he was helping to produce a Youth Hostel Association news-sheet he saw the possibility of doing something similar for the school. I was delighted with the suggestion because while I didn't see a great value in the usual annual

school magazine I couldn't think of an alternative: if something could be produced monthly it could become a newspaper, reflecting the life of the school not a production which cast an eye over a year some months after it had gone.

The other great attraction was that because of Mr. D. Wilkins' new photographic press in Comber it was possible to produce a paper in which photographs and drawings would cost nothing extra. For any other method of printing a block would have to be cut for every single photograph used ... Later we were able to cut costs further by having it typed in school. The transition to the present means of production wasn't accomplished easily; a few issues were difficult to read.

Mr Hammond became the Observer's first editor. Not only did he give it its distinctive character but worked out many of the arrangements — the selling of tokens for example — which still survive ... By the end of 1961 Mr. Hammond's responsibilities in the school greatly increased; in particular he was busy developing the Duke of Edinburgh Award scheme. As a result he had to relinquish the editorship to Mr. J.B. Stevenson. Mr Stevenson ably maintained the Observer's standards: his particular contribution was the building up of a more formal boys' editorial committee."

We thank these Businesses for their subscriptions without which we could not produce this newspaper. Please give them your support.

H.A. Newel, School Outfitters, Royal Avenue.
Inglis & Co., Ltd., Bread, Cake & Biscuit Manufacturers.
Cantrell & Cochrane Ltd., Mineral Water Manufacturers.
S.S. Moore, Sports Outfitter, Arthur Street.
C.A. Gowdy, The School Shop, 121-127, Woodstock Road.
Robert Wilson & Sons (Ulster) Ltd., Food Manufacturers, Newforge
Littlewoods Ltd., Ann Street, Belfast.
Northern Publishing Office, Printers & Booksellers Belfast.
Alfred H. Leitch, Photographic Dealer, Castle Lane.

The *Observer* was the most durable title of the Orangefield Press to hold up a mirror to life at the School in all its diversity. Titles such as *Orange Peal* and *Spectrum* waxed, waned, or found themselves revived in later years. Matt Maginnis recalls the publication of *Cosmos* and its moment in the sun ....

Top left: Fernie Glenfield, Top right: William Shaw, Bottom right: Barkley Campbell

In the late 1960s, the Sixth Form were called Seniors and the vast majority played a role in the corporate life of the school. 6A2 boys were allowed to select an area of involvement where they could help out and work with members of staff. There was a wide range of choice for them which suited the skills on offer. Some helped First Form tutors, in the Library, Duke of Edinburgh Assessment, Clubs and Societies and the School Magazine.

The magazine gave me a clear insight into the school and the social history of the catchment area. It provided an opportunity to work with a full age – range of pupils and abilities. Brian Weston wanted a magazine which represented all year groups. In this endeavour, I was helped by a multi-talented team of juniors and seniors who kept their ear to the ground in the interests of producing newsworthy material and the occasional scoop.

David Craig from the Art Department was a gifted cartoonist, Barry Traynor a skilled photographer, and there were many wordsmiths such as Denis Totton, Barkley Campbell, Fernie Glenfield, Gerald Kane, Gavin Bamford and Michael Andrews. Denis had an acerbic wit and provided most of the edgy satire. I realised from the launch of the magazine that Fernie Glenfield was destined for a higher plane. He was not passed by and he featured on the cover of the new magazine. A star in the making but, in retrospect, he should have been put inside the rocket and sent in search of the Cosmic Dawn or perhaps the Taurus Meteor Storm! At the time of writing, Fernie is a Church of Ireland Bishop.

The Editorial Team covered stories about the Extension, Soccer, House Teams, Staff Leavers, New Staff, Howard Hughes and the Hughes House connection. Some in depth interviews were conducted, e.g. with David Gibbons and his time at Manchester City Football Club, Noel Clingan on his football coaching experience, David Bleakley and his thoughts on Community Relations.

Whinlands and the residential experience were popular sources for junior stories. Football was always a compulsory topic and there were two local scouts at least looking for the next George Best. Gibby McKenzie and Bob Bishop spring to mind. Two boys in 4th Form were spotted and taken to Manchester United in 1971. Victor Moreland and David Vance reached Old Trafford and met Denis Law and George Best.

The magazine was produced and distributed free to all pupils who comprised a readership of over 1,000 pupils at that time. In meeting deadlines for Botanic Printers, I was indebted to Margaret Vance, the School Secretary who had to type the magazine in a special way so that I could literally cut and paste in the photos, titles, cartoons and one line filler jokes. There were no Photoshop or Scanners in 1971.

Margaret always deciphered my handwritten scrawl without an Enigma Code and used her skills, acquired in Miss Elliot's Secretarial School, to good effect in the production of *Cosmos*. Margaret worked with Hilary McCavana and Mavis Scott during the late Sixties and she left Orangefield in 1973 to join the teaching profession.

— 23. —
MEMOIRS: SET 5

"Life is often about perceptions …"

John Grayden [1966-1972] tells his tale of leaving Elmgrove Primary School, joining Form IRK at Orangefield, and some stormy weather …

IN THE EARLY 1960s, to working class parents on the Beersbridge Road area of East Belfast, Orangefield Boys' Secondary School didn't have the appeal of the neighbouring grammar Grosvenor High. However, to the average ten or eleven-year-old boy, Orangefield represented something different again, the chance to play football, a sport ignored by grammar schools in those days.

As I negotiated the final year of primary school, I began to resist the notions harboured by my mother of a potential place for me at Grosvenor, or even the former Annadale at far-off Ormeau. Early stubbornness showed as I dug my heels in after getting the news that I was one of five in my class to pass the 11 plus. Thankfully, 1960s Belfast mothers also had a respect for what they perceived as authority.

Jim Hunter, principal of Elmgrove Primary School — a man she trusted — convinced her that Orangefield was not only a different kind of establishment to the one she thought but one that could secure my future. He explained the alien concept of a school where pupils with an academic bent could successfully rub shoulders in the corridors with those who wanted to pursue a technical or manual career.

So it came to pass in September, 1966, I joined the ranks of Orangefield's 1RK in the charge of Raymond King before being entrusted to form teachers such as the energetic Alan Hunter and the urbane Moore Sinnerton.

Seven years passed in a flash as we collectively enjoyed fun times with teachers such as the blackboard duster-throwing Matt Maginnis who mimicked John Wayne as he kicked in the doors of other classrooms; endured the scathing wit of Ted McClelland who tried hard on a daily basis to hide his concern for the future of his pupils, reversed the traditional pupil-teacher scenario as we caught Noel Spence having a crafty lunchtime fag behind the bike sheds, and embarked on outings to places such as Dublin and weekend trips to *Whinlands*.

It wasn't all bliss though. Like any institution you got to know who to avoid and give them a wide berth. With my latter years at school coinciding with the early days of the Troubles, we had to contend with the external events of a city in turmoil and the phenomena it spawned such as the almost comical Tartan gangs and the more sinister allure of para-militarism which claimed a couple of my classmates.

Facts and figures seeped in all the while, despite the failure of some dedicated guys in the Maths Department to teach me the mysteries of algebra, logarithms and pie charts. Yet Orangefield's biggest imprint on my life involved more than mere classroom learning.

Not long after starting school, music teacher John Ritchie discovered I had a singing voice sparking a lifelong involvement in musical theatre and choral music. Topical discussions in the latter years of school, initiated by the likes of Moore Sinnerton, the gentlemanly Marty Graham, wise old cove David Francis and even Brian Weston, by then Orangefield's Principal, encouraged us to think for ourselves, not to accept things at face value, to question motives and to rationalise arguments.

It was a useful armoury not just for a career in journalism but truly a lesson in life.

John Grayden graduated in 1974 from the National Council for Training of Journalists' course based at Belfast's former College of Business Studies in Brunswick Street. He started his career with the Down Recorder before joining the Belfast Telegraph as a reporter in 1976. John stayed with the Belfast Telegraph until 2005 where for long periods he was responsible for the content of inside news pages and, in his later years, acted for spells as chief sub-editor. John left the organisation in 2005. In the 1990s, John fronted a BBC Radio Ulster programme on musical theatre, and since 2007 has run his own businesses and acted as national adjudicator for the Association of Irish Musical Societies.

Maths is fun!

Ian Simons [1972-1979] writes:

AFTER LEAVING ORANGEFIELD Boys' School in 1979, I attended Stranmillis College where I trained to become a Maths and PE teacher at post-primary level. Enjoyment was always a motivating factor in whatever I did. I enjoyed Maths and wanted my students to do the same. This objective became very clear when I asked all the students in my junior classes to repeat after me *"Maths is Fun!"* and so the lessons began. My philosophy for learning and my teaching style were greatly influenced by my teachers at Orangefield and to them collectively I say a massive thank you!

An appreciation of Maths really began for me in Form 2. Up until then, I had gone through the motions and made some effort to learn the skills, concepts, formulae and techniques but with limited success and no real love for Maths or anything else outside of playing football. I was in Mr Philip Hewitt's Maths class and his approach to teaching the subject suited my natural learning style. At 13 years of age, I was learning to play guitar by practising the same techniques over and over again, I was playing a lot of sport and was practising skills over and over again, so it was fabulous when learning Maths followed the same pattern.

Each lesson began with an introduction of the Maths concept, several examples were worked through on the board and then we were given what seemed like an endless supply of questions to practice. Each class followed the same pattern and I really enjoyed the challenge of getting questions done and right before the class was over. Form 2 was pivotal for me at school because my new found love for Maths soon spilled over to other subjects. I realised that with practice and effort I would become more capable in a technique, skill or subject and so my desire to win followed a path of repetition and for me a reasonable level of success.

For students who wanted to learn, Orangefield proved to be a very positive experience. Although I really only wanted to play sport, I realised the value in learning other skills albeit academic in nature. In time, I was thankful to those wiser and much more learned than me for their discipline, encouragement and patience.

GCE 'O' Levels were difficult and Maths presented challenges for most of the pupils. In a class of 32 boys, the teacher Mr Paul Gibson had his work cut out. Teachers at Orangefield must have been given the same teaching manual because Paul Gibson's approach to teaching Maths was very similar to my junior school experience. The topics were introduced with some whole class discussion, a few worked examples followed for everyone to watch the explanation on the board, and then we were presented with a generous supply of practice questions. At the end of each topic, we were presented with another set of questions which were taken from past GCE 'O' Level examination papers. This approach to learning catered for the whole mixed ability set within my class and everyone responded well.

There was a good fun factor within the class even though the course had its demanding features such as integration, differentiation, trigonometry etc. The *craic* at Orangefield was always mighty with banter between the students and the teachers being the norm. Even teachers who did not teach my class offered assistance with topics and questions we found difficult. On more than one occasion, Mr Alan Campbell held an after-school class for me and some of my class mates to help us with differentiation. Alan was not our Maths teacher, he just wanted us to do well. After the two years, everyone passed his GCE 'O' Level Maths. All the students were over the moon. Mr Paul Gibson et al were joyous – a job well done!

GCE 'A' Levels were a massive step up for most of the students but again we were supported and encouraged to do our best. I sat beside Chris Martin and Gary Hill, and some of our class mates, Alistair Allen, Harry Best and Ken Jackson, were very academic having taken on extra GCE 'O' subjects at the end of Lower Sixth. [At the time, the four Maths subjects were 'O' Level Maths, Additional Maths, Engineering Science and Applied Mechanics]. This was followed by 4 GCE 'A' Levels – several students obtaining 4 As.

However, I enjoyed my sport too much, and so stuck to nine GCE 'O' Levels along with 4 GCE 'A' Levels which included Pure Maths and Applied Maths. I was just as proud of obtaining a Grade 1 in C.S.E. Physical Education, as one of the first boys in Northern Ireland ever to study the subject to examination level at 16 as part of a syllabus devised by Billy Lawther and Walter Bleakley.

Pure Maths at Advanced Level presented a new challenge to me because the teaching style changed dramatically. We were introduced to the topic in the usual way but then were given a six-page, handwritten booklet with examples using first principles. The notes looked as though they were taken from a University course and possibly were. This dramatic change in style, along with having a number of different teachers during the course, left me wondering whether I had made the right decision to study Pure Maths at GCE 'A' Level.

Applied Maths was a very different experience for me. My teacher, Mr Dessie Taylor, had the gift of making difficult concepts very understandable and his skill and expertise helped all of us to succeed and pass well. Mr Taylor's variation in approach appealed to me. Each question was analysed to gather the information, and then in a logical manner the problem was solved using the information gathered after the first or even second reading. I enjoyed the technique so much that it is the style I tried to emulate when I eventually became a Maths teacher.

Mathematics at Orangefield took me on a journey. I found it enjoyable, challenging at times, but usually very positive and rewarding. Teaching is a profession which can have a massive impact far beyond the classroom (for good and bad) so it is vital that all of us involved in the profession love the job we are doing, work with the students to help them overcome the challenges, make learning a positive experience and for Mathematics teachers to remember – *Maths is fun*!

Ian Simons, *formerly head of the ICT Department at Wellington College, is currently Lecturer in Computer Science at Stranmillis University College. Ian has written a standard textbook for A-Level Computer Science, published by Oxford University Press, and in 2015 was the recipient of the Blackboard Teaching Tech Award for teachers in Northern Ireland who have advanced significantly technology teaching in the province. Ian is co-author with the multi-award winning Go Beserk computing resources, and founder of 'Make Code work 4 U', a company to recognise and award computer coding certification.*

— 24. —
CLUBS AND SOCIETIES

Eds. Note: Reading *'Orangefield Remembered'* is to be reminded of the importance the School placed on providing pupils with access to a large range of lunchtime and after-school activities. Constraints of space make it impossible to detail more than thirty clubs and societies created to reflect and nurture the interests and passions of pupils and staff. Below, a small number of clubs and societies are recalled.

Chess Club

Observer Vol 6, No 4, March 1964.

THE CHESS CLUB was very popular for many years, with up to 200 members at any given time. Every new member was given a place on the chess ladder and could challenge the person above him for a game. A win for the new member meant he took the place above him and by a series of steps like this could get higher and higher. The ultimate target was to become Number One on the ladder – the best player in the school.

There were several Orangefield teams entered in the Schools Chess Leagues and they had great success over the years against all types of school, winning many prizes. Mr. Taylor had valued assistance in looking after these teams, especially travelling to away matches by car or minibus. Mr. Graham, Mr McMullan, Mr. Fraser and Mr. Walshe were particularly generous with their time.

In school itself the House matches were keenly anticipated every year, as was the annual match against the staff.

1966 Team: Cantrell and Cochrane Cup Winners

Left to Right: Mr. T.L. Mills (Sales Manager, Cantrell and Cochrane), Sam Mateer (Captain), Sidney Spence, Tom Reynolds, Mr. D. Taylor (Teacher-in-Charge), Alan Harpur, John Ferguson, Mr. A. Long (Ulster Chess Union), Alan Stirrup, and Mr. W.G. Hall (Director, Cantrell and Cochrane).

There were many good players at Orangefield over the years and some of them included Brian Nesbitt, Sam Mateer, Alan Harpur, Alan Stirrup, John Ferguson, Denis Totton, Sidney

Spence, Colin McCool, Alan Patterson, Jim Cowden, Tom Reynolds, Kenneth Adams, Billy Groves, Glenn Millar, Jimmy Whiteside and, last but not least, George Heathwood, who went on to great success in adult chess. However, all the players, weak as well as strong, were valued, and hopefully provided with an enjoyable activity which could be a hobby for the rest of their lives.

CHESS

White to play and mate in 2 moves. i.e. What move must white make so that he can checkmate black with his next move after that, no matter what black does in the meantime?

CHESS RESULTS

In the final of the Form 1 Championship, Ivor Campbell (1MG) beat Paul Meadows (1MG) after a close match.

In the Form 2 Championship Colin McCord (2PS) beat Alan Patterson (2M) in the final.

In the final of the Senior Championsh John Ferguson (6G) beat Kenneth Adams (6GFR).

The Form 3 Championship was won by Glenn Millar (3M), who beat Herbie Black (3T) in the final.

In the final of the Junior Championship (open to boys in forms 1, 2, 3 and 4) John McAvoy (3CL) beat Derek Connolly (3B).

Observer Vol 10, No 7, May 1968.

In memoriam: Paul Gray

Constable Paul Moore Gray

Paul Gray [1965–1972] was an active member of the Orangefield Chess Club. He served with the Royal Ulster Constabulary in Forkhill, Crossmaglen, and Bessbrook. On 17th April, 1979, Paul was killed instantly, along with three colleagues, after a bomb exploded under their Police Land Rover.

The Young Farmers' Club

Jimmy Masterson writes:

ORANGEFIELD YOUNG FARMERS' Club was established in 1960/61 and at the time was the first Young Farmers' Club within Belfast City Boundary. Indeed it may have been the only one to have ever been so. The Y.F.C. evolved from the activities and membership of two successful and very active after-school clubs, Nature Study and Fishing, which had been established in the previous two years and the stimulus of the introduction of the Duke of Edinburgh's Award Scheme.

The Nature Study Club and the Fishing Club were designed to offer boys living in the city the opportunity to learn about rural and countryside activities and to experience the natural environment – its flora, fauna and people at first hand. The success of these two clubs was mainly due to the enthusiasm and commitment of the boys themselves and the understanding and patience of a very supportive Principal and staff.

The boys' natural curiosity, enjoyment of working together and undertaking new as well as challenging activities were probably the underlying reasons for the continued membership and support for the clubs. Boys from all forms were involved and as the membership was not restricted a significant number of boys joined both clubs, which contributed to the formation of the Y.F.C.

Both clubs met in after-school hours on one afternoon each week and the informal meetings offered ample opportunities for a wide range of discussion and activities, which inevitably were of a practical nature. These regularly included enthusiastic planning for future outdoor activities involving nature rambles, fishing and a variety of club outings and visits to appropriate centres. Much could be written about both clubs but a few examples of activities which stand out from the very many happy and stimulating times spent together may help to illustrate the enthusiasm, commitment and companionship experienced by myself, and hopefully club members and staff who willingly assisted.

In the early years Orangefield did not have a secure school boundary or fence and the only piece of ground available for school nature studies was a very well maintained lawn within the central quadrangle and adjacent to the principal's office. A small portion of this lawn was kindly made available for gardening activities.

Members of the Nature Study Club were encouraged to bring in their pets for display, observation and discussion. These naturally included a wide range of animals, birds, fish and reptiles. However, a variety of snakes, baby crocodiles, dangerous spiders, and a monkey created quite an interest. Eventually it was suggested we should keep some pets in school and without delay a rabbit hutch was enthusiastically constructed and erected on the principal's lawn. The principal demonstrated his great insight and understanding of the importance of recognising the enthusiasm of young people [staff and pupils] with a casual remark a few days later, "I see the school garden is producing rabbits."

On another occasion having dissected a badger, which had been killed on the roadside near the school, and disposed of its entrails, it was agreed to cure the skin and make a badger skin rug which was done successfully. All that remained was the skeleton, and to help clean the bones it was agreed to bury them — again with blind enthusiasm – in the principal's lawn. On retrieval eighteen months later, an attempt was made to identify and mount the bones but this proved beyond the ability of members and myself.

The fishing club engaged in regular outings to various lakes, for example McAuley's lake at Spa, Glassdrummond and the Long Lake, both near Ballynahinch, rivers, sea beaches, rocks and piers. While fishing at Bangor pier, a club member got his line and reel in a tangle. He was advised to lay down his baited hook and trace the line back to his rod and reel. While doing so, a seagull picked up his baited hook and soared above him. He grabbed his rod and line and stood reeling in the bird from high above his head and remains the only member to have caught a seagull while fishing. Like many fish caught and returned safely to the water, the seagull was returned safely to the air.

On another occasion, when the club was camping out on a two-day fishing outing at The Spa, members were washed out of their tents during a major storm of wind and rain. Fortunately, fourteen members and myself found accommodation in a small garage for the night. With no access to toilet facilities, never have empty lemonade bottles and Coca-Cola tins been so welcome during a ferocious gale. On another occasion, this club spent the first week of July fishing off the rocks at Newcastle and thanks to Mr Stanley we were permitted to fish for trout in Castlewellan Lake. On that occasion two other members of staff, Jim Leckey and Jim Parker, Head of the Science Department, accompanied the party.

Hopefully, new and necessary safety procedures will evolve and continue to permit children and staff to engage in similar stimulating, challenging activities.

At this time, I was attempting to introduce the Duke of Edinburgh Scheme and as activities of the Nature Study Club and the Fishing Club met the requirements of part of the Award I undertook an overview of the range of activities on offer in existing clubs and societies. These activities also met some of the aims and objectives of the Young Farmers' Club, and so it was agreed to establish an Orangefield Y.F.C. This was welcomed by members of both clubs although each continued with their own individual programmes and activities. Boys who chose to join the Duke of Edinburgh Scheme were able to use club participation to meet the various Duke of Edinburgh requirements and standards. It is worth noting that Orangefield boys who completed the Bronze Level of the Duke of Edinburgh were the first schoolboys to obtain the Award in N. Ireland.

Orangefield School in its formative years provided an environment in which not only pupils but staff, especially young, inexperienced staff, were enabled to learn and develop skills along with life-enhancing values, standards and attitudes. I am acutely aware of how much it has influenced my own development both professionally and personally and like many boys, and indeed other young staff, I can proudly, thankfully and honestly say I am who I am because of the contribution of the early Orangefield Experience.

W. James Masterson OBE taught Rural Science in OBSS from 1958-61. On leaving Orangefield, he went to work in Malone Training School for a time before moving to England and teaching in an Approved School in Kent. Jimmy eventually returned to Northern Ireland to lecture in the Rupert Stanley College in Tower Street before being appointed Principal of North Down Further Education College.

Italic Handwriting and Printing Clubs

CLUBS AND SOCIETIES which met during lunchtime or after-school provided many platforms for pupils to develop individual talents, personal interests or new skills. Italic Handwriting and Printing had their dedicated followers under the guidance of Mervyn Douglas, Head of the Art Department.

Orangefield was very fortunate when Baird's Printing Firm donated two powered presses to the school. The professional installation of an automatic Heidelberg printing press enabled Club members to become involved in a wide range of printing activities. Boys were given a thorough grounding in the basic techniques of printing, particularly useful for those members with ambitions to gain apprenticeships in the printing trade. Drew Evans set up his own printing firm while John Cunningham eventually held the top position in Further Education in Belfast.

The annual tradition of the Orangefield Christmas card was popular with members of staff and pupils.

Early editions of *The Observer,* invitation cards for the official opening of *Whinlands*, and programmes for school plays were printed on site. Boys acquired skills in typesetting and were able to reduce school costs by doing this work themselves. A number of boys entered the print trade as apprentices.

As part of 'Factory Week' when pupils designed and made plant stands, milk bottle containers, desk tidies, and three-dimensional toys, games and puzzles for younger children, sales brochures and share certificates for investors in the boys' products were also printed by the Orangefield Press.

Pupil: Jeremy Russell

Design by Rowland Davidson

Design by Carl Weathers

The Motor Cycle Club

Jim Lecky writes:

THE ENVIRONS OF Orangefield Boys' School in the late 1950s and early 1960s were very different from what they later became. Between the school and the Knock Road was a glorious wilderness of hawthorn bushes, whins, brambles, old trees, old walls and foundations of a ruined house and, best of all, a little stream meandering through a small valley. What a treasure this "waste" ground was to the city boys confined usually to urban streets and manicured parks and gardens. Here was a boy's paradise where climbing trees, breaking off a stick to whack the heads off some thistles, throwing stones and damming the river were not punishable offences; they were not even noticeable.

This was long before mountain bikes were made, but certain daring fellows could be seen from time to time riding on the back wheel, or in the river, or racing across the playground (forbidden) and jumping their machines right from the top to the bottom of the flight of steps leading down to the bicycle sheds.

It so happened a student teacher was assigned to the school the year it opened. As a lifelong motorcycle enthusiast he had been taken to the 1939 Ulster Grand Prix to see the great Dorino Serafini winning on a 500cc supercharged Gilera and the "Blonde Bombshell" Walter Rusk putting in the fastest lap at 100 mph. He noticed the bicycle boys' antics and was suitably impressed. The next school year he was on the staff.

There was no lack of interest when anyone who wanted to talk bikes was invited to come to WW2 to discuss the formation of an after-school club. All attendees were asked what form the club should take and what they would like to do in it. Suggestions and questions came thick and fast and a programme devised which, with few modifications, lasted for the life of the club.

Meetings took place once a week in the craft room. Usefully this had benches, vices and tools which the members could use to tinker at their bicycles, which were obviously the nearest most of them could get to powered transport. Arrangements were made for what became the club's most popular activity – bicycle trials. These involved a number, usually of ten observed sections being marked out over and around natural obstacles as found in the aforementioned wilderness. Devising these "sections" could take a long time and everyone's idea had to be tried out for suitability for a wide range of skills. The object is to ride through the section without putting your foot down. Footing incurs the loss of one mark for each dab. One observer is required for each section but two are even better: one to fix his eagle eye on the competitor in case of a sly dab, and the other to gleefully record the misdemeanour on his clipboard prepared earlier. These events took place on Saturdays, and as well as competitors and observers, attracted quite a few spectators to support their mates, or perhaps laugh uproariously if they happened to fall in the river.

In time some boys acquired a weird variety of motorised bikes, clip-on engines, auto cycles, mopeds, lightweight motorcycles and remarkably at the top of the range a 500cc Triumph Trophy Twin, a proper trials bike, today worth many thousands of pounds but then only a few bob. This impressive vehicle was the cynosure of all eyes, not excluding the master's. It arrived in the hands of Terry Boyd who later became a motorcycle dealer in Donegall Pass. Other club members went on to become well-known in the Northern Ireland motorcycle scene: Terry Patterson, Derek Stewart and his young brother "Wee Willie" who came from the primary school to compete, Robert Walsh, Gordon Bowden, later of Canada, twins Harold and Raymond Dunwoody, Clinton and Leon Agnew, and many others whose names have faded in the mists of the last fifty years.

One which hasn't faded is Alan Rain. He asked if his big brother could come to the trials. His big brother was Gordon Rain, an established trials rider. His prompting led to the master taking up proper trials riding. This development led to a multi-bike trailer being purchased and boys who had progressed to real trials bikes were now taken to ride all over the country in Ulster Centre M.C.U.I (Motor Cycle Union of Ireland) trials.

Much excitement, hilarity and banter followed these events, especially if any of the young riders should happen to outperform their teacher. Hard to believe, but it did happen.

Bicycle trials still continued of course for those without engines. They were so popular that crowds of up to eighty people, competitors, observers, parents and spectators would gather. Luckily present day health and safety regulations hadn't been invented!

The other club activities continued once a week after school. A major dealer, W.J. Chambers, gave us an old engine to illustrate the principles of the internal combustion engine. This engine was disassembled and assembled so many times by succeeding classes of boys

each of which lost some small component, or couldn't remember what it was or where it went, that eventually only a large collection of disparate parts remained, all very clean by contact with many hands, hankies, ties and blazers. Great fun was had by all, but maybe not the mums trying to deal with the mud, oil and grease!

Another well-known firm, Mann & Robb of Ventry Street, donated a collection of cups from the large collection they had won in competitions. Bertie Mann was an Irish Championship grass track rider and Tommy Robb went on to become a Honda works team member. We were grateful for all the wide benevolent interest in our club.

One less benevolent interest, for which we were not grateful, was the interest shown by a representative of the Belfast Education Board who happened upon a trial in full flight one day.

His apoplexy was a fine sight to behold. After expressing full-bloodedly his opinion of the dirty, noisy, smelly, dangerous contraptions destroying flora and fauna and endangering all and sundry on these precious private grounds, he forbade any further incursions upon the sacred soil. The river was piped, the trees were felled, the wild life (including us) done away with and all his sacrosanct soil pushed around until the sterile prairie you see today was achieved. Then the master resigned and after nine years the club was no more.

Eds. Note: Jim Leckey *joined the staff as a Heavy Craft teacher in September 1958 transferring in 1963 to the Special Needs Department. In 1967 Jim was appointed Head of the Heavy Craft Department at the newly-opened Rathcoole Secondary School.*

David McBride writes:

Just as Orangefield Boys' School has always been noted for its football, there has always been a strong motorcycle interest.

Away in the beginning, it was Mr Jim Leckey who began a little club for boys interested in motorbikes. As well as trips to local events, especially trials, competitions were organised for push-bikes around the school grounds.

Arriving in the school in 1971, I revived the club again and a great deal of interest was shown. Visits to events of all kinds, shows, films, quizzes, and push-bike trials around the school grounds kept club members busy.

Highlight of the year was the visit to the Isle of Man in June to see the international TT races. Fifteen or sixteen boys would spend a week just soaking up the unique atmosphere of the "Road Racing Capital of the World", accompanied by Mr McBride, his wife and family, and another member of staff. Mr. Scott, himself a regular motorcyclist, was one of the most enthusiastic helpers here.

In the mid-1970s the school got its own moped from the Department of Environment's Road Safety Branch and this was used by club members to learn proper control and riding techniques.

Over the years many boys have "graduated" from the push-bike events and moped riding to the real thing, taking part regularly, and indeed successfully, in motor cycle sport here in Ulster and beyond.

Derek Stewart was a top trials rider until illness forced his early retirement. Gordon Bowden won the Ulster Motocross title and then moved to the USA where he became East Coast Champion. Phil Martin and Mark Neill won Ulster and Irish Junior titles in trials riding, and as passenger with Mr McBride in 1982 Ivan Wylie became Irish Grass-Track Champion, in the side-car class.

To-day, there are past members of Orangefield Motor Cycle Club competing in every single branch of the sport. Some are involved in the organisation and administration, some in vintage riding, many have their own road bikes, and we even have a couple of "speed-cops" to our credit.

Eds. Note: David McBride *joined the Geography Department in 1972 from Bangor Boys' Secondary School and remained a member of the Orangefield Boys' School staff until 1990. He was a well-known competitor at Motor Cycle trials throughout the British Isles. Later in David's career, he broadcast on radio and television on motorcycle events.*

Film-Making and Cinema

Matt Maginnis writes:

THERE WAS A culture of amateur film-making in the 1960s when Super 8mm camera became commonplace. Brian Weston, Vice-Principal, made a series of one-reelers around the School. Noel Spence, English specialist, filmed many short films around Comber with his brother Roy Spence, mainly in the Horror Genre. They also had their own cinemas for showing their latest releases.

Moore Sinnerton made a film about the Annecy Ski Trip in 1972, and his brother, Henry, also covered a French trip at a later date. Paul Acheson produced a documentary about a typical *Whinlands* residential with 1PA in 1977. The Staff Cultural Club featured many a visit to a variety of downtown cinemas to assess the merits of the latest pop culture after the obligatory 'pie and a pint' in the Crown Bar. These outings often led to some comical pseudo-critiques the next day in the staffroom lunch-break. Bill Comyns, Fred McCracken and Alan Hunter were adept at creating an 'intellectual atmosphere' in discussing the plot, dialogue, music and photography of some mediocre films. They were often elevated to Cult Status and serious Oscar contention because of this largely frivolous dissection designed to counter the 'subtitle' culture at the other end of the staffroom.

I made three amateur films, usually after school, in the school grounds, Orangefield Park and up on the Laburnum Playing Fields. They were designed in a comedy framework and intended to convey a simple message about battles fought in the past. The first film I made was with 1BR, a terrific class, and it was shot as a western with bicycles instead of horses! It was called 'CUSTER'S FINAL GLORY' and it told the story of the Battle of Little Big Horn and the effect on the Sioux nation 100 years later. Two members of staff, Bill Comyns and Sam McCready, had cameo roles. Bill has sadly passed away and Sam went on to higher roles in the Lyric Theatre and the University of Baltimore.

Sam McCready, Courtesy of David Craig, Art Department, 1971.

'DECOY' was a short film made with members of 2JG and it was designed to show four reliable pupils, Brian Smallwood, Willie Duncan, Colin Booth and Kenny Murphy, how a film was put together and shot on a microscopic budget. I needed these four pupils to help organise the more complex scenes in the planned epic about the BOYNE. 'Decoy' was made around the ruins of Orangefield House on a dreary Saturday morning in about three hours! The setting of urban decay suited the film which was about hidden loot. The boys called the grounds of Orangefield House the SCRAPYARD at that time because of the number of scrap cars that were dumped there in 1971. Their only reward for this two-reeler was a meagre bag of chips!

The Battle of the Boyne has always interested me as a battle and my morning journey to Orangefield with Stead Black provided me with the necessary junior historical facts. Stead and I discussed a light-hearted version of the battle. I was fortunate that further support came from Ken Stanley, Brian Weston and John Malone. 1971, and especially 1972, was a difficult time to make any film in Belfast and, with hindsight, it was a miracle it was ever made. Orangefield was that kind of school and help was always available from skilled people inside and outside the school gates. Weapons for the battle scenes were made in the shipyard, costumes were borrowed from female wardrobes and ideas for comedy elements were put forward by the two classes involved, namely 3JG and 2RF.

Brian Weston allowed us a day out to Shaw's Bridge to shoot the battle scenes. Paul Acheson helped to muster the Williamites and Jacobites on our battle site beside the Lagan. There were plenty of stuntmen volunteers on the day and some incidents just happened. For example, Tommy Smith played King James and, when shooting the scene where he is directing his troops, a large Labrador appeared from nowhere and sat beside him. We decided to leave that in the final version! One lady told me in 2014 that she had loaned her best blouse to her brother who was playing King Billy!

I think we all had great fun making the film and that there was a sense of purpose to the madness. When the films were shown to Staff and Old Boys in November 2011 and August 2014, it was gratifying to hear the laughter and the questions about schooldays that are now largely shackled by health and safety risk assessment.

When I was filming the hanging scene in Orangefield Park in May 1972 after school, Mary Peters was training for the Munich Olympics that summer. She often trained with Don McBride and Buster McShane on the school playing fields. It is regrettable that I did not take any film of her training at that time. The P.E. Department were concerned at one stage that some deviate had buried a shot putt in the long jump pit! Fortunately, they found it before any damage was done to hopes of winning a special Gold Medal for a Troubles-wracked Northern Ireland.

J.J. Morrow recalls the revolutionary arrival of video technology:

Over the year, the Film Club has been forced by circumstances to substitute films which have failed to turn up, for various reasons, by video films.

In fact, such has been the success of the video replacements and so convenient is their availability and economical their hire fee, that it has been decided in future to formulate the programme chiefly of video films.

At the same time, we will screen the actual films themselves on more important occasions for larger audiences. This will represent both financial savings and greater reliability; indeed the range of video films is now so wide that we hope to show a number of recent comedy and horror successes which would otherwise not have been available on film.

Among the "successful" films shown have been 'Enter the Dragon', 'The Blues Brothers', and 'Supersnooper.'

THE FLICKS: A. Kennedy, 6DS, writes for Cosmos, 1972:

"Today, with the showing of comparatively recent films on television, and the constant attack of fickle film critics on directors, producers, and the actual films themselves, a lot of people are saying "The Cinema is dying". However, now that the 'Hollywood era' is over, a new era has appeared, termed by some as "Low budget realism". Basically this type of film takes a realistic look at various controversial themes and involves lower production costs.

Belfast today is very much a 'desert' for such films. Most of the main attractions reach us months after their general release, and even when they do reach us, they have suffered terribly under the 'censors' scissors' particularly if they previously have been to Dublin. We must face the horrible truth. Dublin is ahead of us in cinema culture, even if its idiotic form of censorship is not! Though, while being bad, it is not just as severe as the censorship of Italy, where the Pope would appear to have a grudge against this major form of art. The great Italian directors, Pier Paulo Pasolini, Roberto Rossellini, Fellini, to name but a few, have suffered under the censorship laws. The cinema as an art form, and a medium of expression, should be allowed to express itself freely, and not to a restricted audience.

It would appear that the only hope for the survival of the cinema in Belfast today, or for that matter in Northern Ireland, lies with the Queen's Film Theatre, and one man in particular, Michael Open. This man has done so much to revive this 'sleeping dog', and his effort is paying off. He is one of the editors of a new cinema magazine titled "Cinephile". Its main aim is to create an interest in the people of Belfast to go to the cinema, and take note of what they see.

One step in the right direction is the introduction of film study to schools, but this must be taken seriously. If film study to you means an easy time sitting back watching films, you are very much mistaken, you're wasting your time, and taking up a place that someone who is genuinely interested could fill.

So the future of the cinema lies with you and me – the audience. We will determine what happens to it, but rest assured it will not die."

Scripture Union

Philip Hewitt writes:

I REMEMBER WALKING down my school's front drive on the last day of Upper 6th and thinking that I had no idea what I was going to do in life, but I would never be a teacher! However, after spending my entire working life in education, on reflection, it was the massive influence of two Christian teachers at Orangefield — John Birnie and Billy Burnison — and seeing how they impacted on the lives of many of their pupils through their Scripture Union work — that brought about that 180 degree turnaround in my career. So the work of Scripture Union has always had a special place in my heart.

When I joined the staff of Orangefield Boys' Secondary School in 1972, there were two Scripture Union groups meeting after school: a Junior SU for Forms 1-3 and a Senior SU for Form 4 and up. Max Woods, Billy Burnison, Graeme Thomson and John Birnie were organizing the groups at that time, and over the years they were joined by Rowley Davidson, Gordon Topping, Stephen McAteer, Raymie McNeill and Bert Caldwell amongst others. The typical format was that we would gather in one of the classrooms and sing choruses for about 15 minutes and this would be followed by a quiz and a short talk by one of the staff or an inter-active Bible Study.

Over the years we made a few changes to this format to facilitate the pupils, the major one being that we changed the meeting to lunchtime, as some pupils had a clash with other after-school activities. This meant quite a fraught day for the staff involved as there was no break for lunch, especially if the SU was being held on a day when you had no free periods!

Some of the more memorable moments came from our annual SU weekends and the SU canvas camps. Each year the Boys' and Girls' schools had a combined weekend in the SU bungalow in Ballycastle and the arrangement was that if the Girls' School staff took responsibility for the meals, the Boys' School staff would do the talks. This worked well, except that Heather Reid and Hannah Holmes catered for girls' appetites, and couldn't understand how after a good meal of fish fingers, baked beans and mashed potato, the boys were still hungry and the bread was disappearing off the tables like snow off a ditch, no matter how many times the plates were replenished!

The traditional Saturday afternoon activity at these Ballycastle weekends was to go to Portstewart for games on the beach followed by refreshments in Morelli's. At one of these blissful coffee and ice-cream breaks, the tranquillity was broken by a lady's scream as Gordon Topping fainted and fell on her lap after a particularly gory re-telling of one of my rugby injuries. I even suspect, in the commotion, that Billy Burnison got out of paying the bill!

Each year Scripture Union Northern Ireland ran a vast array of summer camps, house parties and CSSMs, and a strong tradition had been built up in Orangefield of supporting the canvas camps in Donegal and Magilligan. There had been one camp for secondary schools and one for grammar schools (how divisive was that!), each with a capacity for around 60-70 campers. Billy Burnison, John

Birnie and Graeme Thomson were leaders at the secondary schools camp, and such was their relationships with their classes that each year more and more Orangefield pupils came on the camps. Eventually the secondary camp was bursting at the seams and we had to divide and run two secondary camps – both of which filled up very quickly, so we then had to limit the number of pupils coming from any one school to 30. This was because our school regularly exceeded that quota, and we had a waiting list for several summers of boys who hadn't got their applications in on time and were waiting for someone to drop out.

Several other of our SU teachers became leaders at these camps, including Raymond McNeill, Stephen McAteer and Paul Thompson, and in years to come, it was a real pleasure and privilege to see quite a few of our SU pupils going on to lead these camps including Alan Carson, Alan McClelland, Philip Kerr, Craig Gallen, George Martin, Alan Galbraith, Mark and Stephen Boyd, Ian (Doughnut) Patterson, Brian and Chris Martin, John Newberry, David Chambers, Tony Ross, Philip McKee, Stephen Campbell and John Fraser. It was exciting to see God touch our boys' lives through these SU Inter-Schools camps and to see several of them come to faith and others grow in their faith. However, the Christian life can be a difficult one for teenagers, and some of our campers had no church connections and couldn't get to the SU in their schools, so we started an evening weekly SU Camp Club in the Brookeborough Hall in Sandown Road, which was meant to be for campers from all schools, but in reality most of them were Orangefield boys.

Orangefield was renowned for John Malone's philosophy that school is about much more than just educating the brain; it was about developing the whole person, and for me, this included the spiritual nature. The SU work in school added a whole new dimension to my teaching life, and it was such a joy to see pupils' lives turned around because of their new-found relationship with Jesus Christ. Some of them went on to become ministers, for example John Coulter and Stephen Boreland, while others, like Philip Kerr (Crown Jesus Ministries), Glenn Miller and Kieran McDougall (both YMCA) went into other full-time Christian work.

Canoeing

FINALLY, Canoeing from the Orangefield Observer, Vol 8, No 2, June 1966 ...

"MR MCCULLOUGH DENIES reports that he has the answer to the shipping strike. A canoe has been in fact been under construction for some weeks in the Woodwork Department. The project began as a result of some 5th formers approaching Mr Comyns about starting a canoe club. A canoe kit was purchased and has been assembled by Mr. McCullough with the help of some woodwork classes, notably 3B, who have been using the project in connection with the Duke of Edinburgh's Award. Andrew Moore, 5S1, helped with some odd jobs and Coffey and Flood of 4S2 did quite a bit of varnishing.

Another canoe, needing repairs, has been given to the Club by Mr Loan. It is hoped that both canoes will be used in Annalong at the end of the month, when there will be canoe and swimming races."

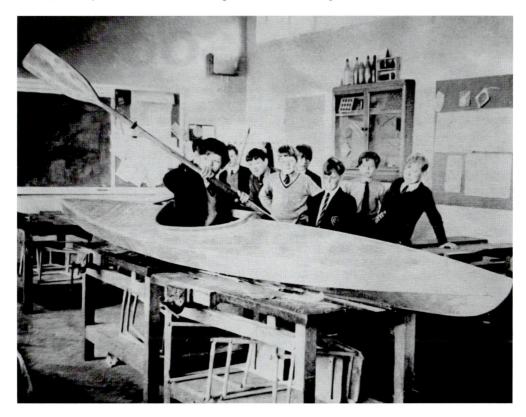

Guitar Making

from the *Orangefield Observer*, March, 1974 ...

'Craftsmen in the Sixth Form' writes Stephen Young, 6A:

"*When an enthusiastic Scottish Woodwork teacher called Mr. Trevorrow suggested, back in September 1972, that the sixth form should be allowed to make guitars for General Studies, most people quietly imagined him to be joking. In fact some of the less kind pupils sneered outright!*

Different kinds of wood were used in construction and everyone tried to use best-quality wood. The back and sides were made of sycamore, a specially grown pinewood was used for the sound-board, and the neck was made of ebony or rosewood. Despite the expense, it was well worth it...

Additional expense arises from "finishing off" the guitar, and this varies as to the type being made. On a guitar like mine – a Spanish style with nylon strings – this would total about £4 (split up between strings, bridge, tuning heads and varnish – the strap is extra). This finishing expense would vary from £4.50 for a steel string acoustic to £20 for an electric guitar although the wood for this costs 50p less.

It these guitars were put up for sale on the open or black market, providing the workmanship was good, an expert opinion priced them at:-

Spanish guitar £30, Steel stringed acoustic £20.30, Electric (minus amplifier) £40."

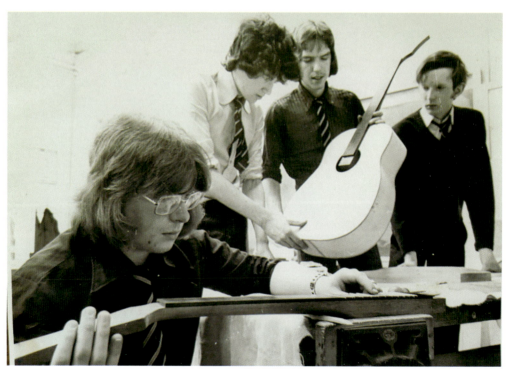

— 25. —

MEMORIES AND APPRECIATION

The Reverend Joan Scott [née Barr] recalls her time teaching at Orangefield during the years 1971 to 1974:

I CAME TO take a temporary post after having worked in the Western Caribbean as an organiser for the Girls' Brigade. I felt that Jamaica was like my second home, but I had had various difficulties with my 'Boss' in England and I came home feeling a failure within myself. Since my five brothers, Jim, Ronnie, Kenneth, David and Hugh attended OBSS, I knew that John Malone's aim was to help those boys who had been deemed 'failures' by our examination system. By the time I was leaving, three years later, I realized that what Mr. Malone had envisioned for the pupils had also been at work in me and I became a stronger person for it. I know that I owe a great deal to Brian Weston and the staff during my time there as well as to all the boys and young men in my classes.

My Form Class

They were a bit disappointed when I arrived in October, because I was a woman, and their previous teacher was male, in a boys' school where most of the pupils had had female teachers in Primary School! However, we all survived it!

Fridays were difficult days for them as I had to teach them for six periods! What to do? Last two periods we set aside for reading, when two boys would chose a book from the store for us to read. When my voice got tired someone else took over. One week the book chosen was a 'Bobby Brewster' story. I'd never heard of it, but in one afternoon we read the whole book, to the amazement of some of the boys who had never finished a story book. One or two joined the local library so that they could find more 'B B' stories.

After conducting a survey for a government youth initiative, I was shocked to learn that only two boys in the class had any hobbies, apart from kicking a ball in the street. We decided to use a double period [also on Friday] for a hobbies class. We listened to music, played some board games, etc., but what I most remember was the cooking we attempted — preparation had to be done in the classroom and then, with staff permission, I took the items to the only cooker in the school … in the staffroom kitchen! The teacher in the next room always agreed to keep an eye on my class. Thanks for all of that.

We ate what we had cooked, and it was good, usually.

One day when I was feeling very discouraged by the behaviour of one of the older boys I took my problem [not the boy] to the Principal. I was a bit fearful that he would suggest I should leave teaching. But that wasn't Brian Weston's way with people. He was an encourager. He listened and we talked together for a while.

Then he took me totally by surprise when he told me that I was a good teacher. I think my mouth dropped open – had he not heard me confessing to failure in the classroom? 'No', he continued, *'a good teacher is one who is interested in the boys and their welfare.'*

It was moments like that that led me out of my own sense of failure to a more realistic assessment of what I could and couldn't do.

Thank you, Brian. The whole school atmosphere was like that. Teachers were prepared to go more than the extra mile. During the summer holidays there were only about two weeks when the school buildings were empty – when the caretaker was on holiday. In the English Department we decided that we would prepare our own worksheets and mark our own exams for the C.S.E. That used up quite a bit of holiday time – no computers, no delete button etc.

There were the full length films on the big topics covered in the English curriculum … my husband gave me a copy of *'The Red Balloon'* at Christmas in memory of my time in O.B.S.S.

Memories to Savour: Trips to Whinlands in Annalong

Being with a first-former, when he discovered that he could see pictures in the clouds as we came down the mountainside.

Two fifth-formers did a tour of the house with my little portable tape recorder, one pretending to be a posh English visitor and the other an 'inmate' of *Whinlands*. It was amusing when they played it back to the class, but more importantly, I was able to use the tape for the spoken English part of the C.S.E. Exam because one of the two lads had a severe stammer and could not have made a speech in front of the class!

A very wet and windy day when we two teachers sat in the minibus and watched those same big lads braving the waves that came over the harbour wall in Newcastle. Then a memory of sitting in the kitchen the next morning with Mr. Cranston having breakfast and deciding to let the pupils have a long lie in after a fairly hectic day and foul weather! On our return to Orangefield a teacher stopped me in the corridor, saying, 'What have you done with those lads?' I feared there may have been a row or something like that, but he told me that he'd never seen them more alive!

I could go on and on with the memories and anecdotes, but will finish with this; many, many of the pupils left the school with a greater sense of their own worth and their ability to achieve their goals in life and I am proud to meet them still.

I left Orangefield with regret, but I had a sense of calling to the ordained ministry in the Presbyterian Church in Ireland. I was accepted for training and had to go.

O.B.S.S. - you provided excellent preparation for me to study and work in what was largely seen as a man's world. Thank you. Thank you all!

— 26. —
THE ORANGEFIELD OLD BOYS' ASSOCIATION

Thompson Steele writes:

THIS ASSOCIATION WHICH was formed in 1966 has planned to celebrate its 50th Birthday by holding a Golden Anniversary Banquet at the City Hall on 17th September, 2016.

The desire to form an Old Boys' Association came about as a natural progression from those initial annual games of Soccer, Rugby and Hockey between school teams and the former pupils. Annual events also included a Dinner Dance, Golf Outing and Barbecue. In those formative years with a membership of around one hundred Old Boys, Rodney Usher and Larry Lannie were actively involved in various activities. An aim of the Association was to encourage an interest in the affairs of the School among its members.

In the Association's early years, a "Club Night" was held on Monday evenings at the School under the watchful eye of Rodney Usher. This consisted of training sessions, followed by optional games, usually three-a-side Soccer, Badminton and Table Tennis. On Wednesday evenings the soccer players held a further training session at the School.

Although the Old Boys' were most appreciative of school facilities it was, nevertheless, their ambition to acquire a home of their own. This desire was achieved in 1984 when the Old Boys' agreed to amalgamate with Cregagh Cricket Club to form Cregagh Sports Club. The demise of the Tennis Club at Cregagh, beyond the cricket outfield, provided enough ground to accommodate a soccer pitch. This is now the team's home ground.

Under the name *Orangefield O.B.* there are now three teams playing Amateur League Football. The 1st XI play in Division 1A of the Northern Ireland Amateur League, managed by Gary Cunningham, the 2nd XI managed by Darren McMillan play in Division 3A of N.I.A.L., and the 3rd XI play in Division 1 of the South Antrim League managed by David Reid.

At present, training nights are now held on Tuesday and Thursday evenings at Knockbreda F.C. on Upper Braniel Road.

There are four Trustees of Cregagh Sports Club, three of whom are former pupils of Orangefield: Roy Archibald, Billy Girvin and Jim Long. The Old Boys' Association is indebted to former pupils such as Derek Wylie, Tom Kerr, Alex McCune and Jim Long for the invaluable service they have rendered to the Club at various times over the last 50 years.

OLD BOYS and SCHOOL SOCCER TEAMS.
1970—71.

Back Row:- S. Jamison; D. McClure; H. Barr; T. Kerr; A. Smallwood; I. Kennedy; B. Thompson.
Middle Row:- E. Howard; W. Dale; R. Nesbitt; K. Wray; D. Wylie; S. Simms; T. Kelly; W. Girvan.
Front Row:- S. Napier; R. Lowry; G. Walker; C. Maxwell; A. McCune; J. McKeag; J. Crone.

OLD BOYS and SCHOOL RUGBY TEAMS.
1972-73

Back Row:- S. Burrowes; A. Redpath; N. Gilmore; B. Petrie; R. Thomas; J. Davidson; T. Cartlidge.
Middle Row:- C. Atkinson; J. Myles; H. Adams; K. Balmer; A. Bremner; D. Hassard; A. Conn; G. Rodgers; Mr. J. Stevenson.
Front Row:- G. Halliday; A. Roberts; L. Colhoun; R. McAlpine; D. Clarke; W. Norwood; R. Roulston; J. Gordon.
Seated:- R. Bell; G. McConnell; A. McDowell; M. Mason; W. McVeigh; J. Young; A. Campbell.

OLD BOYS XI AND SCHOOL 1st XI HOCKEY
1976 - 77

Back Row > N.Sinclair, C.Johnston, P.Robinson, K.Scott, D.Lambe, M.Johnston, D.Taylor, J.Hodgen, P.Brown, D.Johnston, N.Gilmer, T.Sterling, G.Hall
Front Row > S.Taylor, R.Rasoul, P.Monks, R.Nixon, J.Hunter, L.Shilliday, B.Campbell, I.Armstrong, B.Ferguson

OLD BOYS XV AND MODEL SCHOOL OLD BOYS XV
1977 - 78

Back Row > A.Campbell, P.Murray, W.Duncan, R.McClure, A.Braden, A.Ward, E.Ward, B.Dodds, B.Petrie
R.Fullerton, J.Stanfield, M.Simpson, H.Williamson, W.Brown, D.Dalton, G.Bergen, R.Adair, S.Aiken, G.Rodgers, D.Bruce, T.Boyles, L.Craig, R.McAlpine, J.Stokes
Front Row > R.Moore, T.Coulter, R.Magill, M.Clarke, K.Balmer, S.McDermontt, J.Myles, S.Sharkey, G.Martin

— 27. —
STAFFROOM CAPERS

Jimmy Clements writes:

I WAS ON the staff of Orangefield when it opened in 1957 and was there for nine years. Almost sixty years on I find myself very frequently thinking about those days much more than I do about the remainder of my teaching career, because, when I left, it was only then that I realised what a remarkable place Orangefield was. With John Malone at the helm and with his vision and drive the school successfully pioneered, in the classroom and elsewhere, an amazing range of initiatives to ensure as much as possible was available to all our boys. We worked hard and played hard, and when I mention "play" I automatically think of the staff room.

It was there we relaxed, restraint was cast to the wind and we lived it up in spectacular fashion. We were a young-ish staff and were blessed to have amongst us a magnificent selection of wits, raconteurs, jesters, would-be anarchists, practical jokers and reprobates of many kinds thus ensuring that the staff room at lunchtime was an experience in itself. As an example, I found myself, the other day, laughing, yet again, at the ingenious methods used to ensure that the newspaper that Smokey McKeown was endeavouring to read always burst into flames. Ah, happy, happy days. Looking back I suppose it was a form of therapy but all in a very good cause.

Sometimes we had ladies on the staff and, to their eternal credit, they didn't bat an eyelid but accepted the status quo and, I think, seemed to enjoy it – what else could they do? On Fridays we were sometimes invited to the very neat and orderly staff room of the Girls' School for a bread and cheese lunch for Oxfam and I often felt it was like going to church. There were vases of flowers on the tables and saucers and things like that. I suppose we should have returned the invitation but the experience might have been too much for them.

Another memory I have is of the cleaners – Mrs Harris and sometimes Mrs Hamilton – who came in to the staff room after we left at lunch hour. In my mind's eye I can still see her as she surveyed the chaos that confronted her. She never looked appalled but just smiled tolerantly and got on with it. Marvellous woman.

On a more serious note there was a great camaraderie amongst us and still is. When we meet at reunions and funerals it is as if all those years never existed and we were still there in that staff room. All the memories flood back, we ask about one another and are concerned for one another. It's a very heart-warming experience.

So, often in my life I have looked back to those days, and the memories evoked have been my salvation, especially at stressful times. I'm more grateful for them, and the fellows who made them possible, than I can express.

I wouldn't have missed it for anything.

Eds. Notes: Jimmy Clements *was Head of Science from 1961 to 1966 prior to his appointment as Vice-Principal of Newtownbreda High School [1966-1977]. He served as Principal of Ballymena Boys' Secondary School from 1977 to 1989.*

— 28. —

THE ORANGEFIELD LIBRARY RESOURCE CENTRE

Tom McMullan highlights a major episode in the development of Orangefield School (and indeed all schools) – the rapid growth of Information Technology (IT) in the Library Resource Centre. Has this transformation from 'Gutenberg to Zuckerberg' been beneficial, or a 'Pandora's Box', or both?

THE DECISION TAKEN in the mid-1970s for Orangefield to move to mixed ability teaching presented a significant number of challenges to teachers and the school leadership. Not the least of these challenges was the nature of the educational support materials, educational technology facilities and support arrangements which would be necessary to facilitate the new approaches to teaching and learning which mixed ability classes would bring.

It was from these challenges that Orangefield moved to develop what would become one of the most sophisticated educational library resource centres in Northern Ireland and indeed beyond.

In the early seventies, the School had quite a well-developed Audio Visual (AV) unit supported by an AV Technician, David Saunders, who had roamed the school in his white AV technician coat for many years. However, around 1973 David left for wider opportunities and was replaced by Jeff Cundick, a Canadian. Jeff quickly filled the role (but not the white coat) vacated by David and was a key figure as the AV facilities developed to embrace reprographics, computing facilities, and the eventual integration with the Library, to form the Library Resource Centre.

The AV resources available in the '70s and early '80s included audio and reel-to-reel tape recorders, the increasingly popular VHS video recorders, standard slide and film equipment and portable screens – with the potential to chop your fingers off if you closed them incorrectly!

The facilities available were considerably enhanced in 1973 by the introduction of the then first domestic video cassette recorder [Philips N1500 series] which allowed for the recording and playback of video material on an "ordinary" television set.

As Orangefield made time available for groups of teachers to develop teacher-designed resources, (a relatively infrequent and innovative practice in schools of the 1970s), the role and capabilities of the reprographics unit within the resource centre became more and more important to the point that a member of the support staff, Audrey McAuley, was appointed to take charge of an increasingly complex reprographic operation.

Integration with the School Library

In its early years, and as indicated above, the Resource Centre comprised the AV Unit and the Reprographic Unit, so it was primarily a service for teachers. Within the School there was an

Stead Black, Ann Crawford and Tom McMullan.

extensive and well-resourced school Library under the direction of David Francis, one of two Vice Principals.

This Library was used by teachers primarily on an *ad hoc* basis – individuals or small groups could be sent to the Library to facilitate research and it was also possible to timetable regular visits for the entire class.

However, as the range of media available in the Resource Centre expanded the distinction between book and non-book resources became increasingly irrelevant. The possibility and educational advantages of a fully integrated service began to be discussed.

When David Francis was approached with the idea of merging the library and resource centre to form an integrated Library Resource Centre it would have been easy for him to shy away from the challenges and the potential disruption to his peaceful and well-equipped Library such a move might have generated.

However, recognising the policy context where we were trying to better support teachers who were operating in the new environment of mixed ability teaching, David embraced the change willingly and, within a few months of the idea being floated, the Orangefield Library Resource Centre was born.

The team included Jeff Cundick, Audrey McAuley, Sylvia Stewart, Ann Calvert, Mamie Kelso and Geraldine Smith. What these individuals (and indeed the overall Library Resource Centre team) demonstrated was the significant value that they could add to the overall educational process beyond just the fulfilment of their day-to-day jobs.

For Orangefield, the resourcing of such posts was a major challenge, and the credit for overcoming the multiple bureaucratic challenges presented long before the introduction of Local Management of Schools in Northern Ireland in 1990, must go to the then principal Brian Weston, and Michael Rea, an education adviser within the Belfast Education and Library Board.

Whilst the range of media available to support teachers increased significantly during the early years of the Library Resource Centre they were, of course, primarily single medium resources and lacked interactivity. Those constraints would only begin to be addressed with the introduction of the (albeit) embryonic educational Information and Computer Technology (ICT) systems.

The introduction of new technology

The initial provision of new technology – microcomputers – was by way of the loan of an Apple II computer by the then head of the Resources Centre. These Apple II systems, designed at that time by two relatively unknown USA entrepreneurs, Steve Wozniak and Steve Jobs, represented state-of-the-art technology in the late 1970s and early 1980s.

Such embryonic systems in the late 1970s would still have cost about £750, equivalent to about £3,500 in 2016 money – a far from small investment for any school at that time. It is worth noting that a 2016 mobile phone costing a few hundred pounds would have some 4,000 times the memory of those initial Apple II machines!

The key message here is that costs were high and capabilities low by modern standards. Nationally and internationally, the expectations of what microcomputers could do to support learning and teaching were just beginning to be understood when Orangefield made its first steps into what was then a strange, exciting and expensive new world.

In recognition of the high relative cost, and keen to explore the educational potential of microcomputers, the then UK government launched a number of schemes to support the use of computers in secondary schools. Orangefield participated in these initial schemes and acquired a BBC computer and a Research Machines computer – thus increasing its stock to three!

The range of educational software available for those early machines, whilst limited, did for the first time bring together the technical capability to integrate sound, video, graphics and user-interaction. This opened the way for computer-based simulations, educational games, word-processing and computer programming to enter some Orangefield classrooms in a more exciting and educationally invigorating way than was otherwise possible.

In addition to the provision of equipment and support for the development of educational software, government funding extended to creating the 'Microelectronics in Education Programme' (MEP) which established regional groups across the UK to help schools and teachers develop their use of new technology. In Northern Ireland, Orangefield both participated in and benefited from the work of the regional MEP organisation, and also from the support offered via the Teachers' Centre at Queen's University Belfast, which facilitated much sharing of early experiences and underpinned many innovations.

Like many schools, Orangefield's first tentative use of computers was to support the curriculum. It was not long, however, before computer literacy classes became an important additional focus – moving on to computer studies. To address the widening role of the use of computers, a specialist post for computer studies was created and responsibility for this area of the curriculum at Orangefield passed to Anne Preston, a long-serving member of the Mathematics Department.

By the time I left Orangefield the computer lab had about 10 BBC Computers, some provided by central government, many funded directly by the School, and some supported by the Belfast Education and Library Board of the time via the good offices of Reggie Gribben, its first adviser for Microelectronics.

Eds. Notes: *In 1983,* Tom McMullan *was appointed Head of the North Eastern Education and Library Board's Educational Computer Unit. In 1986, Tom was appointed as the first ICT adviser for the South Eastern Education and Library Board. In 1997, he was the founding Director of the £500 million, 10-year, Northern Ireland Classroom 2000 (2CK) project. In 2001, Tom retired from the public sector, and subsequently developed a role as a private sector educational ICT consultant.*

Later, John Reaney, *Head of the History Department, took over the running of the Reprographics Unit. Secretaries, Jennifer Hamilton and Margaret Jordan, coped with the increasing amounts of teacher material which were required as a result of mixed ability grouping of pupils and other curriculum developments.*

29.

RETROSPECT:
BRIAN WESTON (1957–1988)

Robert Crone writes:

A first former in 1962, my earliest memories of Brian Weston are of his physical presence at morning Assemblies. Huge in stature, neatly-moustached and arms folded, he stared out over the hundreds of boys present. The tightly-squeezed throng silenced, music master John Mercer began a prelude on the piano. From stage-door left, John Malone, of slighter build with spectacles and begowned from shoulder to foot, made his way to the podium.

A Bible reading, or *'Thought for the Day'*, and a song from the School's hymnal – my fraternity was *Bryson* so at House assemblies this was always *'For all the saints who from their labours rest'* – were followed by prayers and the sports results as well as a listing of clubs and societies meeting at lunchtime or after school hours: *"Young Farmers' Club ... Duke of Edinburgh Award ...Radio Club ... Chess Club ...Photography Club ... Table-Tennis Club... Aircraft Recognition Club ... Oxfam Group ... Motor Cycle Club ... Stamp Club ... Fishing Club ... Tennis Club ... Modelling Club ... Film Society ... Weight-lifting ... Debating Society ... Judo Club. "*

A profile of Brian Weston appeared in the *'Orangefield Observer'*, Vol 6, No 3, February 1964. Interviewed by *nom de plume,* Ivan the Terrible, GBW informed readers, *"I was born before 1929 in the village of Belmont."* When asked about any strong memories of boyhood, he replied, *"Only one. I was chasing my big brother round the side of a house, when he released the handle of a grass roller which sprang up and hit my nose. I thanked him*

"GBW was a pipe-smoker. This craft brings with it a complete set of actions and rituals that generally betoken someone who aspires to be mellow and thoughtful. Someone who draws metaphorically a languid draught of Condor after hearing a pupil say something silly and allows the heat of it to dissipate in a cloud of smoke."

Class of '72.

Photograph: *Spectrum Magazine*, Orangefield Press, 1970

afterwards for making it such an imposing member – after all he was older and bigger than I."

In response to *"Have you any strong memories of school?"* GBW, an Old Instonian, reflected, "They were nearly always girls at my first school. I recommend this for all boys." For the standard question of apprentice journalists, *"Do you think young people of today are worse or better than in your day?"* the Vice-Principal replied:

"Much better; they are more adventurous and they haven't the respect for adults we had. I think we respected our Elders just because they were older. Young people today are more discriminating. I like, too, the way young people take short cuts to things.

For instance, when I wanted to go to a dance, I spent hours learning dance steps, and paid for this, and hated it. I always felt as if I was walking on my partner – probably because I was. Nowadays, anyone can "shake" without a single lesson, and you never get near enough your partner to stand on her."

Colleagues of Brian remember him as a big man, in body and presence: *"Young teachers – barely older than their pupils, and struggling with their own inadequacy – relied on his sympathy and support ... When John Malone was on Olympus, Brian Weston was his representative on earth, protecting him from trivial distractions – and comforting the trivial distractors. His laughter was a metronome of sanity."*

Brian Weston and John Malone first met as assistant teachers in Edenderry Secondary School on the Crumlin Road. Brian also taught in Ashfield Boys' School, where John Malone served as Vice-Principal [1953-57], prior to his appointment as Headmaster of Orangefield. A founder member of staff, GBW on the teaching list, he was put in charge of the Social Studies Department. In 1961, following Bill Stirling's appointment to the headship of Ballyclare Secondary School, Brian Weston was appointed Vice-Principal.

> *"GBW could well have been a squadron leader in a World War 2 film. The noble chief leading his men into battle while maintaining a cheerful camaraderie and sense of purpose.*
> *Class of '72.*

In time and circumstance, GBW's eighteen years as Acting Principal and Headmaster, 1970-1988, were very different from John Malone's tenure 1957-1969. 'The Troubles' took hold of the Province, and, for almost three decades, the city of Belfast found itself scarred by frequent bouts of civil disorder and terror. David McKittrick et al's monumental *'Lost Lives: the stories of the men, women and children who died as a result of the Northern Ireland Troubles'*, Mainstream Publishing 2007, records how much of the mayhem and violence was centred on Belfast. From an overall total of 3,720 deaths, *'Lost Lives'* documents 1,687 fatalities in the city alone. Orangefield, like all schools, strived hard to remain a citadel of civility and order, but also suffered from the blitz on the city.

Therefore, it was during the best of times and the worst of times, that Brian Weston led teaching staff and guided pupils in their care. Life was not always secure or easy for families with teenage boys making their transition to adulthood in several neighbourhoods served by the School. East Belfast's historic industrial base, reflected in the names of the Orangefield House system – Hughes, Musgrave, Davidson and Bryson – continued its post-war decline. Today, film studios, located in a contemporary theme-park, *Titanic Quarter*, are the home of an acclaimed, international drama series *Game of Thrones*. The film studios are emblematic of the radical cultural, economic and social re-configuration of Belfast that took place in the decades Brian Weston served as Vice-Principal and Headmaster.

The style and tone of Brian Weston's annual 'Report to Parents', 1978, display a directness of speech and honesty of thought far removed from the advertising copy that fill school supplements of local newspapers today. GBW spoke, and wrote, in a language that was authentic as well as persuasive to parents, pupils and teachers. From the beginning, the style and tone of the closely-typed, nine-page Report, adopt an un-patronising, plain-speaking mode of address:

"It doesn't seem like a year since I last wrote this annual report – perhaps it is true that time accelerates with age. It was a year marred to some extent by appalling weather, the breakdown of the heating system, the Saturday night vandals who smashed our musical instruments, and industrial action by teachers in support of a pay claim. As well, we suffered the unusual experience of three senior teachers absent through illness for very long spells, so you will appreciate the year's end was greeted with some relief."

The Headmaster's unvarnished account of school life continues with the names of former students obtaining Bachelors' and Masters' degrees as well as university post-graduate diplomas: Kevin Adair, Kenneth Brown, Paul Brown, David Catherwood, David Clarke, Adrian Farlow, William Halliday, Alan Jebb, Alan Kirker, William McClune, Howard McCrea, Michael McCully, Andrew Neagle, Philip Peattie, George Russell and Leslie Tipping. Listed too, are pupils attending the School achieving noteworthy examination results in GCE 'O' and 'A' Levels: Clive Calderwood, George Clarke, Robert Emerson, Stephen Gordon, Robert Hanna, David Mackey, William McDowell, Nigel McIlwrath, John Sparks and Samuel Clarke.

From the beginning, Orangefield entered as many pupils as possible for public examinations. This proved an effective strategy in building the School's reputation: conventional attitudes towards secondary intermediate schools within officialdom as well as among parents soon found themselves challenged; boys of all backgrounds, abilities and aptitudes found their potential nourished and their expectations raised; an educational orthodoxy of the time that labelled four out of five children as 'failures' at eleven was shown to be false. Historian Ferdinand Mount reminds us in his book titled *'Mind The Gap'*, CPI, 2013:

"It is not until 1955 that the Oxford English Dictionary records the first British use of 'loser' to mean an unsuccessful or incompetent person, a failure in life. This notion that there is a whole category of people who are doomed to flop in all significant departments of existence was originally American. Over here we would once have felt it indecent to brand people this way. Not anymore."

In the early 1970s, the **C**ertificate of **S**econdary **E**ducation [CSE] was introduced, locally, as part of a UK-wide system of examination reform. This reform sought to extend accreditation in public examinations to at least 50 per cent of all pupils in secondary education. In a number of subject areas, Orangefield teachers along with colleagues from other secondary intermediate schools, played a major role in pioneering the new, Northern Ireland Certificate of Secondary Education [NICSE], a teacher-led, subject-based examination reform aimed at those pupils for whom the more academic GCE 'O' Level courses were unsuited.

Ken Stanley, Vice-Principal at the time, saw at first-hand historians John Reaney, Bob

McKinley, Ivan Armstrong and Drew McFall become deeply involved within and beyond the School, in producing CSE syllabi, setting examinations, marking scripts, and training colleagues. Other subject departments, in both the Humanities and Sciences, were no less committed to making a success of the CSE examination reforms. In 1974, the Physical Education Department, advised and guided by specialist staff from the Ulster Polytechnic at Jordanstown, offered the first CSE syllabus in the subject to be examined publically in Northern Ireland. In its first year, the CSE Physical Education syllabus attracted enough candidates to make it necessary to timetable two classes. Today, Physical Education examination courses exist at GCSE, GCE 'A' Level, and degree Level.

As ever, Brian Weston gave clear guidance to parents about the importance of boys taking public examinations:

"It is very important to remember that more modest grades are also often the result of very hard work by those less gifted academically and that we are just as proud of the young man who pushes himself hard to raise his C.S.E. Grade 5 to Grade 4. After all, the average C.S.E. examination for the United Kingdom is a Grade 4."

Memories have faded of how the different methods of classroom learning and pioneering assessment techniques teachers experimented with as part of CSE examination courses, influenced subsequently the making of the **G**eneral **C**ertificate of **S**econdary **E**ducation. GCSE, first introduced in the mid-1980s, made possible a single system of public examinations at 16+, and replaced the old dual system of GCE and CSE. Today, GCSE remains the predominant public examination taken by pupils attending all types of post-primary school within Northern Ireland's culturally divided, socially selective *systems* of post-primary schooling.

> *"Westy had a sense of humour with a kindly tone. He was a tall man with a deep, resonant voice. It was not his teaching style to belittle with sarcasm those pupils who erred-and-strayed. A humorous remark could shoot-down a rebellious pupil without having to draw blood."*
> Class of '72.

Brian Weston listened to teachers' dispatches from daily life in the classroom. On occasion, innovation in school derives as much from the need to survive as any theory. GBW was persuaded of the urgency to reach out to particular groups of boys who, for various reasons, remained unmotivated by public examination courses of whatever kind. GBW's advice to parents was unambiguous:

"Although this year in most subjects the examination results were marginally better than last year, we still get a 'tail' of about twenty boys who seem to have given up very soon after starting the exam courses. I am convinced that our internal School Certificate course is a much more useful introduction to adult working life than that provided by working in a half-hearted way through C.S.E. syllabuses and ending up with five or six "U" grades. I propose this year to ask Mr Burnison who is Head of the School Certificate course, to talk to boys in 3rd Year, and subsequently during the Parents' Subject evening, to explain more fully what the course has to offer."

The Orangefield Certificate course, designed specifically for school leavers, saw Billy Burnison, Sam Preston and colleagues, devise a written record providing the evidence of success achieved by senior pupils undertaking a variety of learning activities in different working environments. The teachers' positive approach to engaging pupils outside the constraints of the school classroom was viewed favourably by the Department of Education. In future years, the Certificate course provided a model for other secondary intermediate schools.

As part of a *Belfast Telegraph* series titled 'The Schools of Ulster', 22nd January 1982, Brian Weston made clear the educational priorities and values of Orangefield: *"It is a very open system, and it does not exclude people. We get about 25 coming back for A-Levels, and some are from CSE backgrounds. It is important that children of ability, and the eleven-plus doesn't catch them all, should not lose out."*

Individuals were encouraged to grow in various directions and in different ways. Uniquely perhaps, the School also recognised a boy might choose, or have to make, progress at his own time and pace. GBW stressed Orangefield did not just put the emphasis on the top 20 per cent at the expense of the other 80 per cent of pupils by adding bluntly, *"It is not just a matter of getting O-Levels – we are aware of the rat-race, but producing happy, contented and fulfilled human beings is just as important."*

Brian Weston recognised above all other considerations that a teacher had to teach a child as well as a subject. In the life of the School, inclusion not exclusion provided the motivation for staff relationships established with boys inside and outside the classroom. Many past pupils would corroborate Billy McKee's remark in *Orangefield Remembered* that while we belonged to the School, it also belonged to us.

Brian Weston's belief and confidence in young people, and that of many staff, expressed an admirable optimism. GBW's willingness to reform the traditional system of appointing School Prefects, inherited from the 1950s/60s, is just one example of a willingness to listen to pupils as well as experiment with new ways of doing things.

> *"Around 1971, a group of about eight representative Sixth Formers were invited to GBW's house for an evening. We were in effect a Sixth Form Council. The purpose was to discuss school matters in a homely setting. In this Camp David we were listened to among the sausage-rolls, sandwiches and cakes provided by his First Lady. How many Headmasters do you know who have ever opened-up their house to pupils?"* Class of '72.

Few institutions today are without a School Council. The 'First Lady' here was Mrs. Weston who, like Tina Malone before her, supported her husband as Headmaster in every endeavour. Moyra Weston shared the destiny of many Orangefield wives, finding that she married a community that frequently and generously gave time and expertise in support of numerous causes: fund-raising; helping with field trips to *Whinlands*; sharing in travel visits abroad; accompanying sports teams on tour; and, on occasion, working in the School itself.

Inside and outside the classroom, teachers continued to explore ways of engaging the imagination of as many senior pupils as possible. As a result, non-examination courses of study devised were often based on teachers' own interests and passions as well as those of their pupils, and included film studies, photography, gardening, yoga, glass-fibre technology, and guitar-making. Tom McMullan's account of the development of the Orangefield Library Resource Centre provides just one more example of Orangefield's well-established track record in the field of educational innovation.

In 1982, twelve years into Brian Weston's principalship, with school enrolment just under 1,000 pupils, a General Inspection was carried out by the Department of Education. Inspectors noted Orangefield's attendance rates in *all* year groups were *"remarkably high."* The conclusion to the Inspectors' Report was generous in its praise: *"The school has maintained its reputation for innovation and service to the community and its standing in the educational life of Belfast is as high as ever. It is fortunate to have a dedicated teaching staff, ably assisted by an efficient office staff and by zealous technicians.*

Much of the credit for the school's high standing belongs to the principal. His relaxed but effective leadership over the years has helped to calm the school in troubled times and to inspire staff and pupils to greater effort. As the school's main public relations officer, he is well-known as conscientious, sympathetic, humane and tolerant. He is fortunate to have the assistance and support of very able vice-principals and senior staff."

Brian Weston retired in 1988. The following year saw the introduction of the 1989 Education Reform Order, with its centrally prescribed school subjects and programmes of study describing what *every* child should know, do and understand at the ages of 5, 7, 11, 14 and 16. The Northern Ireland Curriculum was buttressed by statutory assessment arrangements, and set out to measure individual pupil performance on the basis of pre-defined Levels of attainment numbered 1 to 10. It has to be said, this standardisation of the secondary school curriculum was antithetical to the *Orangefield Way*.

> *"We suspected that GBW would be a participant in any darts tournament that would be held in the Aladdin's Cave that was the Staffroom. A place from where gales of laughter frequently escaped as the door opened and shut with the traffic of teachers. A place seemingly of mischief and hilarity."*
> Class of '72.

Paul Witt's artistic impression captures Brian Weston's last Assembly, December 1988.

I remember when the 1989 Education Reform [NI] Order was first introduced, a comment made to the effect that the ERO legislation marked an end to laughter in the staffroom. *The Rest is History*, to steal a title from Gerry Dawe. Meanwhile, the passage of time has seen 'insider' information emerge from *Aladdin's Cave*:

"*In the staffroom, at lunchtime, Brian dined at 'the top' – the table furthest from the door. His company was a Colloquy of Elders – Dai Francis, William Stirling, and Jim Holland, with Larrie Lannie, Tony Fleck, and David Hammond. The 'other end' – beside the dart board – was romper room, where newspapers frequently burst into flames, cartoons of staff appeared on lampshades, and an unforgiving timepiece proclaimed Ted O'Clock. Brian watched it all with equable amusement, like an oriental monarch indulging the clowns.*"

In 1982, already an 'Old Boy' at the age of 31, I wrote a laudatory article of my time at school

Brian Weston died on 13th May, 2001.

for the *Orangefield Observer*. On the back of a school-crested 'Compliments of the Headmaster' slip, Brian Weston wrote in pencil, "Thank you Robert. Welcome to the fast growing number of my friends with untrustworthy memories." Decades later, the humour and grace of these few, handwritten words remind me of the *Orangefield Way* of teaching, lessons in life from which I have never stopped learning.

Robert Crone *[1962-1968] co-authored with John Malone, 'Continuities in Education', National Foundation for Educational Research, 1979, and 'The Human Curriculum', Farset Co-operative Press Belfast, 1983. He spoke about 'The John Malone Effect' as part of the Eastside Arts Festival, 2014.*

— 30. —
A VIEW FROM THE SCHOOL OFFICE

Administration is an essential part in the running of any school. Orangefield was well-served in this respect by secretarial and clerical staff who sought to support the Principals and teaching staff in provision of a good educational experience for the boys. Margaret Vance, Ann Crawford and Hazel Beesley *remember ...*

MURIEL CRAIG WAS the first school secretary and resigned her position when she got married. She was followed by Margaret Vance. Margaret Vance was one of the first secretaries who worked alongside John Malone as Principal, and his successor Brian Weston, until 1973. Ann Crawford then took over as secretary and remained in the post until 1990. Such was the influence Orangefield had that Margaret went on to qualify as a primary school teacher, while Ann acquired further qualifications at evening classes which enabled her to obtain a future position working with the CLASS Project set up to procure a computerised administration system for schools.

As pupil numbers increased, it was necessary to take on more administrative staff. Over the years, we were fortunate to be supported by Mavis Scott, Evelyn Woods, Hilary McCavana, Patricia Morrow, Rosemary Barry, Lynda Young, Connie Clarke, Lynne Scarborough, Rae Steele, Norma Weir and Ann Aiken who all showed remarkable patience in dealing with the large number and variety of situations a school of that size could generate.

Still in the mind, are a range of memories: sympathizing with a second former very upset because his budgie died the previous night; arranging cover for the teacher whose rabbit escaped and had eaten the cabbages and was being hotly pursued to prevent further mayhem; attending to a white-faced first-former bravely holding out his finger where the spring from inside a ball-point pen had lodged itself, contacting with difficulty his father before having the boy whisked away to hospital [he returned several days later to tell the tale]; on the phone continuously to anxious parents as reports filter through that the boats are due to go on strike, while their children were still enjoying themselves with the P.E. staff on a football tour in Liverpool.

Again, its lunch-time, and the rain is bouncing off the playground. Wouldn't you know it – the majority of boys are outside dancing in the puddles! All that's needed now is for one of the three diabetic boys to have a reaction. The Ribena and Dexterol are at the ready anyway, for it usually happens on days like this. On occasion, of course, our good will was taken advantage of as when a boy reported to the office that his granny had died. He was sympathetically driven home, only for it to be discovered a few days later that his granny was alive and well!

As you can imagine, with at one stage an enrolment of more than a thousand boys, drawn mainly from East Belfast, this was an environment that produced many amusing encounters embracing the local vernacular. For instance, the boy who needed a dressing for his arm because his boil had 'busted', and another who was very amused when the secretary directed him to the Geography department for a map when what he really wanted was a 'mop'. One teacher, on trying to correct a boy who had used the term 'the marra' for 'tomorrow', asked him what was the 'marra' to which the boy replied, 'Thursday'. One morning, a secretary got a great surprise when a boy brought a fox he thought she would like to see into the office!

The 'Troubles' in Northern Ireland during that time brought huge unrest to East Belfast, and the school suffered greatly with endless broken windows and bomb scares. At one stage, the offices were the subject of an arson attack. The secretary, to eliminate her from the police enquiries, was required to have her fingerprints taken, which she 'claimed' was a new experience. A similar incident was averted earlier in the life of Orangefield when a School Inspector threw a cigarette into the waste-paper basket in the secretary's office.

We think the boys in Orangefield are very privileged to be educated in an establishment where *"we do not make a drama out of a crisis."*

Being secretaries to such dedicated men as John Malone and Brian Weston called for some jobs beyond the call of duty. When John Malone was laid up in Newtownards hospital in traction, Margaret Vance was called upon to attend his sick bed bringing mail and notes. In order to raise funds for the purchase of *Whinlands*, Mr Malone had the great idea for Margaret and some boys to sell ice cream one 13th July at the entrance to the Sham Fight in Scarva. Unfortunately, it poured with rain on the day, and the fund-raising event had to be called off, though the sun shone in other years of fund-raising events at Scarva. Brian Weston obtained a street map of East Belfast with numbered housing. He then asked Ann Crawford to insert a pin in the house of each boy enrolled at the School, using different colours of pin for each year group (over a 1000 pins), so that he could observe the change in intake from year to year.

Again, growth in the use in education of visual aids and technology, led to the setting up of a Resource Centre. Evelyn Woods, who had worked in earlier years with Margaret Vance in the office, returned to help staff in the early stages of the Resource Centre's development. Indeed, it was through ancillary staff's involvement in the full life of Orangefield, helping with school productions, concerts, fund-raising activities and *Whinlands*, that many friendships were made and sustained over the years. Fond memories remain of a special place and time.

— 21. —
MEMOIRS: SET 6

Moving On

Alan Galbraith [1986 – 1990] recalls drama, sport, poetry and moving on:

I BECAME A pupil of Orangefield Boys' School in 1986. Prior to this I had attended Elmgrove Primary School. During my time at Orangefield I was taught English by Eileen Gardner, Maths by Jeff Turkington, History by John Reaney, Bob McKinley and Drew McFall, Religious Education by Philip Hewitt and Economics by Ted McClelland.

Outside the classroom I was a squad member of various school soccer teams and also, for a time, showed an interest in rugby. When in 4CN, I was co-author with Mark Harvey of a poem published in a school magazine edited by Eileen Gardner. I was also in the cast of Michael Fieldhouse's production *'Thompson in Tir-na-nOg'*, the last play to be performed in the Boys' School. On completing my GCSE studies at Orangefield, sadly I had to transfer to Grosvenor High School to study for GCE 'A' Level. On completing my 'A' Levels I went to Stranmillis University College where I specialised in Religious Education. Presently, I am teaching that subject at Breda Academy where I am Head of Year 8.

To Be In The Mournes

When Donard in Spring is clothed all in green,
And the Whin's golden flame makes Binian so bright,
The quiet lake waters reflect silver sheen
To be in the Mournes is my heart's delight.

When I think of the hills and dark leafy glens
And the rivers all dappled in light,
The sheep all secure in the dry stone pens,
To be in the Mournes is my heart's delight.

When the blackbird in willow sings loud and clear
And beech buds burst forth in the light,
The signs all around you shout summer is near
To be in the Mournes is my heart's delight.

Alan Galbraith, 4CN
Mark Harvey, 4CN

The Last Homework

Richard Beckwith entered Orangefield as a first-former in 1987. Richard's memoir names his form teachers and charts his way through secondary schooling, Further Education and beyond.

Mr. R. Black (1BL):

The year was 1987, 1st September. I was leaving primary school to move on to the big school – a secondary school called Orangefield Boys'. I was totally unprepared for the shock of entering a new place. I was only an 11 year old kid and entering a class full of other 11 year old boys. I was with a great class teacher called Mr Black who was a very clever guy – he taught three subjects (Geography, History and Religious Studies). During the course of the first year I found it hard to settle in but Orangefield grew on me. The highlight of the year for me was to head for *Whinlands*, a big house bought by the late Mr John Malone. While there, the class experienced a cattle market, a midnight bonfire on the beach, and endless games of hunt (hide and seek in the dark). What blew me away was the quietness and the sheer darkness. Then back to Belfast on Friday afternoon.

Having difficulties with Maths and English as a result of being dyslexic, I was given extra help by a fine teacher called Mr Ritchie who supported me through the difficult times ahead primarily in showing me how to make coherent sentences and improve my spelling. He also threw in extra Maths for good measure. I found nearly all the subjects difficult due to the fact that I could not relate to them except for Technical Drawing, CDT, Art and Computer Studies. However, when the topics in Geography turned to planting trees, top soil erosion and crop rotation, I could relate to these due to the fact that my mother was brought up on a farm and so I could relate these topics to some first-hand knowledge of farming practices. I felt really excited that I knew something useful and relevant about this subject area.

Another great thing I learnt was outdoor skills through the Duke of Edinburgh Award scheme. I spent two weeks at *Whinlands* learning First Aid, Navigation, carrying a rucksack and learning the value of interpersonal relationships. This was a very relaxing fortnight. We even managed to call Mr Campbell by his nickname but alas all good things come to an end. As we parked up in the school car park, Mr Campbell politely turned to us and said, '*Lads, we have had a really good time away but we are now back, and so remember it's Mr Campbell and not Soupy.*'

It was during this year that we started to learn French with Mrs Leonard. I found this subject very hard but I tried, and to this day I can say 'Hello'. However, French was not for me, though I did try other languages and can now speak good but basic Norwegian.

Mr J. Chambers (2CH):

I was given a new class but this time it was different. The teachers had to figure out who was going to make GCSE and who wasn't (high band and low band). Low band were the boys who were going for a slightly different qualification. Their goal was to gain City and

Guilds in English, Maths, CDT and a Science subject. This was better for me as I liked the more practical subjects, not forgetting the Technical Drawing supplied by Mr Eaton in first form and Mr Moore in second year.

I went on to complete my Duke of Edinburgh Silver Award practice hike in the heart of the Mournes which was a welcome break from school work. Here I saw the wonders of wildlife, felt the silence and the pitch blackness. Taken together, these were new experiences for me. In Belfast, there was always a car driving past, street lights, and people talking in the distance. All too soon, we were back in school again and more lessons.

Then there were House games. My House was Davidson, also known as Sirocco, where they made industrial fans originally for the tea industry, and then for other purposes.

Mr D. Walshe (3DW):

I now found my stride and I tried to get stuck into my class studies in English, Maths, Science, CDT, Technical Drawing, IT, PE and RE. After the first month or so, I got used to the smell of the Science Department – a fine cocktail of acids, alkalines, metholated spirits, and of course, the whiff of gas from the Bunsen burners. This was the last year of Orangefield Boys' School and the baptism of fire lay ahead with the merger with the Girls' School.

During the course of this year, I learnt quite a lot in Science owing to Mr Walshe's superb handling of our form class. We covered Boyle's Law, Charles' Law and how we could boil water in a paper box and why the paper didn't ignite, and how to extract gas from powdered coal. Little did I know how relevant these Laws would be to me in my working life as a Scuba diver and welder.

Dressed for a 180 minute dip (working dive at 15 metres) Denmark nightshift

It was during this year that Mr Walshe decided to decorate his classroom and we were warned not to get paint on our uniforms. Also in this year, Mr Fieldhouse, our English teacher, produced a play where he managed, in some way, to gel us together and formulate what was an enjoyable event. I learnt how a play is prepared and rehearsed not forgetting the backroom guys, the props and how they were made, the costumes, the lighting, and if that was not enough, we had a prompter should one of us forget a line. Then it was the opening night, and to tell the truth, I was too focused on the job to notice the 300 eyes gazing up at us.

Mr J. Allen (4JA):

During my final years, we had exams at the end, and work experience one day a week (Wednesdays), Technical Drawing with Mr Cranston, CDT with Mr Baird, English with Mrs

Ferguson, Maths and Careers with Mr Allen. It was during this year that I was inspired by the teaching and encouragement of Mr Cranston and Mr Baird in developing Technical Drawing and CDT skills. I had asked Mr Cranston to help me build a model yacht only to learn that he had yachts in his garage at home and was an experienced yachtsman.

This was a more settled time when I was more focused on what I might do when I would leave school. Little did I know that twenty years later, I would be phoning the school seeking dress sizes for Mrs Ferguson who often said how she loved Chinese dresses and now I was in China working 650 miles off Hong Kong helping to fix an oilrig!

On leaving school, I started my apprenticeship as a Pipefitter/Welder at Millfield Tech.

After completing my NVQ2 in pipefitting, I went on to gain my Advanced City and Guilds in Pipe-Welding and Oxy-Acetylene Welding. Further courses in Welding, together with my training in Scuba diving have given me an interesting and challenging career.

The OBS Bard

Stuart Laffin *was a pupil at Orangefield Boys' from 1987 to 1990. He titled his poem, 'The OBS Bard', and in his own words described it as being dedicated to the memory of the School and to all the staff who "inspired many a generation of bright Belfast boys."*

My first trudge to Orangefield Boys
An imposing building
Under rain-filled clouds
Sat aloft moat-like fields
Track, football and hockey
Ranged as far as I could see

Pushing through the heavy doors
Wood panelled and marbled floors
Left was the assembly hall
Right the hatched reception
Staring at my sodden shoes
With fear and apprehension

Welcomed by an opening assembly
Introduced to all the teaching staff
Mr Stanley's softly spoken compassion
Mr Hutchinson's endeavoured self-belief
Mr Eaton providing levity
While sorting self-inflicted grief

I roamed cavernous, sun-soaked corridors
And quickly found my way
All woes soon turned to wonderment
Now this school I want to stay
First assigned to Sirocco house
Then expected games to play

My first year passed lightning fast
All those lessons learnt at last
Then in the autumn of 1990
The wheels of progress turned
Now another story altogether

Eds. Notes: *On leaving school,* Stuart Laffin *worked in a voluntary capacity for Action Cancer, before obtaining paid employment with Oxfam. Stuart, pictured, is currently a deputy manager in their retail shop in Dublin Road, Belfast.*

I Remember …

Rodney Brown [1964-1971] graduated from QUB, Cambridge, Manchester and the Open University. Rodney taught for 36 years at Sullivan Upper School, Holywood, County Down, where he became Head of History, Senior Teacher, and served for sixteen years as Vice-Principal.

WHEN I STARTED Fourth Form in September 1967, a teacher asked me what I wanted to do when I left school. I indicated that I hoped to go to university to study History and then become a History teacher. What struck me most about the encounter, and why it has stuck in my mind, was the teacher's response, *"Well then, we must do all that we can to help you achieve your ambition.'*

He didn't say, as so many adults did, that getting into university was difficult, or that I would be competing against grammar school pupils, or that perhaps I was aiming too high, or that I would have to work very hard, even though all of these points were true.

Instead, his response encapsulated in the 1960s what fifty years later is now considered the essence of a good school: not organisational structures but rather high expectations of all pupils, the crucial role of the teacher in helping pupils to achieve their potential, and the celebration of success. But then, OBS was always ahead of its time.

I remember the commitment and interest of the staff and their consistent encouragement; the pupil induction booklet we were given in First Form with its St. Trinian's style illustrations; playing on the School's first successful Cup-winning Hockey and Tennis teams; the innovative English course in Fourth Form which introduced us to the study of English Literature through the use of film, television and theatre visits before moving on to the texts; the Mock School Election in 1969 and the sense of excitement at the break-time hustings and casting my vote.

I remember the excellent drama productions, whether Mr. Horner's staging of Molière's plays or Sam McCready's *The Enemy Within* which won so many amateur competitions.

I remember *Whinlands*, particularly the activities of pupils to raise £1000 towards the cost of the house. For example, each day at lunch-time, my own class opened a 'Coffee Shop' in one of the labs. We made the tea and coffee (or perhaps our mums made them), and we had a rota for serving tea behind the counter.

I remember the School Orchestra playing in Sixth Form Assembly and the annual Music concert which was reviewed on at least one occasion by Rathcol in the *Belfast Telegraph* – a rare honour for a school.

I remember the School magazine, *The Observer*, and the attempt to have a school radio station which broadcast at lunch-time and suffered so many technical difficulties that one frustrated announcer, after a particularly long break in transmission said, *"That pause in transmission was brought to you by courtesy of OBS Radio Station and will be repeated at irregular intervals this afternoon."*

I remember the quality of the teaching: in History Jonathan Bardon's graphic descriptions of events; Ken Stanley who, because of staffing problems when I was in Fourth Form, had the unenviable task of covering the entire GCE "O" Level course in less than a year and still managed to make it interesting; and David Thompson who, at GCE "A" Level, honed our skills in argument and debate through discussion of the issues raised by the course; in Geography, Matt Maginnis, who taught us how to study as well as the details of the syllabus; in Economics, Ted McClelland, for his quirky sense of humour and clear explanations of economic theory; and English teacher, Alan Hunter, for his enthusiasm for books and literature.

We were often referred to as *'late developers'*, a term rarely used today, and what we *gained* most from OBS was a *'second chance'* to acquire a broad and balanced liberal education which included both academic and practical subjects and was as good as that offered by any grammar school. It provided a hinterland of cultural interests which has lasted a lifetime and enabled many of us to proceed to university after GCE "A" Levels. But we didn't just cover the examination syllabus; we were taught how to think about the material and how to study, something with which many contemporaries at university struggled.

What OBSS achieved was an innovative and progressive school with a forward-looking staff and a willingness to embrace new ideas. In the 1960s, the School attracted pupils from a wide range of social and academic backgrounds and developed an ethos which delivered a positive, encouraging and caring environment where success, in whatever activity, was valued and celebrated. The concept of the self-fulfilling prophesy was no empty formulation of words; it was a conscious strategy to enable many pupils to access and realise their potential.

The *'second chance'* provided by the school was grasped by many so-called *'late developers'* for whom life at OBS resembled a more benign version of the *Pygmalion* effect in the classroom.

The Abbot, Todaiji, Japan.
Casein Tempera on Card.
25.5 x 26.25cm

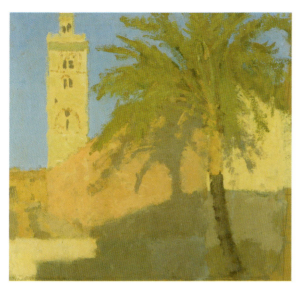

Koutoubia Minaret, Marrakech.
Casein Tempera on Card. 37.5 x 40.5cm

The Channel. Casein Tempera on Canvas. 101.5 x 139.5cm

Eds. Note: *Colin Watson [1977-1984] is a Fine Art graduate of the University of Ulster and has exhibited at the Royal Academy in London as well as the Royal Ulster Academy and the Royal Hibernian Academy. Colin was given the Ireland Fund of Great Britain Annual Arts Award in 1999. In October 2008, he was invited by HRH The Prince of Wales, to accompany him on a Royal tour of Japan, Brunei and Indonesia, as the Official Tour Artist. An award winner with both the Royal Ulster Academy and Royal Hibernian Academy, he provided illustrations for David Park's novel, The Poets' Wives, Bloomsbury, 2014. Colin has held six solo exhibitions in London and also exhibited in Dublin, Northern Ireland and Morocco.*

— 32. —
EPILOGUE

by Ken Stanley

IN TIME AND place, *Orangefield Remembered* tells a story familiar to other secondary intermediate schools built as a result of the 1947 Education Act. By the 1980s, the role played by *not-selected* post-primary schools across Belfast had altered radically. Various factors contributed to this change: the corrosive effects of 'The Troubles' on civic society; declining school enrolments to post-primary schools; urban redevelopment and population drift out of the city; the emergence of an 'integrated education' movement and its flagship, Lagan College; from 1977 onwards, revised transfer arrangements at eleven enabled grammar schools to select higher percentages of pupils; and the diminished social status accorded to local secondary intermediate schools.

In 1982, David Francis retired as Vice-Principal, and was succeeded by David Hutchinson from Deramore High School. Reference has already been made to the very satisfactory general Inspection Report of the same year which recorded Orangefield's enrolment of nearly 1000 boys, and observed that despite ongoing civil unrest, attendance rates in all year groups were *"remarkably high."*

Across the city, many *not-selected* schools were faced with amalgamation or closure. The 1980s was a decade which saw the closure or amalgamation of more than a dozen secondary intermediate schools across the city of Belfast. Michael Fieldhouse recalls that '*the final curtain fell for Park Parade*' in 1984. Along with a number of his colleagues from Park Parade, Ken Jackson, Dorothy Kerr and Albert Patterson, Michael transferred to Orangefield, and he became Head of English and a Senior Teacher. All were a decided asset to their new School. Michael Fieldhouse remembers:

"Ken Jackson joined BTech/City & Guilds Courses for senior pupils. He contacted local businesses and arranged placements for the boys to gain work experience and supervised them in these positions. He organised boys running the school Tuck Shop introducing them to money management and book-keeping. Dorothy Kerr set up a school bank in conjunction with the Northern Bank and managed the School Fund. Albert Patterson became Head of Hughes House, and was found out only when he tried to pick football teams of 12, only to be corrected by a small boy who pointed out there were only 11 a-side. His reputation was repaired when he led Hughes House to a clean sweep at all levels in the Cross Country!"

Already, on the grapevine, speculation had begun about an amalgamation of the two Orangefield Schools, and contributed to a climate of uncertainty as well as anxiety about the future. Over the first five years of the 1980s, Orangefield's admissions numbers averaged 146 boys; during the remainder of the decade that figure declined to 109 pupils.

Following a series of meetings held between representatives of the Belfast Education and

Staff Photograph of 1989-90

Kneeling: Jack Cranston, Maurice Johnston, Jim Chambers, Alan Campbell.
1st Row: Rodney Usher, John Ritchie, David Hutchinson, Ken Stanley, Jack Eaton, Edward McClelland, John Allen, Albert Patterson.
2nd Row Standing: Philip Hewitt, Billy Lawther, Billy Murdoch, Edna Stanley, Eileen Gardner, Dorothy Kerr, Valerie Meadows, Anne Preston, Dessie Marley, Carl Weathers, Henry Blakely, Ken Smyth, Brian Christie.
Back Row: Stephen McAteer, Randal Drury, Jeff Turkington, David McBride, John Reaney, Yvonne McKelvey, Henry Sinnerton, Bob McKinley, Stead Black.
Not Present: Rowland Davidson, Michael Fieldhouse, Paul Gibson, Ken Jackson, Allan Kilgore, Drew McFall, John McLaughlin, Thompson Steele, Dessie Walshe.

Library Board and delegations from Orangefield Boys' and Girls' Schools, the Board decided that an amalgamation of the two schools would take place beginning in September 1990. The name of the merged school would be Orangefield High School and the Principal-Designate would be Mr. W. Hyndman from Deramore High School. Mr. Brian Weston had announced his intention to retire as Principal of the Boys' School at Christmas 1988, and Mr. Ken Stanley was appointed Acting Principal until August 1990 when he would take early retirement. Shortly afterwards, Mr Jack Eaton was appointed Acting Vice-Principal.

Members of staff continued to work tirelessly on behalf of the boys in their care. Excellent productions of Paul Acheson's 'Oliver' and 'Titanic', along with Michael Fieldhouse's 'Our Day Out', had preceded the final drama performances held at the School. On the 4th and 5th April 1990, Michael Fieldhouse directed 'Thompson in Tir-na-nOg', a one-act play about an Orangeman transported to the Land of Youth when his gun explodes in a sectarian affray.

The double-bill also included a performance of David Campton's 'Look-Sea'. Pupils read a selection of 'Poetry and Verse or Worse!' The Programme provided an explanatory note: *"Some insights into the anguish of youth and school days. Read by members of the cast."*

Residential visits to *Whinlands* remained popular and a large extra-curricular programme of sports and activities was maintained. Success on the sports field continued with the Under 15 XI winning the Irish Cup for the sixth time in 1989-90 thereby maintaining the high standard of football achievement documented elsewhere by Mr. Lawther. Pupils and staff raised large sums of money for a number of charitable causes which included appearances on BBC's *'Children in Need'* and ITV's *'Telethon 90'*.

The Orangefield Press, whose titles over the years included the *'Observer'*, *'Spectrum'*, *'Cosmos'* and *'Orange Peel'* continued with the publication of *'33: 1957-1990 Orangefield Boys' High School ['33 OBHS]*. This informative booklet, produced by Miss Gardner, Miss McKelvey and Mr McAteer supported by others, recorded the various School activities taking place at the time. As ever, the 'Orangefield Press' kept abreast of current events reporting in its section titled 'News of Former Pupils':

"As some people may well know, Brian Keenan, one of the hostages currently being held in the Lebanon, is a former pupil of the School (1962-1969). Brian also taught for a time at Orangefield ... We were all shocked to hear of his kidnapping and it is our fervent hope and prayer that Brian and the other hostages will be released soon."

In *Orangefield Remembered*, acknowledgement has been made of the many fine teachers, dedicated ancillary staff and faithful friends who contributed to the School's success. For many years, an active Parents' Association, led by Mrs Given, Mrs Scott, Mrs Dornan and Mrs McGookin, provided tremendous support and help in various ways. For example, the Parents' Association contributed significantly to the Orangefield School Fairs held in 1966 and 1967. On many occasions, sales of work were organised to raise money for a variety of school projects, while members of the Association and other parents, alongside members of staff, spent countless hours making costumes and undertaking make-up duties for numerous drama productions.

Over the years, school technicians Jack Thorpe, David McClean, Sam Meneely; Science laboratory assistants Charley Stewart, David Owens, Billy Anderson, Graham Stanex and Brian Johnston; Art technicians Jennifer Baxter and Margaret McIvor all made a huge contribution to the efficient running of their departments.

The extensive sporting life of the School played out on the Orangefield Laburnum was ably supported and sustained over many years by groundsmen Jim Fisher, Tommy Foster, Ernie Morgan, John Glover, Harry Carson, John Griffin and Andy Stewart. The School bursars, Lucas Hardy, John Compton and Billy Downes, played a vital role in the day-to-day life of Orangefield. Another group that must be acknowledged were the School caretakers, of whom the first was Mr Stewart, and included John McKinney, Bobby Orr, Rab Fletcher and Ivan Thompson. Over the years, they were supported by members of the cleaning staff, Mrs Hamilton, Mrs Harris, Mrs McVeigh, Mrs Warnock, Mrs Pinkerton, Mrs Scarborough, and Mrs Flack. Here, too, were to be found many 'characters' who more than brightened up a dull morning!

The School community also enjoyed the co-operation of individuals who were representative of the wider community including Jim McMullan, from the Community Division of the RUC, and Orangefield Park rangers, Billy Edgar, Dickie Anderson and Jackie Mills.

Finally, I should like also to pay tribute to the various School Management Committees (later Boards of Governors), who over the years, gave generously of their time and expertise to advise the Headmasters and Senior Staff in so many ways. In 1990, Mrs Dorothy Dunlop, Chair of the Board of Governors, wrote a *'Fare-Thee-Well'* message for *'33 OBHS*:

"All of us at Orangefield Boys' High School, Governors, Staff and Pupils alike, must have greeted 1990 with trepidation. We all knew that the School, our School, would be radically changed before the next school year began, and indeed would no longer exist in the eyes of the Education Board. Yet we also retained in our hearts a belief and determination that all that was best in the School would not be diminished or diluted by the changes ahead. Particularly we were determined to preserve the spirit and ethos that had been breathed into it by John Malone, and the good reputation for sound schooling and friendly guidance which grew and flourished under Mr. Weston and his staff.

Now the time has come to say goodbye to that particular era on the Orangefield Campus, and to prove that those very qualities can be carried over and built upon in the new Orangefield High School. Although we inevitably do it with sadness, we have a great deal to look forward to, together with our counterparts among the girls.

On behalf of the Governors, I wish to thank all staff members, both academic and ancillary, who are leaving Orangefield. To all the boys who are leaving we wish every happiness and success. And to all who are staying to join the new school I would wish a very happy and refreshing holiday, so that we may all meet together in August with a new strength and enthusiasm to build another fine school at a time of great challenge and opportunity."

Looking back over the decades, it was a pleasure and privilege to have worked in Orangefield Boys' School from start to finish (as did Rodney Usher), and to have been fortunate enough to have been guided by men of the calibre of the late John Malone and Brian Weston. Likewise, my thoughts turn to those former members of staff, who gave so much to the School, and sadly are no longer with us.

The buildings may largely have gone, but Orangefield lives on in the hearts and minds of many teachers and former pupils who passed through its doors.

– 33. –
ELEGY

The Bright Field

by Douglas Carson

June 2015

To know fully even one field is a lifetime's experience.

Patrick Kavanagh, 'The Parish and the Universe', 1967

September, 1957.

Somewhere or other, a school is beginning. But I am in a different field.

I am lurking in bracken, looking at hares.

The hares are romping on a holy mountain, beside a river called the Flux.

Their ancestors were here six thousand years ago, when our forefathers started building a temple.

Today it is a Giant's Grave, a cluster of persistent stones.

The hares enjoy their patronage.

I join them as a History Student and trespass on the ebb and flow.

I think about another holy mountain, where History became a burning bush.

> *And God said unto Moses,* I Am That I Am.

Moses had grown up in Egypt, at court.

His *amness* was a pictogram.

The verb 'to be', beside the Nile, was conveyed by the hieroglyph of a hare.

I watch the generations on the run, and wonder at their grace and poise.

The iambs of the silences. The rhythm of the gaps and joins.

❖

Somewhere or other, a school is beginning.

New uniforms, new pens, new schoolbags.

Van Morrison is leaving Hyndford Street and pining for the final bell.

> *With my pen I'll write my song*
> *Among the rolling hills*
> *With my pen I'll write my song*
> *Among the rolling hills*

Somehow or other, on mountain and meadow, on linen-mill and platers' shed, a sudden miracle of brightness.

❖

A hot autumn.

1960.

I am digging holes in boulder-clay, foundation trenches for a byre.

I am 22.

I live in a stone cottage in the Antrim Hills.

No telephone. No television. No electricity.

I am privileged. I've had sixteen years of schooling, mostly on scholarships.

But I need room to breathe, and I'm fed up with classes.

I want big spaces, silence, mountain hares – a view of Slemish
and a cairn. I read aloud to Neolithic tombs.

A car arrives. Two men with glasses. I take them for inspectors
from the Min of Ag.

They introduce themselves. Malone and Stirling. They run a school
in Belfast. I have never heard of it.

A new term is starting and they're one teacher short. My name has been
mentioned. Could I come in October?

I explain I have no qualifications – no teacher-training, no
experience. I sit on a mountain talking to stones.

Maybe they think this is good preparation. They say they will
pay me £10 a week – and find a replacement as quickly as possible.

I like the look of them. I want to help.

A month or two of child – minding won't hurt.

And £10 is a lot of money.

❖

When the day dawns, I'm up with the larks.

In 1960, few teachers had cars.

A green bus takes me into town, at Smithfield. A red bus decants me on the Castlereagh Road.

I walk into a building which looks like a school. It turns out to be the Hughes Tool Company.

A House in the real school is named after it.

We don't know the owner is losing his reason, will vanish in a darkened room, and bottle his body-waste for posterity.

We take our models where we find them.

❖

I am welcomed to Orangefield by Brian Weston – as merry and avuncular as Christmas.

He introduces me to 1C, who look as virginal as I am.

He gives me a yellow book about grammar, and tells me to enjoy myself.

I put the grammar book away and make up stories about mountain hares.

Another room, another class. The pimply ones, in 4P2. I tell them about the Black Death. And tombs.

❖

By lunchtime, I am ready for retirement.

I have totally exhausted my knowledge of everything.

I am also catatonic – completely incapable.

I'm not used to crowds, movement, and noise.

And half the day is still about to happen. Four periods. Four centuries. Millennia. An infinite continuum of hares.

I'm not minding children.

The children mind me.

They minded me, in the end, for six years – enormously to my advantage.

I taught very little, but I learnt a great deal.

Today, suddenly, I am 77.

I still talk to stones. But I'm better at listening.

> Those who knew what was going on here
> must give way to those who know little.
> And less than little.
> And finally as little as nothing.
>
> In the grass which has overgrown
>   reasons and causes
> someone must be stretched out
> blade of grass in the mouth
> gazing at the clouds.

Wislawa Szymborska, 'The End and the Beginning', 1993

Orangefield was an extravaganza. A revelation. Or a mirage.

The fountainhead, of course, was John Malone.

For all his earthiness and his humanity, in memory he shines like a mosaic, a timeless voyager to Byzantium.

His travels inspired and sustained a community.

A Benedict. A Bernard of Clairvaux. Or maybe a St Francis, teaching birds.

John's vision was panoptic and satellic.

His tolerance was (almost) inexhaustible.

He created a universe of targeted anarchy where ordinary mortals escaped the mundane — and nobody felt equal to his expectations.

The sixties were an age of optimism. We thought the world was getting better, and hoped we were contributing to that. We had no apprehension of the sub-human sequel.

By moving when I did, in 1966, I left the aftermath to others. I tried to help them from a distance — a padded cell in Bedford House.

But all my memories are summers, and shapes that Grecian goldsmiths made.

John Malone moved out in 1970 — and he, too, ended up in Bedford House.

We pursued him for the rest of his days. And beyond.

The children minded us, and we responded. As our charges were growing up, we grew down.

When Edward McClelland entered the staffroom, he was greeted by forty frogs croaking *Ted!*

When Bill Comyns heaved a dart at the board, he was aided by forty simultaneous grunts.

David Hammond cleared the staffroom with a hosepipe.

Don McBride repeatedly laid eggs and perfected a repertoire of animal noises.

My coat was hoisted on the flagpole and lowered with full military honours. Jake Gallagher wiped a tear from his eye and said it was a sad movie. It was.

We were bonded by rituals of affection.

The last words of Seamus Heaney's last poem, 18 August, 2013:

> *Energy, balance, outbreak*
> *At play for their own sake.*
> *But for now we foot it lightly*
> *In time, and silently.*

The names are still resonant, fifty years later.

> *Maureen and Thompson Steele*
> *Edna and Ken Stanley*
> *Celia and David Craig*
> *Eileen and David Hammond*
> *Doreen and David Francis*
> *George Hayes*
> *Tony Fleck*
> *Jonathan Bardon*

I cannot express what these syllables say.

> *I would need a gold pen,*
> *as big as a gun,*
> *filled with heart's blood,*
> *to put down the rehoboams*
> *of praise.*

W.R. Rodgers, 1955

The final scene of Cameron's *Titanic*. The cast is reassembled in the Stairwell. The living and the lost. Together.

I am walking the corridors in my head, intruding on the rooms and tenants:

> *John Allen ... Bob Ashe ... Stead Black ... Bert Caldwell ... Sam Campbell ... Ernie Cave ... Connie Clarke ... Jimmy Clements ... Bill Comyns ... Muriel Craig ... Alec Cunningham ... Mervyn Douglas ... Jack Eaton ... Menna Gallie ... John Gowen ... Bob Hoffmann ... Jim Holland ... Ronnie Horner*

'When I left Orangefield,' John Malone said, 'it was like a death in the family – you try to avoid continually recalling your loss.'

Our staff-lists are a genealogy.

> *Raymond King ... Larrie Lannie ... Jim Leckey ... Frank Loan ... Ronnie McCracken ... Sam McCready ... Smokey McKeown ... John McKinney ... Bob McLean ... Jimmy Masterson ... Renee Maxwell ... Barney Megarry ... John Mercer ... Raymond Mills ... Jim Parker ... Sam Preston ... Alan Price*

When Van Morrison gave his Orangefield concert, old men came up to me and said: 'You taught me history in 1961!'

Their presence – like the concert – was proof of survival.

> *John Ritchie ... Duncan Scarlett ... Maurice Scott ... the Sinnerton brothers ... Brian Sloan ... Jim Stevenson ... Charles Stewart ... John Stewart ... Desmond Taylor ... Jack Thorpe ... Eric Twaddell ... Rodney Usher ... Margaret Vance ... Nick Watson... Yvonne Williams ... Linda Young*

When Robert Crone was lecturing on John Malone, he quoted Samuel Beckett's *Worstword Ho*:

> *Ever tried. Ever failed. No matter. Try again, fail again. Fail better.*

We are back in the Stairwell, failing better.

❖

> *From the window of the Return Room*
> *I see the childhood city,*
> *acres and ogres away,*
> *lying open like a monster eye,*
> *staring up at the soft sky*
> *and the wet Atlantic winds,*
> *and crying:*
> *'Weep, weep, weep —*
> *weep for Polyphemus*
> *and the once-was.'*

W.R. Rodgers, 1955

❖

On Parents' Night, we meet the families.

Their trust is humbling, even frightening.

They want a brighter future for their sons, and hope we have a masterkey.

We wish we had. But we are failing better. We cannot disabuse or disappoint them.

Instead, we stumble forward. To the seventies. And none of us is fleeing the wrath to come.

Our only oracles
*   foretold*
*   the walls of jasper*
*   and the streets of gold.*

We missed the trailers
*   for the Hunger Games:*
the walls in rubble
*   and the streets in flames.*

❖

The sixties are untravelled lands. Their margins wobble when we move.

A thousand mothers, now long dead, are packing lunches, ironing shirts, and saving for a fortnight at the shore.

A thousand fathers, now deceased, are working overtime for football boots and shiny bicycles at Christmas.

A thousand adolescents, now on pensions, are tuning to the Mersey Sound and dreaming about Jenny Agutter.

A thousand loners, now immortal, are hugging fundamental truths and priming thirty years of slaughter.

> *There lies the port: the vessel puffs her sail:*
> *There gloom the dark broad seas.*

❖

The older staff have been to war. But most of us are used to peace.

It's fifteen years since Hitler shot himself.

'The War' is a gas-mask in the attic, a memory of searchlights on the hills.

We are climbing on Winston's broad, sunny uplands – and buying a base at *Whinlands* in the Mournes.

❖

The earliest centres of learning in Ulster are mountain megaliths – Giants' Graves.

They were built by the first farmers in Ireland, a thousand years before the Pyramids.

We call them tombs, but they were sanctuaries – theatres and schools and community centres, the pivots of a new society.

Two hundred generations later, we tried to make a Welfare State. With all the resources of the twentieth century, we raised a megalith at Orangefield.

By chance I left the Antrim Hills and found the magi on a different campus.

Their histories were histories of the future, their geographies geographies of hope.

The parish would embrace the universe, and John Malone was Captain of the *Enterprise*.

❖

The school has vanished in a single lifetime.

A necessary act of pragmatism? Or a gross violation of human endeavour?

The Giants' Graves have held their ground.

I am back where I started, talking to stones.

They testify to aspiration – a parish reaching for the cosmos.

❖

The Wild Places, 2007.

When Robert Macfarlane was climbing in Cumbria, he passed the night beside a pool. He reached down and lifted a stone from the bed.

> *I sat on the bank, holding the stone, and tried to list to myself the motions that were acting upon it at that moment: the earth's 700 - miles – per – hour spin around its axis, its 67,000 - miles – per – hour orbit about the sun, its slow processional straightening within inertial space, and containing all of that, the galaxy's own inestimable movement outwards in the deep night of the universe.*

> *I tried to imagine into the stone, as well, the continuous*
> *barrage of photons – star photons and moon photons and*
> *sun photons – those spinning massless particles which*
> *were arriving upon the stone in their millions, hitting it*
> *at 186,000 miles – per – second, as they were hitting me,*
> *and even with the stone still solid in my hand, I felt*
> *briefly passed through, made more of gaps than of joins.*

Our touchstones put us in our place.

❖

Talk and chalk.

I'm begowned in Room 7, with a new box of colours.

Today, it's elementary geology.

> When I was your age – hundreds of millions of years ago – I used to
> go swimming in a tropical sea. It was swarming with creatures –
> oysters and sea-snails: sea-lilies, coccoliths, and corals.
>
> When they died – in their billions – they sank to the bottom.
> Their bony bits became the ocean bed. Today we find them on
> dry land. Their skeletons have turned to rock.
>
> This chalk-box is a tiny coffin.
> Our limestone is a giant grave.

I spread it on the Antrim Hills. I spread it at Orangefield, on
a blackboard.

❖

I'm drawing a Roman legionnaire, in colour.

While Paul was posting his epistles, this man was marching to
the Irish Sea.

He brought the art of writing in his kit.

I practise it with 4P2. The chalk – dust puts them in their place.

But scientists have made us restless.

A particle can lurk in the back of my hand, and
romp simultaneously at the edge of the universe.

I watch the Roman soldier taking shape, and wonder who is
drawing him, and for whom.

❖

October. On a bleak peninsula.

The summer has been ripped away by storms.

A priest is visiting his parish. His white hair shines like a mosaic.

He finds a battered thicket, and goes in.

The wood is blasted, but was not consumed.

> It was alive with goldcrests.
>
> The air purred with their small wings. To look up was to see the twigs re-leafed with their small bodies.
>
> Was I invisible?
>
> Their seed-bright eyes regarded me from three feet off. Had I put forth an arm, they might have perched on it.
>
> I became a tree, part of that bare spinney, and for a timeless moment the birds thronged me, filigreeing me with shadow, moving to an immemorial rhythm.
>
> Then suddenly they were gone, leaving other realities to return ...
>
> Where had I been? Who was I? What did it all mean?
>
> When it was happening, I was not. Now that the birds had gone, here I was once again.
>
> I realised I was other, more than the experience, able to stand back and comprehend it ... to recognise myself not as lived by, but as part of, the infinite I Am.

The birds are preaching to St Francis.

R.S. Thomas, 'A Thicket in Lleyn', 1984

Our former pupils are still minding us.

Robert Crone is pastoral and hears Confessions.

Trevor Poots arrives with Christmas.

Bruce Cardwell takes us to Milk Wood.

And tonight it is Van Morrison's birthday.

Another sunset, on another Avalon.

Maybe we imagined it, this mirage — an urban legend about Prester John.

If so, it is benign mythology, enough to sustain us here for a lifetime — and big enough to reach a wider world.

It can hardly be coincidence, after all, that the best histories of Ulster in print were written by a former teacher at Orangefield.

His next publication is about the Messiah.

Sir — what use is history?

It passes time.

I walk the demolition site at Orangefield and pick up a stray brick from Room 7.

Our histories are grass and nettles.

I have seen the sun break through
*   to illuminate a small field*
for a while, and gone my way
*   and forgotten it. But that was the*
pearl of great price, the one field that had
*   treasure in it. I realise now*
that I must give all that I have
*   to possess it. Life is not hurrying*

on to a receding future, nor hankering after
*   an imagined past. It is the turning*
aside like Moses to the miracle
*   of the lit bush, to a brightness*
that seemed as transitory as your youth
*   once, but is the eternity that awaits you.*

R.S. Thomas, 'The Bright Field'

The painting of hares in an orange field is copyright of Lara Harwood www.laraharwood.co.uk and courtesy of Simon Barnes and *The Sunday Times Magazine*, 13th March, 2016.

W.R. Rodgers, *The Return Room* (1955), was published by the Blackstaff Press in 2010.

Patrick Kavanagh, 'The Parish and the Universe,' was printed in *Collected Pruse,* Macgibbon & Kee, *1967.*

An early version of 'The Bright Field', by R.S. Thomas, was published in *Laboratories of the Spirit*, Macmillan, 1975.

R.S. Thomas wrote 'A Thicket in Lleyn' for a symposium – *Britain: A World by Itself* – published by Aurum in 1984.

Robert Macfarlane, *The Wild Places*, was published by Granta Books in 2007.

The translation of Wislawa Szymborska is from David Rieff, *Against Remembrance,* The Liffey Press, 2011 (p. 109).

Van Morrison, *Lit Up Inside: Selected Lyrics,* edited by Eamonn Hughes, was published by Faber & Faber in 2014.

Michael Longley, *The Stairwell*, was published by Cape Poetry in 2014.

Michael Allen, 'The Parish and the Dream: Heaney and America, 1969-1987' (1995), is printed in Michael Allen, *Close Readings: Essays on Irish Poetry,* edited by Fran Brearton, Irish Academic Press, 2015.

Jonathan Bardon, *Hallelujah*, was published by Gill & Macmillan in December 2015.

ACKNOWLEDGEMENTS

THROUGHOUT THE MAKING of *Orangefield Remembered: A School in Belfast 1957-1990*, the Editors have been indebted to the guidance and support given by many individuals. Without the unfailing co-operation of numerous former members of staff, pupils and friends of the School, we would have been lost for words and much more.

There was sufficient material collected for two books. All contributions made, spoken and written, have helped to shape and inform *Orangefield Remembered* for the better, even where they do not appear directly in the text. The following list of names, by no means exhaustive, represents our wish to thank everyone, named and unnamed, who gave of their time and thought responding to requests to provide information or technical support in the preparation of the book over the past three years:

Kerry Adamson, Michael Adamson, Marshall Addidle, Alan Campbell, David Coffey, James Coffey, Jeff Cundick, Ian Davidson, Bill Duff, Stuart Duncan, Willie Duncan, Andrew Emmett, Samuel Graham, Eileen Hammond, Don Hawthorn, Jim Holland, Neil Hunter, Maurice Johnston, Jim Long, Charlie Ludlow, Ivan Martin, John Mercer, Joe Miles, Peter Murray, Don McBride, Drew McFall, Anne Preston, Michael Rea, David Robinson, George Robinson, John Ritchie, Trevor Scott, John Shepherd, Wayne Spence, Brian Stirling, Jim Stokes, Dessie Taylor, Raymond Thomas, the Trevorrow family, Jeff Turkington, Carl Weathers, Philip and Mary Weston, Derek Wylie, Winston Young.

Special mention is needed of artists Colin Watson and Ken Hamilton for their selection of paintings as well as the Royal Ulster Academy for providing images of the work of the late Sam Mateer. Likewise, our thanks to goldsmith and silversmith Billy Steenson.

Van Buren, Church Lane, were the official sports photographers for team games. *The Belfast Telegraph* and *The Newsletter* have been very generous in allowing us to use a wide selection of photographs from their coverage of major events and sporting triumphs during the lifetime of the School. Without their collaboration *Orangefield Remembered* would have been a lesser memoir.

Other sources drawn on, books, photographs and artefacts, have been acknowledged with deep gratitude throughout the book.

Inevitably, our subtitle, *A School in Belfast*, found us indebted to many institutions and organisations within the wider community. In particular, we acknowledge assistance provided by EastSide Partnership, EastSide Arts Festival, Malone Rugby Football Club, Cregagh Sports Club, the Belfast Operatic Company, Castlereagh Hills Golf Club, Public Record Office of Northern Ireland, local Churches and businesses in East Belfast, and the Arts Council of Northern Ireland.

KS, TS, JE, RK
14th September, 2016